In Harm's Way

TERESA THORNHILL

In Harm's Way

The Memoir of a Child Protection Lawyer

HarperCollins*Publishers*

HarperCollins*Publishers*
1 London Bridge Street
London SE1 9GF

www.harpercollins.co.uk

HarperCollins*Publishers*
Macken House, 39/40 Mayor Street Upper
Dublin 1, D01 C9W8, Ireland

First published by HarperCollins 2024

1 3 5 7 9 10 8 6 4 2

© Teresa Thornhill 2024

Teresa Thornhill asserts the moral right to
be identified as the author of this work

A catalogue record of this book is
available from the British Library

ISBN 978-0-00-865784-0

Printed and bound in the UK using 100%
renewable electricity at CPI Group (UK) Ltd

To Isaac, with love

Author's note

To protect the confidentiality of the children, parents, grand-parents and other relatives I came into contact with as a child protection lawyer, and to comply with the rules to which I am subject, all the cases related in this book are fictitious creations. To invent them I've combined, for example, elements of the background of real family A with elements of the trauma suffered by the child or children of real family B with a little of the courtroom experience of real client C. In the process I've altered names, ethnicity, ages and genders of children and adults, as well as the attitudes of parents.

The physical appearance, mannerisms and words of all the lay people who appear in the book are entirely fictitious. Here I've given free rein to my creative imagination.

I've also invented the names, appearance, personality and attitudes of the judges, magistrates, lawyers, social workers, court clerks, doctors and psychologists referred to in the text; but the characters I've created are deeply rooted in my real-life experiences.

In Part Two I describe my experiences working in a number of local authorities – on their permanent staff in some, as a locum in others – over a period of years. My descriptions are not based on any one particular authority; rather they are intended to depict the working conditions in which local authority lawyers typically operate and the stresses inherent in the work.

Contents

PART TWO – LOCAL AUTHORITY LAWYER

PART THREE – LOCKDOWN

PART FOUR – LAST DAYS AS A LAWYER

Preface – Alice G

'Morning, Teresa!' calls a male voice as I push open the door to the robing room. A fresh-faced young man sits at a table, two ring-binders of court papers neatly stacked to his right and a fountain pen in his hand. He looks like a rugby player in a pinstripe suit. 'We're going to have some fun today, aren't we?'

His thick blond hair and neatly trimmed beard strike me as familiar, and as I drag my wheelie bag to the coat rack and kick off my trainers I return his greeting.

As I pull on my smart black shoes, it dawns on me that he's Simon, a junior member of my chambers. I ask if he knows which courtroom our case is listed in. We're in front of a lay bench today (lay 'justices' or magistrates, to the general public), which is presumably what he means about anticipating fun. No self-respecting lawyer ever *chooses* to argue a care case before a lay bench, even if, like Simon, they're representing the local authority. For me, representing the mother, a lay bench spells disaster. I'll put up a fight for my client, but my chances of persuading justices not to place her child for adoption are virtually non-existent.

Justices who sit on care cases are volunteers who are not required to have legal qualifications. There's a selection process, following which they're provided with basic training in child protection law and policy. Once in court they operate under the guidance of a legally qualified adviser; but he or she can only guide them as to the law, not the making of value judgments about the factual evidence they hear. As an individual who can afford to work for free, the typical lay justice is over sixty and white, and, in my experience, most appear to hold socially conservative views. In recent years, efforts have been made to address the lack of ethnic diversity, particularly in London and other big cities; but in the regions where I've mainly worked, an all-white lay bench remains the norm.

The use of lay justices to make life-changing decisions about the future of children is one of the most bizarre anomalies of the English and Welsh system of family justice. A decision to remove a child from her birth family against the parents' will and allow the local authority to place her for adoption, for example, should surely be made with the utmost care by a tribunal with all the relevant training and experience. But no, in England and Wales, in the less complex cases, we ask lay justices to shoulder the responsibility for making these decisions. During thirty years of practice I've come to the conclusion that the explanation is relatively simple: most of the children who come before the Family Court in care proceedings are born into the poorest echelons of society[1] to parents whose voices are the least likely to make themselves heard. These parents don't vote in elections. The use of lay justices to decide their children's fate is relatively cheap.

Simon's grinning. 'Court 9, it's always a lay bench in there.' He stands up, walks to the mirror and slowly, deliberately, straightens his tie. 'Your lady's mad, isn't she? I did an interim hearing on this one a few weeks back and she came across as barking.'

Now it dawns on me that his suggestion that we're going to 'have fun' is an insulting reference to my client's supposed mental health difficulties. I stare at him coldly and his grin becomes a smirk.

'Right,' he says, 'I'll see you up there. Court 9, fifth floor.'

He lays a tattered copy of the Red Book – the family lawyer's bible, otherwise known as *The Family Court Practice* – on top of his ring-binders, perches the entire stack on his left arm and strides to the door. I bristle as I complete my transition from rural lone mum to city-slicker urban brief by painting my mouth with professional-looking lipstick (inoffensive pale pink), straighten the skirt of my black suit and button up the jacket. How dare he describe Alice G as 'mad'? What does he understand of the pressures in the life of an inner-city lone parent whose ex-partner is a junkie and whose own mother was schizophrenic?

There's not a lot about Alice's background in the court papers, but it's clear she grew up on the streets of the roughest area of the city, going home from school – on the rare occasions she attended – to a mother who was in and out of psychiatric wards. The social worker's summary of Alice's mental health is a muddle, claiming in one paragraph that she's bipolar and in the next that her mental health has never been assessed. I spent the last hour before midnight highlighting the inconsistencies in the statement, for use today in cross-examination. And even if Alice is bipolar, so are lots of other mothers, and some take medication and their parenting is seen as 'good enough', to use Donald Winnicott's famous phrase.[2]

Simon's comment has pissed me off. Bloody barristers, I mutter to myself as I steer the wheelie bag towards the door. The family bar is littered with people who lack insight into the lives and struggles of the parents who provide them with a livelihood. And it's not just the men. Plenty of female barristers see the mothers in their cases as belonging to an alien species. 'Us and them' is the deep, unspoken value system that underpins the practice of public family law. 'We' are the 'normal' people, the ones whose lives, relationships and parenting skills provide a baseline against which 'they', the least privileged parents in our society, are measured. 'We' are the 'good enough' parents – and, by implication, the good enough human beings – against whose parenting the neglect and abuse perpetrated by 'them' falls to be judged.

We avert our eyes from the uncomfortable fact that many of us work such long hours that we rarely see our own children, leaving them in the care of nannies and childminders or even home alone (I put my hands up to this last one, but my son is nearly fifteen), and some of the more 'successful' among us send our children to boarding school.

When I'm stressed and short of sleep, like I am this morning, I often rant to myself about my colleagues and the system. Now I enter the lift in a crush of anxious parents and besuited lawyers, and I press the button for the fifth floor. A strong whiff of alcohol emanates from a haggard, unshaven man in torn trousers and a parka. After stealing the briefest of glances at him, I fix my face in a neutral expression and stare at the ceiling. What will Ms Alice G be like, I wonder. Will she, literally, bark at me? I'm half excited, half nervous at the prospect of meeting her. I hate to encounter the client for the first time on the morning of the final hearing, at which the fate of their child will be decided, but my schedule is mostly out of my control.[3]

The moment I step out of the lift, my phone rings. 'Mu-um,' says the newly broken voice of my beloved offspring. When I set off for court this morning, he was still asleep in our cottage in the small country town where we live. Now I feel shocked at how adult he sounds. 'I've just woken u-up …' Adult, but half asleep.

'Oh blimey,' I reply. 'You'd better get your skates on.' I glance at my watch: 9.10. 'What's your first lesson?'

'RE.'

He thinks the way the subject's taught, with a disproportionate emphasis on Christianity, makes it a total waste of time. I'm inclined to agree.

'Well, just get down there as quickly as you can.'

I picture him sauntering along our garden path towards the road, spewing crumbs down his blazer as he munches on a piece of toast. He's not going to hurry for RE.

'Can't you phone school for me? I don't want a detention.'

I've done this before, but no, today I can't. 'I'm about to meet my client,' I protest. 'Just apologise, smile sweetly.'

'Huh!' he snorts. 'OK, Mum, see you later.'

Putting away my phone as I turn into the lobby, I'm immediately aware of a commotion. A large white woman, dressed in a military-style trench coat and with a profusion of ginger corkscrew curls streaked with grey, stands at the door of Court 9. She's hissing and spitting at a group of professionals, her broad forehead puckering into deep, vertical frown marks. I'm unable to pick out her words, but I get the gist: somebody has let her down very badly. Simon stands in the middle of the huddled group, cool and calm as a glass of mint tea, while a petite young woman in a pink skirt, whom I take for the social worker, cowers behind his back. A middle-aged woman solicitor in dull brown, the representative of the child, stands uncomfortably close to Simon. She's murmuring in a low voice to a worried-looking man, the children's guardian, who gives her instructions on behalf of the child. I note that his face is lined, his skin grey and his corduroy jacket has seen better days. He carries a briefcase and a steaming Starbucks coffee cup.

Simon's trying to catch my attention. When I make eye contact, he gives the faintest of nods towards the woman with the corkscrew curls, and for a split second a look of amusement flits across his face. Acting as if I haven't seen it, I approach the woman and hold out my hand.

'Ms G? I'm Teresa. I'm representing you today.'

'No, you're not!' the woman retorts with an anger so hot that it singes my cheeks. 'Mr Randall's my solicitor, he always does my hearings.'

'Mr Randall couldn't make it today,' I ad-lib. 'He's sent me instead. He's told me all about your case and I'm very happy to represent you.'

Unless, of course, you want to sack me, I think to myself; but what a waste of all that prep! I spent at least nine hours over the weekend reading the papers and preparing a line of attack. I force a smile.

'Don't you smile at me!' Ms G hisses. 'This is serious! I haven't seen my daughter in seven weeks!'

'I know, I know.' I banish the smile and drop my voice to a near whisper, so that Ms G has to take a step towards me to hear what I'm saying. 'Please come with me to somewhere we can talk privately. You don't want the other side overhearing what you're saying, it really won't help.' I gesture at a row of doors on the far side of the corridor, which open onto small, claustrophobic consulting rooms. 'Come on, let's sit and talk, and you can tell me how you want me to approach this.'

Unable to resist this offer of attention, Ms G follows me into a room, but she's still furious. 'I just want Mr Randall. He promised me he'd be here. He said he'd meet me downstairs at quarter to nine.'

I pull out a chair for her and sit down across the table. 'Look, I don't know what's gone wrong, but Mr Randall's not here. And I am.'

My brief arrived late on Friday afternoon, so perhaps Mr Randall was planning to do the hearing himself, but made a last-minute decision not to. Alice is still standing, the trench coat falling stiffly from her shoulders, the muscles of her pale face twitching and shifting. Her skin has the quality of fine paper, and if I didn't know she was forty-two I might have taken her for fifty-five.

She studies my face with an anxious, doubtful look.

'I've read all the papers and I'm ready to represent you,' I go on. 'If you don't want me to, you're free to sack me; but then you'll be on your own.'

And they'll eat you alive for their elevenses, I think to myself. Possibly right now, Simon's calling for security to sit in the back of the courtroom. What a great covert message to the justices that will give.

'I want to see my daughter!' Suddenly Alice G lets out a wail and I watch as her large body collapses onto the chair like a punctured inflatable. 'It's been seven weeks, I've not seen her once!'

She rests her elbows on the table and drops her head into her hands. I hear a strangled sob and suddenly I, too, am on the point of tears.

'I'm really sorry you've not seen her,' I say when she looks up. 'That must be so painful.'

The daughter, Poppy, was taken into foster care six months ago following an incident in a supermarket, where, it's alleged, Ms G threatened to hit a cashier over the head with a bottle of soy sauce. It was the culmination of a long series of incidents in which Ms G lost her temper in Poppy's presence. Her anger was never directed at Poppy herself, but the nursery, and then the school, were worried about the impact on the child of witnessing her mother's repeated losses of control. They'd also noticed that Poppy sometimes came to school hungry, often appeared acutely anxious and frequently arrived late or not at all.

A referral was made to Children's Services, who called a case conference. The police disclosed that Ms G was on something akin to a war footing with her next-door neighbours in the block of flats where she and Poppy lived. She had a string of convictions for minor assaults on members of the public, dating back over the last ten years. She'd even assaulted Poppy's father, a recovering heroin addict on a methadone script, in front of Poppy. He attended the case conference, saying he wanted to offer his daughter a home but didn't dare because he knew Ms G would never leave them in peace. The conference made Poppy subject to a child protection plan[4] under the category of emotional abuse and urged the social worker to seek legal advice.

I reach in my handbag, pull out a wad of paper tissues and slide them across the table. 'Has the social worker told you why she stopped the contact?' I ask gently.

Local authorities are under a legal duty to allow children in care 'reasonable contact' with their parents, and are not allowed to stop contact for more than seven days without the court's permission.

'Nope.' Alice G blows her nose so loudly I imagine you can hear her on the floor below. 'She never speaks to me.'

When she was first in care, Poppy was given supervised contact with her mother twice a week after school. But one morning, according to the foster carer, Poppy intimated that she was afraid of her mother and didn't want to see her that afternoon. When the foster carer asked what she was afraid of, the little girl allegedly said, 'Sometimes Mummy shouts. I want to see my friend Carol at after-school club.' And on the strength of *just that*, the local authority stopped the contact.

'Did Mr Randall ask the social worker to reinstate your contact?'

This is delicate: although I've never met him, Mr Randall is my instructing solicitor, and I have a sneaking feeling that what Ms G is about to tell me may not put him in a good light.

'Dunno. I told him I wasn't getting no contact. He said he'd bring it up at the final hearing … which is now, isn't it?'

The rage has vanished from Alice G's face, replaced by a look of exhaustion and despair. I wonder when she last had a square meal and a good night's sleep. She locks her eyes onto mine, imploring me to help her. I feel we've established a degree of rapport.

'It is, Alice – can I call you Alice?'

She nods.

'We're listed for three days: today, tomorrow and Wednesday. I'll do my best to get your contact reinstated, but for now we need to look at the bigger picture.' Steeling myself inwardly, I take a deep breath. 'The local authority's care plan is adoption. They say your care of Poppy is causing her emotional damage and apparently there's nobody else in your extended family ...'

This, as I feared, produces more hissing anger, followed by more tears. I don't want to cause so much distress, but I have to be sure that Alice grasps just how high the stakes are. While she weeps, I double-check Poppy's date of birth. It's as I thought; she'll turn six in just four months. In the local authority who have brought the proceedings, current social work thinking is that the age of six is a cut-off point for adoption. According to this thinking, up to the age of six, most children have the potential to bond with and settle in an adoptive family; whereas, from six onwards, a successful adoption is much less likely.[5] And it's much harder to find an adoptive family willing to take an older child. So, even if the local authority gets its care and placement orders[6] on Wednesday, their plan for Poppy involves a race against time.

We've been speaking for over an hour when a black-robed usher taps on the door. Their worships are ready, he says, can we make our way into court? I suggest to Alice that she removes the trench coat, but she shakes her head. 'Nah, T'reeza, I never take it off when I'm out and about. It's smarter than what I got on underneath.' The lines of her mouth form into something close to a smile, convincing me that beneath all the swirling emotion there's a warm and likeable human being.

As we set off towards Court 9, Simon appears from nowhere and touches my elbow. 'Got a moment?' he murmurs, glancing uneasily at Alice. I ask her to wait and we take a few steps down the corridor.

'Bit embarrassing,' he begins with a worried look, 'but the sodding local authority have cocked up, big time.'

'You don't say, Simon!' I smile faintly. A local authority cock-up may be just what Alice needs. 'What's up?'

'The social worker's on long-term sick and the legal department weren't told.'

'*What?* So who was that woman standing behind you, in the pink skirt?'

'My instructing solicitor. She's been on the phone for the last half hour, trying to locate the social work team manager.'

'And?'

Simon grimaces. 'No joy, so far. Seems like she may be on annual leave. We're waiting to hear back.'

I note, with a certain satisfaction, a tinge of pink spreading over Simon's ears. 'So what are you going to do?'

'Ask for more time. Don't see what else I can do.' He looks at me dejectedly.

I glance at my watch: 10.20. 'What about the other witnesses? The teacher, the health visitor, the contact supervisors? We've only got three days, you know, there's not much time to spare.'

Simon draws breath. 'I'm not sure we're going to get to them. If I haven't got a social worker or team manager, the hearing may have to be adjourned.' He tilts his head to one side and looks at me hard. 'Unless your lady would like to chuck her hand in?' He drops his voice. 'She's not got a cat's chance in hell of winning this before a lay bench, as I'm sure you're aware. Perhaps she'd concede the making of the care order? You could always give her a little bit of advice …'

I stare at him in incredulity. '*No way!* I'm not advising her to concede when you can't prove your case!'

An adjournment would be a godsend for Alice. The court lists are hopelessly congested, making the chances of a new listing in the near future unlikely. With a few months' delay, Poppy will be, according to local thinking, too old for adoption. I glare at Simon. 'The failure to tell us the social worker's on long-term sick isn't the only cock-up by your clients, you know. They stopped my client's contact without going back to court to get permission. She hasn't seen her little girl for seven weeks! Will you take instructions, please, as to what the hell's going on?'

Now it's Simon's turn to get exasperated. 'I can't bloody take instructions, can I? Who from?'

When I hurry into court a few moments later, closely followed by Alice G, the magistrates are already seated on their podium. I apologise for our late arrival, dump my papers on the table and make space for Alice to sit beside me. This is the only advantage of being in front of magistrates: your client is allowed to sit next to you, rather than behind, which makes communication easier. I'm half expecting the bench will order Alice to remove her coat, but no. They're more bothered, it seems, by the fact that Simon is standing in the door of the courtroom, talking on his phone.

I've warned Alice that she must keep the lid on her feelings in the presence of the bench, and thus far she's rising to the occasion. While we wait for Simon I lean across and whisper into her ear that the hearing may have to be adjourned. Her curls tickle my cheek. 'That would be very good,' I add, 'It would give us time to play with. And in the meantime I'll do my best to get you some contact.' She knits her brows and shakes her head. I hope she's got my meaning. For if the hearing goes ahead, we're on a losing wicket. Alice is so volatile that I'll be very nervous about putting her in the witness box. If it gets adjourned, on the other hand, and I'm able to swing some contact, it could be a different story. The care plan might have to change from adoption to long-term foster care, and Alice would have a chance of the contact continuing. In theory, in the fullness of time, if she could sort herself out, she might even get her daughter back.

Long-term foster care, despite its name, is always a temporary arrangement. The local authority remains under a duty to permit 'reasonable' contact between the child and the parents unless it has obtained a 'no contact' order on the basis that contact is not in the child's interests.[7] Given the passage of a certain amount of time following the making of the 'final' care order, a parent can in theory apply to discharge the order and resume care of the child, but she or he will only succeed if she can demonstrate that it's in the welfare interests of the child to return home.[8] Adoption, by contrast, severs the legal relationship between birth parent and child. The birth parent has no right to contact[9] and, except in the rarest of circumstances, cannot apply to revoke the adoption order. 'Open' adoptions do exist, where the parent has ongoing contact, but they are rare. Usually the only contact is by letter: the adopters are encouraged to send a letter to the birth parent once a year via the local authority's 'letterbox' scheme,[10] describing how the child is getting on. In some cases the birth parent is permitted to send an annual letter too, via the same scheme, but this does not always happen and is difficult to enforce.

Now Simon marches to his seat, thrusting his phone into his jacket pocket and delivering a grovelling apology to the bench for keeping them waiting. The chairwoman, a thin lady with bifocals perched on the end of her nose, looks at him coldly. 'Are you ready to proceed, Mr Fairbanks? We heard you were in difficulties.'

Simon now confesses that the whereabouts of his clients (the social worker and team manager) are unclear, which elicits a lot of tutting and frowning from the chairwoman and her two wingers, one a short bald man whose stomach is about to pop the buttons on his navy blue suit, the other an older woman in a bright orange dress. She wears her blonde hair in a bouffant and I muse that she wouldn't look out of place opening a church fête. All three justices are white – in this town where over 40 per cent of the population are Black or Asian.

After conferring with the wingers in a hushed but irritated tone, the chairwoman tells Simon she'll allow him half an hour to track down the errant team manager.

My eyes are on Alice. Her eyebrows are zipping up and down at extraordinary speed, and she's muttering beneath her breath. I lean towards her. 'It's fine,' I whisper. 'They're the ones in a pickle, not us.' She glowers at me and I can tell she's about to hiss, 'I want to see my daughter!'

Luckily, at that moment the usher shouts, 'All stand!' and Alice's voice is drowned out by the scraping of chairs on the wooden floor. The bench troop out through the door behind the podium, and the rest of us make for the lobby.

Asking Alice to wait in the consulting room, I march up to Simon. 'If the hearing gets adjourned,' I say, 'she's got to have some contact. You can't just stop it, unilaterally.'

I'm taking a risk, for what's to prevent Simon asking the court to make an order permitting the local authority to refuse contact? But he can't do that, I tell myself, without instructions from his clients, though neither can he agree to contact resuming. We're in a cleft stick, both of us.

Simon's friendliness in the robing room has completely evaporated and he looks at me with an air of annoyance as he pulls his phone out of his pocket. 'One thing at a time, if you don't mind,' he tells me sharply. 'I'm trying to make an urgent phone call.'

I return to Alice in the consulting room. She sits hunched in her chair, clearly too hot in the trench coat, her brow furrowed and beaded with sweat. I take out the stainless-steel flask I always carry, pour a cup of tea and push it towards her, but she shakes her head and slides it back. 'If you'd prefer,' I say, 'we can go out for tea. There's a café next door.'

Before the credit crunch in 2008, most large court buildings had their own cafés, but these were axed in the early days of austerity. A parent can spend seven hours a day in a court building, watching the state convince a court to sanction the permanent removal of their children, with nothing to eat or drink.

'Alice,' I begin, 'if the local authority barrister can't track down the team manager, the hearing will be adjourned; and I'm hoping to get your contact restarted.' She turns her large green eyes on me, and the lines on her forehead separate and regroup. 'The thing is,' I go on, 'Poppy hasn't seen you for seven weeks.'

'Nearly eight!' Alice clicks her tongue and I notice for the first time that her breathing carries a rasping sound.

'Nearly eight,' I repeat. 'Far too long. Have you spoken to her on the phone?'

'They won't let me!' The rasping gets louder.

'How ridiculous,' I reply. 'All based on one little thing that the foster carer claims she said. But we have to think of it from Poppy's point of view. She may be worrying about you. She may not know what she has to say, to be allowed to see you.'

The furrows on Alice's forehead deepen, and she rocks herself to and fro on the plastic chair.

'What I think would be good,' I go on, holding firmly to eye contact, 'is if you could go out at lunchtime and buy her a card. Bring it back here and I'll help you write something. Just a simple message – tell her you love her, that sort of thing.'

Alice's expression is dubious, almost suspicious. 'I don't like writing,' she replies.

Before I can respond I see Simon peering through the glass panel in the door. 'Just a minute,' I say to Alice. 'Something's up.'

I open the door and step outside, where Simon tells me that the team manager's in Mallorca on annual leave, but a colleague of hers is coming to court at two o'clock to explain the situation to the bench. The colleague knows nothing about the case, so the hearing will have to be adjourned.

As we're talking, the solicitor for the child walks up, with the children's guardian in tow. She catches my eye and rolls her eyes to heaven, as frustrated as I'm elated. 'Hmm,' I say firmly to Simon, turning to the solicitor and guardian to include them in the conversation. 'My lady hasn't seen Poppy for seven weeks, which puts your clients in breach of their statutory duty to provide reasonable contact. I'm going to make a song and dance about this when we go back in.'

The guardian gives his solicitor a meaningful look. He's still clutching his Starbucks coffee, which must be cold by now. 'What's your view about contact?' I ask him. 'Surely it's not right for this little girl to lose all contact with her mum. She's not even been allowed to speak to her on the phone.'

Now that I have an excuse to study the guardian's face, I see a look of intense weariness. It's in his slightly bloodshot eyes and the way his cheeks droop towards his jawbone. There's been an epidemic of exhaustion and ill-health among guardians this last couple of years; the ones I know well say their case-loads are intolerable. Yet there's kindness in this man's face.

'Yes,' he says slowly, 'I think she could have some contact. Not quite sure why it was stopped, really.'

Should I tell him, I wonder, or wait for somebody else to show him the passage in the social worker's statement? 'Something Poppy said,' I reply. 'Or rather, which the foster carer *alleges* that she said. A highly ambiguous remark; and the local authority were only entitled to stop contact for seven days without coming back to court, as you know.'

The child's solicitor leans towards me. 'But given that they didn't, your solicitor could have brought it back to court, couldn't he?' I totally agree, but it's not good form in front of other lawyers to criticise the solicitor who instructs you. I turn my gaze on her and raise my eyebrows silently.

Twenty minutes later, the case is called back on. I fetch Alice, warn her of what she's about to hear and explain it's vital that she remain very calm in the courtroom. Keeping my eyes firmly on Alice, I barely listen while Simon explains to the bench the predicament he's in. If she loses it now, that could screw up my plan to get her contact reinstated. Her forehead's twitching and she's drumming her fingertips on the sides of her chair, but she keeps her mouth shut. The bench are furious to learn that the team manager is in Mallorca – almost anywhere would have been preferable, it seems – and with a lot of huffing and puffing Madam chair adjourns the hearing till 2 pm. I fancy I see her mouth the words 'wasted costs' at the legal adviser and feel a frisson of glee. A wasted costs order is the only means the court has of punishing the local authority for wasting everybody's time and a lot of public money; but it's very rare for a court to make one in a care case.

Before we rise I tell the bench that if the case gets adjourned, I'll want a firm commitment by the local authority to the reinstatement of contact, which has been improperly withheld. Madam chair tells me briskly that I mustn't jump the gun. She's hoping that the hearing can still go ahead, but the besuited winger shakes his head with an air of disbelief while the one in the orange dress frowns and looks confused.

It's five to twelve when we come out of court. I explain to Alice that this is all looking good, the hearing's highly likely to be adjourned and that may give her a chance to re-establish her relationship with Poppy. I don't point out that a four-month delay would make it much less likely the local authority would pursue a care plan of adoption, as I don't want to raise her hopes. One thing at a time. But I'm in buoyant mood, and she seems relatively calm. I open my wallet. 'Here, Alice,' I say, pulling out two £1 coins and thrusting them into her hand. 'Please go and buy that card, and be back here at 1.30. It's really, really important.' Then I wonder if she's got any money tucked into an inner pocket of the trench coat. Quite possibly not. 'Are you hungry?' I add. 'Can I buy you a sandwich?' But she shakes her head, mumbling something about intending to eat her dinner when she gets in tonight, and we go our separate ways.

I spend the next hour and a half in an empty consulting room on floor two, eating my packed lunch, reading some papers for a hearing later in the week, and sending a WhatsApp message to my son reminding him to feed the cat and take some sausages out of the freezer when he gets home. I'm knackered. I consider lying down on the floor for a snooze, but the carpet's stained and filthy, and people passing in the corridor can see me through the glass panel. Last night, after I'd finished my prep at midnight I lay awake for at least an hour with the details of today's case churning round in my head. It was clear from the papers that Alice wasn't going to be the easiest of clients.

I drink the last of my tea and reflect on how quickly she became calm and reasonable once she clocked that I was taking her seriously. I've taken a shine to the woman and I'm hoping I'll get the brief for the adjourned hearing.

At 1.30 I make my way back to the corridor outside Court 16, where Alice is waiting for me. There are raindrops on her shoulders and clinging to her hair. Without speaking, she thrusts a card wrapped in cellophane into my hand, together with a 50p piece. On the front is a drawing of a little girl with red hair, scattered with glitter, and the words 'To my darling daughter'.

'Well done!' I exclaim, surprised that she's accepted my suggestion. 'Great, let's go somewhere to write it.'

We sit down on the nearest bench and Alice tears the cellophane from the card, letting it drop to the floor. She accepts the biro I offer her and stares at me with anxious eyes. 'What you want me to write?'

If the message is other than very neutral, chances are the social worker will construe it as emotional pressure and refuse to show it to Poppy. 'Something very simple,' I say. 'Don't mention that you want to see her. Just tell her you love her, perhaps that you miss her, that sort of thing. A few words will do.'

Alice sits very still, holding the biro awkwardly, as if writing's not a familiar activity. Oh shit, I think, what if she's illiterate and I've forced this on her? I'm wondering if I should offer to act as scribe, when her hand starts to slide unevenly across the page. I force myself to look away; now I see the guardian trudging purposefully towards us. He's the man I most want to keep onside, so I lift my hand in a friendly wave. A moment later, Alice thrusts the card at me, and I read:

Dear Poppy
I miss you
I love you
Mum xxxx

'Brilliant! I cry, beaming at her. 'That's perfect, couldn't be better.' Now it's Alice's turn to grin. She takes the card and, with a struggle, slides it back into the envelope. She's about to lick the flap when I ask her not to. 'Best to leave it open,' I explain. 'The social worker will want to check what you've written.'

When the guardian sits down beside me, I explain that Alice is keen to resume contact but understands that she will have to take it slowly, at a pace that Poppy can cope with. 'She knows it's got to be indirect contact first, so she's gone out and bought her a card. Would you like to see it?' Before the man has time to demur, I whip the card out of the envelope and thrust it under his nose. As he reads, I glance at Alice.

'Yes,' he says, 'that looks fine. Frankly, I can't see why the contact was stopped. I can see it needed to be supervised, but it shouldn't have been stopped altogether.'

'Exactly,' I reply.

'Has anyone turned up from the local authority?' he asks. 'Shocking, isn't it, that they don't send a social worker to a final hearing! Appalling waste of public money.'

When we're called into court at ten past two, Simon's already seated, with a bearded man in jeans and a denim jacket slouching at his side. This must be the colleague of the errant team manager. I glance at Alice and raise my eyebrows. The magistrates are going to love the way he's dressed.

By the time Simon has finished explaining to the bench that Rod Carrick knows nothing about the case and cannot possibly give evidence in place of the sick social worker or her manager, Madam chair's mouth has formed into a tense, flat line. The winger in the tight suit looks as if he's had one too many in the pub over lunch, but the woman in the orange dress is sitting on the edge of her chair. She's jiggling about as if she needs the toilet, which I interpret, rightly or wrongly, as fury.

The chairwoman turns to the legal adviser and asks him to check the diary for the next available three-day hearing slot.

Now's my moment. I remind their worships of the local authority's duty to provide 'reasonable' contact for children in care with their birth parents and, very slowly and deliberately, rehearse the local authority's failings. If the local authority had followed the law, they would have taken the matter back to court, alerted the bench to the highly ambiguous statement the child had *allegedly* made to the foster carer and asked the court to authorise the cessation of contact. The mother's lawyer would have had an opportunity to oppose the application, and the lawyer for the child would have put forward the view of the children's guardian. It's six and a half weeks, or forty-six days, since the local authority should have made that application; and the court might well have refused it. To a child of five, forty-six days without seeing her mother must have felt like a lifetime, and potentially it has caused – and is causing – untold emotional damage.

When I pause to draw breath, the chairwoman leans towards me, her mouth still tight. 'What exactly are you asking us to do, Ms Thornhill?'

In response I produce the card and ask the legal adviser to pass it up to the bench. What I want, I say, is a commitment from Mr Carrick that the card will be shared with Poppy at the earliest opportunity; and that first telephone and then face-to-face contact will be reinstated, within two weeks. Any other course of action, I claim, will prejudice the mother's case to such an extent that she may have a claim against the local authority for damages under the Human Rights Act for breach of her right to family life.[11] This last flourish on my part produces a murmur of discomfort from the chairwoman and the man in the tight suit. I've gone too far, I tell myself: most magistrates will only brook moderate criticism of a local authority, however richly deserved it is. But I'm wrong. Mr Carrick sits up straight in his chair, leans across to Simon and tells him in a loud whisper that yes, why not, the card can be shown to the child with a view to reinstating the contact.

At rare good moments like these I always find it difficult to maintain lawyerly decorum. Without turning in my seat, I stretch out my left hand towards Alice, hidden by the table top, and raise my thumb.

PART ONE

LIFE AT THE BAR

1

Secrecy, Confidentiality and Why I'm Writing This Book

Both of my parents were visual artists: my mother a painter, my father a potter and sculptor. Some of their creative production was fantastic, but neither of them was willing to compromise with what was fashionable in the art world of their day. By and large their work didn't sell.

Having grown up in the comfort of middle-class families, and survived the war, my parents were naive enough to think money unimportant. My father professed that art was the only thing that mattered and turned down a salaried post in my grandfather's business. My mother would have liked him to earn some money, but accepted his decision. My sister and I were fed a diet of potatoes with corned beef and dressed in the cast-off clothes of the children of Dad's well-off friends. On high days and holidays he drove us in his barely roadworthy Hillman van to west Wales or Sussex, where the same people lent us their second homes.

As is often the case with artists, my parents' marriage was troubled and my father became abusive. After many unhappy years my mother left, taking my sister and me with her. I was eleven. We were nothing like as poor as the people living on the council estates in the part of south London we'd left behind, but Mum was now a lone parent, somewhat fragile, and dependent on Dad for a very meagre income. Our house was cold, Mum's car on its last legs and the quarterly arrival of the electricity bill always precipitated a crisis. Meanwhile, the girls I met at my new comprehensive school lived in two-parent families with dads who drove smart cars and mums who visited the hairdresser.

I'm relating all this because it goes some way to explain why I went into family law and why I approach it the way I do. The strain I endured supporting my mother through her long-drawn-out divorce overshadowed my childhood. I left home at eighteen in a vulnerable state of mind and with very little idea of what I was going to do. Travel seemed the best option.

After nine months volunteering in a Peruvian shanty town, I went to university and became involved in the women's movement. Feminism spoke to me because of what I'd seen my mother go through and it made sense of my experiences at a male-dominated university. Moving to London, I continued my activism, became a supporter of nationalist women prisoners in Northern Ireland and took a job campaigning for police accountability in a north London borough.

I enjoyed working for the causes I believed in, but after a time it wasn't enough to go on the streets and shout that this or that was 'all wrong'. I began to wonder about studying law, to give me more authority to challenge the system. I was still suffering the after-effects of my emotionally chaotic childhood and, on a deeper level, perhaps I was looking for a set of clear rules and boundaries. Beyond that, having witnessed my mother's struggles, I knew I wanted financial security.

But it wasn't an easy decision to become a lawyer. Having grown up writing and painting, I had my doubts about moving into a world in which creativity wasn't valued. My mother was broadly supportive, but my bohemian father made no secret of his disapproval. His objection wasn't just that barristers and solicitors lived more conventional lives than he did: he thought most lawyers were crooks.

When I rang to tell him my plans, he groaned loudly. 'Christ, Teresa, that filthy profession! Do you *have* to?'

In the two years I spent at City University in London and then the Inns of Court School of Law, it was clear to me that I didn't fit the standard mould of the barrister-to-be. Many of my fellow students had parents who were lawyers; one or two had judges in the family. To them, legal language and legal jokes came like second nature, whereas I felt like a stranger in a foreign land. And while I wandered around the college with my activist badges pinned to my denim jacket and my bike panniers under my arm, many of the women students wore business suits and carried Gucci handbags.

After a couple of bad moments when I nearly gave up, I scraped through my exams and applied for pupillage.[1] I was accepted by Garden Court, the chambers of the late Ian Macdonald QC and Owen Davies QC (now KC),[2] which specialised in immigration, criminal and family law. Chambers had an ethos of fighting injustice and defending human rights, generally on behalf of the poor and the marginalised. To my new colleagues, my advanced age of twenty-nine and my history of activism stood me in good stead, and I was made to feel welcome.

Over the next year my clerks sent me off to cut my teeth on magistrates' court criminal defence work. I represented people I would never have met in the normal course of life and thoroughly enjoyed it. After becoming a tenant[3] in the same chambers, I graduated to Crown Court work and won a series of petty crime jury trials – I put this down to female barristers being, in the late 1980s, something of a novelty – and again I enjoyed the work.

Some months later, after securing a 'not guilty' verdict for a man who had allegedly attacked a cab driver from the back seat of a cab and of whose guilt I was convinced, my enthusiasm for criminal defence work waned. From that point on, my clerks funnelled me towards family law, in those days a common lot for women barristers.

Although I liked many of my colleagues at Garden Court, I still felt like an imposter in the legal world. I kept wondering what I was doing there and whether I shouldn't have pursued a career as a writer and activist instead. Part of my problem was social. Although I was white with a middle-class accent, coming from what in those days was called a 'broken home' and a family without money made me feel quite different from the privately educated barristers I met in court.[4] In this ambivalent frame of mind, initially I accepted a diet of domestic violence injunctions, custody battles and family money disputes without complaint. But the work was deeply depressing. After some months I was briefed to represent a lone mother in her forties who was trying to get financial support from a husband who'd abandoned her and their teenage children. The woman was seriously ill and the husband, who had a new, younger partner, was doing all he could to hide his assets. The situation sickened and distressed me.

With hindsight this sort of case was just too close to the bone. Like many of the other family disputes in which I was briefed, it triggered bad memories of the miserable years I'd lived through as my parents' marriage fell apart. I grew to hate such cases.

Then one Friday morning in 1990 my clerks sent me to represent a south London borough on a care application in Camberwell Magistrates' Court. In those days there was no specific training in care work for newly qualified barristers. When you were asked to do something you hadn't done before – or rather, informed by the clerks that it was in your diary for the following day – you were simply expected to read the papers, look up the law and work out for yourself how to approach the case. You could ask for advice from a more senior member of the family team in chambers, who were generally very helpful; but if, despite that, you went to court feeling unsure of what you were doing, it was tough – you simply had to muddle through as best you could. If the client got a rough ride as a result, that was tough too.

The following Friday I was sent back to Camberwell Magistrates (or 'Mags', as lawyers call these courts with open derision) on the same case. My clients were a female social worker and a male team manager, and I rather enjoyed the way they looked up to me, apparently not noticing that I had no idea how to run the case.

Soon after that I was sent to Balham Mags to represent a different borough. The case involved a lone mum whose three children had been taken into foster care some months back because of her drink problem. This was before the coming into law of the Children Act 1989, and I still remember the few flimsy sheets of typed paper containing the entirety of the social work evidence. I read it through a couple of times the night before, but my mind was in a fog as to how I should approach the hearing. When the court sat and the mother gave her evidence, I found myself immediately fired up with a sense of deep empathy for her. I believed every word she said about having given up the booze; despite my role as local authority counsel, my overwhelming feeling was that I wanted her to get her kids back.

It was beginning to dawn on me that I preferred care cases to disputes between separated parents. In care cases the evidence was often disturbing, but it rarely made my stomach churn in the way that accounts of one parent beating up the other or refusing to pay maintenance did. I felt empathy with lone mothers on housing estates being criticised by social workers; but their lives were outside my experience and I was able to maintain a level of detachment.

I had so much to learn about care work. Just how high the stakes were in these cases finally came home to me when I was sent to Tower Bridge Mags one Thursday morning to represent a mother of four. I was feeling emotionally wobbly at the time and my client, a young Black woman, was herself in a troubled state of mind. The local authority had already removed her two older children, and when we got to court they announced that they also wanted to take the baby and the toddler, both of whom she had with her in a double buggy. As is often the case in care matters, the local authority were present in force, with two social workers, a team manager, and their barrister and in-house solicitor. The fathers of the children were of 'whereabouts unknown', and the guardian was supporting the removal. So there were seven professionals arrayed against just me and the mother. I panicked. My distraught client had her back to the wall and I knew I was too green to argue successfully against the removal.

As luck would have it, before we went into court the local authority learned that the foster placement they'd intended to use was no longer available. When I explained this to my client, she burst into tears, grabbed the double buggy and made for the street door. I too felt like running away. The case was adjourned for a listing later in the week, and I went back to chambers and told my clerks I had a vital dental appointment that day, which I'd forgotten to write in the diary.

Representing mothers was too much for me, I decided. Representing the local authority was okay, because you were a cog in a big machine with the odds stacked in your favour; if you messed up, the chances were it wouldn't be the end of the world. But representing a mother was like having to fight for her very life; if you got it wrong, and she lost her kids, you were responsible for the most unthinkable tragedy.

I didn't understand then that even the most skilled and experienced of care barristers are unable, in most cases and most of the time, to prevent the removal of their clients' children.

My aims in writing this book are relatively simple. First, and broadly speaking, I want to make the reading public aware of the miserable and damaging circumstances in which many children are growing up in contemporary England and Wales, and of the failure of our child protection system and universal services (health, housing, children's social care, education) to provide them and their families with sufficient help to turn their lives around. This failure has deepened dangerously during the years of austerity, the pandemic and the cost of living crisis, due mainly to government policies that have starved the public sector of adequate funding. Poverty is not the only root cause of child neglect and child abuse, but it plays a major role.[5]

My second reason for writing the book is that during my thirty years in public family law I've had umpteen thoughts about the child protection system, many of them critical, but till now have not found a satisfactory forum in which to air them. I should clarify here that *public* family law is the generic term for care proceedings and adoption, where the state intervenes in the upbringing of a child, as opposed to *private* family law which addresses disputes between separated parents. This book is about the former.

Most family lawyers who do public law work are so ground down by the pressure and the sheer misery of the work that when they get a free moment to chat they don't want to think about it. Waiting outside court for a care case to be called on, they're more likely to speak about their recent holiday or their child's allergy to peanuts than about what's wrong with the system.

Many would say their energies have been depleted by the daily struggle of managing one harrowing case after another in a queue of work that never ends, and they are drained by the effort of trying to stay on top of the ever-changing practice directions and case law handed down by the judiciary. The pressure of work leaves little room for looking at the bigger picture and asking whether the child protection system as a whole really operates in the best interests of the nation's children.

It is said that after a few years in public family law you become 'case-hardened', meaning you develop a kind of emotional numbness that enables you to ignore the extreme pain you're dealing with on a daily basis. Most lawyers work full-time and do a much greater volume of work than I've ever done. I admire my colleagues' grit and stamina, but I've always been clear that I simply can't do the job full-time as I don't want to become emotionally numb. Perhaps being under less pressure has given me the space to stand back, look at the system through critical eyes and ask awkward questions. This book is the result.

Central among my worries about our child protection system is the issue of social class. In my experience, cases of emotional, sexual and physical abuse and neglect of middle-class children rarely result in care proceedings. Such cases undoubtedly occur, but our system tends not to pick them up. Question – is it right that social workers should be allowed to focus on the deficiencies of the most impoverished parents, while our political and economic systems make their lives ever harder and austerity has deprived them of the public services that could help them?

In modern Britain, parents who are impoverished include people from every ethnic group. I personally have not observed racism as a determinant in which families come to the attention of social workers; but children from certain ethnic groups are over-represented in the care system (see page 32). What I have observed, in some cases involving refugee families, is a level of ignorance on the part of the social worker about the experiences the parents have been through in their country of origin and a consequent lack of insight into how this is affecting their ability to parent in the UK. This is an issue which could be addressed by training.

Whether or not they are migrants, many parents who are accused of damaging their offspring have themselves experienced trauma as children; yet there is precious little on offer to a person living on state benefits to help them recover and move forward. Provision of psychotherapy by the NHS is notoriously patchy and inadequate; so one of my awkward questions is this: why does the Family Court not have the legal power to order a local authority to fund high-quality psychotherapy from the private sector for a parent whose parenting might improve if their own trauma were addressed?

And why is so little of the knowledge and insight developed by professionals working in child development and mental health employed in the training of social workers and the handling of children in care? For whatever trauma a child may have been through in the care of his or her parents, it is very common for further emotional trauma to be inflicted on them once they enter the care system. This may be as a result of being placed with unsuitable foster carers or put through several changes of placement; denial of contact with family members; a failure to arrange play or other types of therapy; and long periods of uncertainty while a case wends its way through court, to name but a few of the things that can and do go wrong.

And, regarding a different but related issue, is it right that the Family Court regularly orders the permanent severing of family ties by means of adoption, when with timely and skilled support the parent might have been able to overcome their difficulties sufficiently to continue caring for the child? The UK is one of only three countries in Europe where stranger adoption is widely used as a solution for the care of neglected and abused children.[6]

Another thing that has bothered me for years is this: why is there no system of research and judicial follow-up, enabling family judges to learn about the impact on a child of the decisions they made about that child's life some five, ten or fifteen years earlier? Without this kind of information, how can judicial decision-making improve?

Some facts and figures

In 2023 there were 83,840 children in care in England,[7] compared with 64,400 in 2010[8] – an increase of 30 per cent in just thirteen years. In Wales in 2022 there were 7,080 children in care,[9] compared with 5,160[10] in 2010 – an increase of 37 per cent. In terms of ethnicity, and based on government figures, children who are Black, of mixed ethnicity or from 'other' ethnic groups are over-represented among children in care, relative to their numbers in the under-18 population; Asian children are under-represented.[11] Little research has yet been undertaken to establish the reasons for the over-representation of Black and mixed ethnicity children in care, but socio-economic deprivation is likely to be a factor. It is well known, however, that Black children waiting in care for adoptive placements wait longer than white children and are least likely to be adopted at all.[12]

Statistics tell us that a lot of 'care experienced' children, of all ethnicities, will face bleak futures. Thirty-nine per cent of care leavers between the ages of nineteen and twenty-one are not in education, employment or training, compared with just 13 per cent of their peers; it's estimated that 25 per cent of the homeless have been in care at some point in their lives; care leavers are estimated to represent between 24 and 27 per cent of the adult prison population; and adults who spent time in care as children are 70 per cent more likely to die prematurely than those who did not.[13]

Secrecy and confidentiality

It's over twenty years since I first thought of writing a book about child protection. In the past I worried that saying what I really thought could bring my practice to an untimely end. I feared getting struck off by the Bar Standards Board or that my solicitors would stop briefing me, or both. I was also unsure what to do about the complex issue of confidentiality. How could I talk about individual cases without breaching the rules?

All care lawyers are subject to strict rules of court that forbid us from revealing either documents from our cases, *or the contents of documents* or other information gained in the course of the proceedings, to anybody who is neither a party to the case nor the legal representative of a party.[14] And even if there were no such rules, I would not want to breach the trust that clients have placed in me over the years by revealing their personal affairs in public.

The attitude of the family judiciary to the level of secrecy that's appropriate in the Family Court has changed in recent years. Up until the end of 2022 the Family Court heard all cases concerning children in private, with only the parents, the lawyers and the judge present. Over the preceding fifteen years there had been a growing clamour that such secrecy wasn't appropriate in a democracy. Thanks, principally, to the vigorous efforts of campaigning journalists,[15] pressure built from 2008 for the court to be opened up to public scrutiny. This resulted in a gradual, limited acknowledgement by the judiciary that the practice of conducting family justice behind tightly sealed doors was no longer acceptable. Allowing full public access was not seen as an option, so a compromise was reached, permitting court access for journalists under a strict regime of reporting restrictions. The aim seems to have been to dispel public fears and allay curiosity while continuing to protect children's right to privacy.

In practice, the media-reporting regime introduced in 2011 made relatively little difference to the privacy accorded to parents and children. Although 'accredited' journalists and bloggers were permitted to sit in the back of care courts and were even allowed to see a limited number of court documents, the restrictions on what they could *report* were so tight that it was rare to see a journalist sit in on a care hearing.

A new policy also initiated in 2011 encouraged judges to publish carefully anonymised versions of their judgments on the website of the British and Irish Legal Information Institute (BAILII). Arguably this represented a small dent in the right to privacy of children and parents; but judges have not been enthusiastic about publishing their judgments, and it's not easy for a non-lawyer to find cases on BAILII.

Initially, for most lawyers and judges, the tokenistic nature of the 2011 measures was a cause for relief. But certain journalists kept demanding greater transparency and the problem remained: members of the public who had never been hauled before the Family Court in public law proceedings, whether as parents, lay witnesses or professionals, had next to no idea what goes on in it; and ignorance breeds fear and suspicion. Whether or not we are now parents, once upon a time we were all children; and the enormity of a child being forcibly removed from the care of its parents stirs difficult emotions in us. If we don't work in the system, what can we do but piece together fragments from the information that escapes?

Recognising that the demand for greater transparency would not go away, in October 2021 the most senior Family Court judge began moves to open up the court's work to a greater level of public scrutiny. He declared: 'The level of legitimate media and public concern about the workings of the Family Court is now such that it is necessary for the court to regard openness as the new norm.'[16]

A pilot scheme commenced in February 2023 for twelve months in three court centres in England and Wales in which accredited journalists and bloggers are permitted not only to attend hearings but also, for the first time, *to report on what they hear and see*. Strict rules require that they refrain from giving names or other identifying information about the children and families concerned.

In January 2024 it was announced that the pilot scheme would be extended at the end of that month to a further sixteen courts in England.

In the context of the new judicial thinking about transparency, it feels much easier for me to write about my experiences as a child protection lawyer than it would have felt in the past. But let me be absolutely clear – I'm not planning to relate real cases in which I've been involved. As a lawyer rather than a journalist, I'm still bound by those strict rules of court to maintain confidentiality; and I have no wish to override the privacy to which I believe children and families are morally entitled.

In case this statement causes confusion, I should explain that I have reservations about the pilot scheme described above. It's my belief that traumatised children should be afforded absolute privacy about their experiences, if that's what they want when they're of an age to make an informed decision – which may be many years after a court case has finished. Anonymisation is good, but for some children it will not feel like enough. A number of consultations have been carried out with children and young people who have been through the care courts. For example, in September 2014 the Association of Lawyers for Children and the National Youth Advocacy Service commissioned research by Dr Julia Brophy of Oxford University. The young people interviewed by her researchers were unanimous in their opposition to media attendance at Family Court hearings and to the media being given access to court documents.

They were particularly concerned that, even without the use of names in published cases, 'jigsaw identification' might reveal the identities of children who were the subject of proceedings.[17]

Personally, I'd have preferred that the current bar to the media reporting even anonymised real cases be maintained. What I think lawyer-writers and journalists should be free to write about is the type of *processes* that go on in the Family Court: I see no good reason for these to remain secret. In the same vein, it's important that the roles played in our child protection system by social workers, police, children's guardians, lawyers and judges should be well understood by the public.

I hope that this book will help lift the veil of secrecy that hangs over the work of the Family Court *without breaching confidentiality*. I also hope to enlighten those who are not already aware of the miserable and damaging circumstances in which the most deprived children in England and Wales are growing up; and to raise a number of questions about the system. What I do not intend is for any parent facing care proceedings to use this book as a source of advice on how to run their case. Faced with proceedings, the only sensible thing to do is to instruct an experienced care lawyer. Legal aid will pay their fees, regardless of the parent's financial circumstances.

2

Who's Who in Child Protection

For readers who are unfamiliar with the world of child protection, I'm going to explain the basics of the system that pertains in England and Wales. I'll try to keep the jargon to a minimum, but if you get confused you can look up acronyms in the glossary towards the end of this book. And if you work in the field you may want to skip this chapter altogether.

The two routes into care

There are two routes by which children present in England and Wales can arrive in the care system. Some enter on a voluntary basis and are described by lawyers as 'accommodated' under Section 20 of the Children Act 1989. An 'accommodated' child is one who has entered the care system without going through a court process and – generally – with the consent of the parent who has cared for them most recently. The largest group of 'accommodated' children are those whose carers are currently *'prevented, whether or not permanently, and for whatever reason*'[1] from caring for them. The potential reasons include every type of crisis an adult can get into, but common ones are physical illness, mental health breakdown, severe drug or alcohol addiction and domestic abuse. Accommodation under

S20 is also used for children whose parents are dead or have abandoned them, and for unaccompanied children seeking asylum in the UK.

In some S20 cases the parent actively requests that the local authority take the child into care; in others the parent reluctantly agrees to S20 in the knowledge that, if they don't agree, the local authority is likely to issue care proceedings.

The second route by which children enter care is as a result of a care order made by the Family Court. In these cases the local authority applies for a care order, asking the court to approve the removal of the child from its parents, regardless of whether the parents consent. In 2022, 16,058 public law applications were issued.[2]

The crucial difference in the two routes into care is the legal concept of 'parental responsibility' or 'PR'. PR is defined by law as *'all the rights, duties, powers, responsibilities and authority which by law a parent of a child has in relation to the child and his property'*.[3] The mother of every child has PR, by virtue of having given birth to them. Fathers do not get PR automatically, but can acquire it by a number of different routes, the two most common of which are being named on the birth certificate or being married to the mother at the time of the child's birth. The court can order that a father should have PR.

When a child is accommodated under S20, the local authority does not acquire PR for them, although the foster carer caring for the child can make day-to-day decisions such as what to give the child for supper and whether to take them to the GP when they're unwell. The parent with PR has the legal right to withdraw their child from care on giving very little, if any, warning. So, although the parent has temporarily handed over day-to-day responsibility for the child to the local authority, in theory, at least, she retains the upper hand. (I say 'she', because among the children who come to the attention of local authorities, it's more common for the mother than the father to be the hands-on parent.)

When a child is made the subject of a care order, on the other hand, the order places the child in the care of a specific local authority and that local authority *does* acquire PR for the child. The parents don't lose their PR, but from that point on the local authority can decide to what extent the parents can exercise it if the local authority thinks this is necessary to protect the child's welfare.[4]

To sum up, and to over-simplify: if your child's accommodated, and you don't like the way the local authority are treating them, in theory you can take your child home on giving a few hours' notice. (In practice, where the concerns are serious, there's a possibility the local authority will swiftly issue care proceedings in this situation.) If, on the other hand, your child is subject to a care order, you cannot simply decide to take the child home. You have largely lost control over the way the child is treated, and over their medium-term future.

Working together

At the core of our child protection system is the idea of 'working together to safeguard children'. This is spelled out in guidance of that name issued by government to health, education and social care agencies and updated every few years.[5]

In any given local authority area – borough, city, county – local organisations and agencies are expected to collaborate to identify children and families who may be at risk or in need of help. The bodies involved include GPs, health visitors, nurseries, schools, police and children's centres. Where serious concern is identified, it's the legal responsibility of the local authority to investigate; that work is carried out by a qualified social worker.

Social workers

All local authorities employ a number of social workers who specialise in working with children. They operate from departments variously named 'Children's Services' or 'Children's Social Care' or 'Children and Families', some of which also encompass education or health. Within each such department there are specialist teams that deal with what's known in the trade as 'front-line' child protection work, as well as teams responsible for 'family finding' (recruitment of foster carers and adopters) and teams that help disabled children.

Social work training involves either a degree in social work, a postgraduate qualification or an apprenticeship.[6] The starting salary for a newly qualified social worker is in the region of £30,000,[7] while an average social work team manager's salary is £50,000.[8] The majority of social workers are female, and Black and ethnic minority social workers are under-represented in senior and managerial positions.

In my view, to be a good and effective children's social worker requires a rare combination of personal qualities and skills – a fact which, until recently, was recognised neither in the recruitment process nor in the training and which is still not recognised in the low pay on offer. You have to be both intelligent and intuitive, with exceptionally good interpersonal skills that enable you to communicate well with everybody from a parent with a learning disability to a distraught toddler to an emotionally disturbed teenager to a High Court judge. You'll require the physical and emotional stamina for long hours of hard and stressful work, which you'll be expected to undertake with very little support. In addition, you must be able to think clearly, especially when under stress and sometimes when under personal attack; to read and digest large amounts of information at speed; and to write clearly. And you'll need the personal resources to enable you to process the human suffering that you'll witness on a daily basis, without going under.

Local authorities have great difficulty retaining children's social workers. Many social work students quit during training and many qualified social workers quit in the early years of practice.

Family support workers

The work of social workers is supplemented in most local authorities by the employment of very low-paid, unqualified staff known as 'family support workers' (FSWs). Again mostly women, they're given basic training in child protection principles and are often tasked with close face-to-face work with parents and children. This is necessary due to the huge caseloads many social workers carry, the large amount of paperwork they're expected to complete and the fact that many social work teams are permanently short-staffed. An FSW may be tasked with teaching a parent how to budget or how to improve domestic hygiene, for example; or with assisting him or her to get children to school on time. FSWs also supervise contact sessions between parents and children who are in foster care. I've known an FSW to be tasked with holding sessions with a parent, which are tantamount to counselling or therapy, despite their lack of appropriate qualifications.

Alice G was the sort of woman who would have benefited from a skilled FSW working with her very closely, to help her see how her outbursts of anger were likely to affect Poppy. (She might also have benefited from some form of therapy, but it would have taken a highly skilled practitioner of a sort that's rarely available to parents in care cases.)

Placements

When a child goes into care, the local authority is under a legal duty to try to place them with a relative or 'connected person' (usually a family friend) who is able to care for the child safely. This is called 'kinship care'. If such a person is available they should be assessed with a view, initially, to becoming a foster carer for the child, with the financial and other support this entails; and in the long run it may be appropriate for the child to be placed with them under a special guardianship order.[9] Where no such person is available, then the next option is to place the child with a 'stranger' foster carer.[10] In some circumstances, older children entering care may be placed in children's homes[11] or bespoke placements.[12]

Referrals

When a referral with regard to a particular child reaches a child protection team, the law requires that it be allocated to a social worker, who will make enquiries and decide what action if any needs to be taken. Some referrals result in 'no further action'. If there are concerns but they are relatively low level, the social worker may recommend some form of support to the child's family (which may be carried out by an FSW) and the child is categorised as a 'child in need' (CIN).

If the concerns are more serious but still at a moderate level, the social worker may call a case conference, inviting a range of professionals (headteacher, GP and health visitor, for example). At the end of the conference a vote is taken on whether the child or children should be placed on a child protection plan and, if so, under what category. A child who is on a plan should be monitored more closely than a 'child in need'.

If the concerns are very serious, then the social worker will refer the matter to their legal department. If the legal department considers that the available evidence establishes on the balance of probabilities that *the child is suffering or likely to suffer significant harm* and *that the harm, or likelihood of harm, is attributable to the care given to the child or likely to be given to him if the order were not made not being what it would be reasonable to expect a parent to give to him, or to the child's being beyond parental control*[13] then they will tell the social worker that *threshold* is met. This means that the local authority can establish the factual basis to apply for a public law order in respect of the child. A public law order is either a *care order* under which the child can be removed from the care of the parent(s) or a *supervision order* that does not entail removal but gives the local authority the power to 'assist and befriend' the child.

Where a public law order is sought in the course of care proceedings, in other words prior to the final hearing, it will be termed an 'interim' order and the local authority only has to establish that 'interim threshold' is met. This means that the test set out above is prefaced with the words *'There are reasonable grounds to believe that ...'* [the child is suffering or likely to suffer, etc.]. This is a slightly lower threshold, which allows local authorities to obtain interim care or interim supervision orders before they have amassed all the evidence.

When considering whether to make a public law order, the court has to bear in mind the relevant articles of the European Convention on Human Rights.[14] The key provisions are Article 8, the right to family life, and Article 6, the right to a fair trial.

If threshold is met and the matter is really urgent, the legal department may advise that an application should be made for an emergency protection order (EPO), under which the child can be removed from their parent(s) for up to seven days while further enquiries are made and, if necessary, care proceedings are issued. If the situation is less urgent, a legal planning meeting will be called at which a decision will be made as to whether to enter what is called the 'pre-proceedings process'. A case conference is also likely to be called, and in some cases a strategy meeting with the police and, if appropriate, health professionals.

Pre-proceedings process

The pre-proceedings process was introduced in 2014. Having had advice that threshold is met, the social worker can decide to enter this process. He or she writes a fairly alarming letter to the parent(s) spelling out why the local authority is concerned about their child and warning that, if improvements are not made, the local authority may issue care proceedings. It goes on to invite the parent(s) to a 'pre-proceedings meeting' to discuss how they can improve their parenting and to explain that they are entitled to free legal aid for a lawyer to attend with them. At the meeting the message is reiterated, and the parent is asked to engage in assessments and, often, to sign a 'Schedule of Expectations', which sets out what it is the parent is being asked to do and/or refrain from doing to keep their child safe.

In some local authorities a Family Group Conference[15] (FGC) is called at this stage. FGCs are family-led meetings that bring a network of family and friends together to make a plan for a child, supported by an independent coordinator. A recent study has shown that FGCs are effective in reducing the number of those children subject to the pre-proceedings process who are subsequently subject to care proceedings and/or taken into care.[16]

Children's guardians

A children's guardian has to be appointed by the court in every set of care proceedings, tasked with safeguarding the interests of the child or children.[17] This is a vitally important role. Local authorities are heavily constrained in what they can do for individual children by their tight budgets, and this has got worse during austerity. Thus, however good the child's allocated social worker is, she or he is likely to be under pressure from management to come up with the most inexpensive available solution for the child. In some cases this is at odds with the child's best interests, which is where the guardian comes in. Being independent of the local authority and the parents, in theory at least, the guardian has only one concern: to work out what the child needs – regardless of resource considerations – and advocate for it.

If the plan she comes up with is at odds with the local authority's plan, the guardian cannot oblige them to change course; but her views carry a lot of weight with the court, which in some circumstances does have the power to reject the local authority's plan. In many cases the guardian accepts the main plank of the plan – that the child should remain in long-term foster care, for example – but disagrees with the level of family contact proposed by the local authority or the amount of support to be offered to the child.

The guardian instructs his or her own solicitor, who attends all hearings (or briefs counsel to do so) and is referred to as the 'solicitor for the child/children'. The guardian also attends all hearings unless she or he has two or more hearings at the same time in different courts.

There's considerable variation in the way guardians operate. Some are prepared to stick their necks out for the sake of a child and incur the annoyance and sometimes downright loathing of the local authority in the area where they work; others opt for a quiet life and generally support the local authority's plans without scrutinising them too closely. And many tread a line between these two extremes.

The vast majority of guardians are former social workers. In the past they were self-employed, which afforded them a good level of independence. These days, however, they're all employed by the Children and Family Court Advisory and

Support Service (CAFCASS). There are a great many complaints about the size of guardians' workloads and the working practices of CAFCASS; many of the best guardians leave after a few years in a state of exhaustion and frustration.

Police

Every police constabulary has a specialist child protection team. Police have powers to temporarily remove a child from his or her carer in certain circumstances[18] in a process called 'taking the child into police protection' (TIPP).[19] The police sometimes use these powers in emergency situations at weekends or during bank holidays, when social workers are less available and access to the Family Court is restricted.

Where it's suspected that a criminal offence may have been committed against a child, or that there's been criminal activity affecting a child by someone in the household where the child lives, social workers will ask the police to investigate and there's supposed to be close cooperation between the two agencies. Common offences against children include sexual and physical assault and ill-treatment, neglect and abandonment.[20] Offences occurring in the household might be drug-dealing by a parent or parent's partner, domestic violence, people-trafficking or county lines activity, to name but a few possibilities.

Police are responsible for the arrest and interviewing of alleged perpetrators of offences against children and the provision of information to social workers. Sometimes criminal proceedings *and* care proceedings arise out of the same set of facts. Where a child alleges sexual abuse by an adult, for example, care proceedings may be issued to protect the child and criminal proceedings will be issued to deal with the adult.

Police are sometimes called upon by social workers to assist in the removal of a child or children from a parent after the court has authorised it, in circumstances where the parent is thought likely to resist removal.

In some areas there's good cooperation between children's social work departments and local police; in other areas the relationship is fraught. The squeeze on resources for both social workers and police during the years of austerity has created a lot of pressure, which can lead to mutual frustration at the level of service provided.

Lawyers

As to lawyers, it's important to grasp that in England and Wales the legal profession is split between solicitors and barristers, and that would-be lawyers must choose to qualify as one or the other. The level of training required is comparable, but with differing emphases. Once they're working, most barristers specialise in court-room advocacy, whereas most solicitors are office-based, and do a mixture of paperwork and meetings with clients. In the Family Court, however, a lot of solicitors[21] also do their own advocacy at the shorter ('interim') hearings, but instruct barristers ('counsel') for longer hearings. In general, family law solicitors operate from high street offices, whereas barristers operate from sets of 'chambers' – often housed in buildings near the court.

A 'brief' or set of 'instructions' is a document written by a solicitor setting out the background to the case and indicating what they want the barrister to try to achieve at the hearing in question. Barristers refer to the solicitor sending them work as their 'instructing solicitor'.[22]

Lawyers who represent parents in public law cases are paid by the Legal Aid Agency, at standardised rates. Broadly speaking, barristers earn a lot more than solicitors. A public childcare barrister working full-time in a conventional chambers may earn, gross, around £100,000 per annum. Out of this sum, they have to pay around 20 per cent to chambers, to cover clerks' fees and chambers overheads; and they have to pay for their travel, continuing professional development, computer kit and any other expenses. By contrast a solicitor specialising in public care work will earn between £35,000 and £45,000 (outside London).

A parent whose child is subject to the pre-proceedings process and/or care proceedings gets legal aid automatically, without means testing: their legal costs are paid in full by the state.

The Family Court

The single Family Court (FC) was created in April 2014. Previously there had been three types of court that heard both public and private family law cases; the creation of the FC formally united them all in a single institution.

Within the FC there are three tiers based on the former three courts, each one presided over by a judge or judges of a different level of seniority. As in the past, the lowest-tier tribunal is presided over by lay justices/magistrates, assisted by a legal adviser, as in the case of Alice G related in the Preface; the middle tier is presided over by a district judge (DJ) if the case is relatively straightforward, or a circuit judge (CJ) if it's more complex. The top tier is the preserve of High Court judges.

Judges

Judges are appointed by the Judicial Appointments Commission, which in recent years has taken steps to recruit from a more diverse demographic than in the past. Any solicitor or barrister qualified to practise in England and Wales can apply once they have a minimum of seven years' post-qualification experience. On appointment, judges who are to work in public family law are sent on a four-day residential training course, followed by continuing education.

The role of the judge

The legal framework for public family law work is set out in Part IV of the Children Act 1989, as amended by subsequent legislation and as interpreted by the Court of Appeal and Supreme Court in a vast body of jurisprudence. This is known as 'precedent' or 'case law'.

In many hearings in care proceedings, both interim 'case management' hearings and final hearings, the judge's work is largely done by the lawyers. The lawyers for each party spend long periods in discussion prior to the hearing, considering how to move the case forward. They will ask the judge to decide any points on which they are not all agreed, but much of the time they present the judge with an agreed 'draft' order. It's open to the judge to reject it, or reject parts of it, but in practice busy judges rarely interfere unless they think that what has been agreed will cause delay or other difficulties.

The role of the judge becomes more interesting where the parties disagree. This will happen, for example, where a parent opposes a local authority attempt to take their child into foster care on an interim basis; or where a children's guardian applies for a psychologist to be instructed to assess a parent and another party objects. At final hearing, the most common head-on conflict is where a parent opposes a local authority care plan of adoption, which can result in a 'contested' hearing of many days' duration.

I never heard what happened to Alice G and Poppy. After the hearing described in the Preface, I sent a detailed attendance note to my instructing solicitor, relating what had happened. I was hoping he would brief me again so that I could see the case through to a conclusion, but he did not. Whether he represented Alice himself at the adjourned final hearing, or briefed another barrister, I'll never know. A lot is said by family lawyers and the Family Court about the importance of continuity of representation, but in practice it's not always achieved. Alice must have concluded that I, too, had abandoned her.

3

Dwayne

I speed-walk from the train station to the court, dragging my wheelie bag behind me, bumping it off kerbs and skirting round piles of dog shit and discarded chips.

My client today, Dwayne F, is a thirty-five-year-old man of African Caribbean descent with a long history of crack cocaine use. He's father to Lawrence, the eldest of three young children who've recently been removed from their mother Rosie, who is white.

The father of the younger two, Jez, is a serving prisoner. Rosie's a long-term heroin user who's always struggled to provide adequate care for her children; over the last few months she has got into the habit of leaving them alone at night while she goes out to visit her dealer and his brother. Three weeks ago Lawrence, aged six, set a J cloth on fire while trying to heat up milk on the gas stove for his baby brother. He ran to a neighbour, who got the younger children out of the flat and called the fire brigade. Nobody was hurt, but the fire brigade called the police, and all three children were taken into police protection and placed in foster care. Up to now Rosie has made no attempt to get them back.

That's it, in a nutshell. L City Council issued the proceedings five days ago with only a Form C110A[1] and a statement from the social worker – I assume they were in a hurry to get the matter before the court. The statement says that on the morning after the fire, when Rosie learned what had happened, she agreed to the children being accommodated under Section 20. Allegedly she admitted to the social worker that her drug-abusing lifestyle had become increasingly chaotic and that she wasn't currently in a position to care for the children. She's now disappeared with her dealer's brother.

As I explained in Chapter 2, Section 20 allows for a child to be 'accommodated' when *'the person who has been caring for him is prevented (whether or not permanently, and for whatever reason) from providing him with suitable accommodation or care'*. The children were in their mother's sole care at the time when she abandoned them, and neither Dwayne nor Jez was in a position to step in. So the three children are in care and, however emotionally traumatised they may be by their mother's departure, from the local authority's point of view, they're 'safe'. Dwayne's son Lawrence is on his own with a single foster carer; the younger two are in a foster placement with a couple.

Local authorities are not supposed to leave young children 'languishing' in care under S20 for months or years on end for the very good reason that S20 holds the child in a kind of legal limbo, where long-term plans are not possible.

Dwayne wasn't named on Lawrence's birth certificate and he wasn't married to Rosie, so, although nobody doubts that he's the father, he doesn't have parental responsibility (PR) and he's therefore not at liberty to remove Lawrence from S20 foster care.

Whether Dwayne would actually *want* to remove Lawrence is one of the first questions I'm planning to ask him.

From the information about Dwayne that the social worker has found time to put in her statement, it's clear to me she thinks Dwayne is unfit to care for Lawrence. When I read the document last night, I got the clear impression the social worker was trying to paint as negative a picture of Dwayne as possible. Undoubtedly his situation's not great: his long history of crack cocaine use and a relatively recent conviction for drug dealing will both go against him. On the plus side, he's just completed a detox in a residential drug rehabilitation centre. Currently he's homeless, sleeping on a friend's sofa.

After hanging my coat in the robing room, I take the lift to Court 8. I spot Dwayne easily. He's tall and thin in a donkey jacket and jeans, with dreadlocks trailing over slightly stooping shoulders. When I introduce myself, his eyes light up and he shakes my hand with warmth. We find a consulting room and sit down face to face on plastic chairs across a scratched Formica table.

'This is a difficult situation,' I begin. 'You must be concerned about Lawrence.'

He flinches. 'Yeah, well, what's happened's happened. I told her she shouldn't leave the kids alone. But she didn't listen …' He raises his eyebrows with a look of suppressed anger.

'It could have been much worse.'

He flinches again, closes his eyes and shudders. 'I can't even think about that.'

'No, of course not.' I pause. 'Had you seen much of Lawrence in the last year?'

'Before I went into detox I'd take him to the football on a Saturday. And I helped her out with the little ones now and then. When I was clean, that is. There were times when I was off my head and couldn't help her.'

'But when you could, you cared for the little ones?' The baby boy's eleven months old and the girl just three.

'Not what you'd call often, but every now and then she'd send me a text and if I was free I'd go over.' He smiles. 'Lawrence loved it when I was there with the three of them. Gave him a chance to show off his little brother and sister to me.'

'Lovely kids?'

'Beautiful. All three of them.'

'So you and Rosie were friends?'

He turns his eyes on me as if he thinks the question's a bit odd. 'I'm Lawrence's father, aren't I? And the other two are his sister and brother. And she was all alone after Jez got sent down for dealing. Heavily pregnant with the youngest one. It wasn't easy for her.'

I'm impressed by the force with which Dwayne speaks; he clearly has a strong sense of family and a loyalty to Rosie, despite the fact that the two younger children aren't his.

I know from the social worker's statement that Dwayne himself had a horrible childhood. After his parents split up when he was four, he witnessed his mother being beaten up by a string of boyfriends. Some of the assaults left her so badly hurt that he and his sister had to stay home from school to look after her. Dwayne's behaviour deteriorated in his early teens and he was taken into care, but shunted through four unsuccessful placements with foster carers who struggled to contain his angry outbursts and his growing use of cannabis. Eventually, aged sixteen, he went home to his mum, got into drug-running for older friends, and after a couple of cautions was remanded into 'secure accommodation' by a criminal court.[2]

At seventeen Dwayne was released, but by then his mother had a new partner and said she wanted no more to do with him. Not surprisingly, he turned to Class A drugs and a life on the streets. In his mid-twenties he spent two years in prison for dealing crack cocaine.

When Dwayne and Rosie first met, they were both using crack. The adopted daughter of a middle-class family, Rosie dropped out of school at fifteen, ran away from home and spent the next ten years in relationships with a string of drug-abusing older men, experimenting with any and every drug she could get her hands on. At some point along the line, Rosie's adoptive parents bought her a flat. Dwayne moved in and for about a year the pair pursued their drug-abusing life-style together, attracting frequent visits from the police, who suspected Rosie was dealing.

Once Rosie fell pregnant, however, Dwayne became concerned about the likely impact of her drug use on the unborn baby. He was now twenty-eight, this was his first child and he was determined that the baby would have a better start in life than he'd had. He signed up with a drug support agency and urged Rosie to do the same. Over a period of a few months the pair came off crack, and by the time Lawrence was born their only drug use was a nightly spliff.

Lawrence was born without any symptoms of drug withdrawal.[3] The midwife and Children's Services were aware of the parents' histories, but on the face of it Lawrence was doing well and there was no reason to intervene.

Things went fine for about a year. Then Dwayne got it into his head that Rosie was having an affair. This was too much for him and he ended the relationship. It wasn't clear whether there was any basis for Dwayne's suspicions, but his departure sufficiently upset Rosie that she started using again. This time she shifted from crack to heroin and within a few months she was in a relationship with her dealer, Jez. Children's Services were worried about his influence on Rosie. Each time they visited they took Rosie to task about the unhygienic state of her flat, the fact she hadn't registered Lawrence with a GP, and her reluctance to take him to parent and toddler groups. But Rosie was a feisty woman who wasn't easily intimidated by social workers. She had answers to all their questions and put up a show of having her habit well under control.

Over the next four years Rosie and Jez went on to have two children together, Lawrence's half siblings. Rosie was heavily pregnant with the second child when Jez was arrested in an early-morning drug raid and a large quantity of heroin was found in the flat. He was remanded in custody, charged with possession of a Class A drug with intent to supply and later sentenced to eight years in prison. Rosie was left alone to cope with three small children and her now very significant heroin habit.

Over the following year Children's Services became increasingly concerned that all three children were being neglected. Lawrence had headlice and often turned up late for school, with ill-fitting clothes and no lunchbox; the younger two looked dirty and tired when Rosie came to collect Lawrence with the double buggy. One night the little girl was rushed to hospital, having consumed cannabis resin she'd found down the back of the sofa. The child recovered, but the local authority took legal advice and started the pre-proceedings process.

Just a week before the pre-proceedings meeting, Rosie left the children alone and Lawrence caught the J cloth on fire.

I reach in my bag for my laptop and boot it up. Then I sit back in my seat and look at Dwayne. I've got to grill him about his drug use, but it's important to choose the right moment. 'So,' I begin, 'how do you see the future?'

Dwayne doesn't hesitate. 'I want to care for Lawrence. He's my son, we're close, he's shattered about his mum disappearing and he should be with me.'

'Yes, of course.' Dwayne mostly stayed off drugs for three to four years after leaving Rosie, but earlier this year he had a bad lapse with crack cocaine – hence the admission to residential detox.

'Are they letting you see Lawrence at the moment?'

'Once a fortnight, for an hour.' The indignation in his tone is clear. 'With a supervisor sitting in.'

'How *is* Lawrence?'

'He's ... upset. What you'd expect from any kid whose mum's disappeared. I don't think he really gets it yet. Sometimes he talks as if she's gonna come back any minute and take him home.'

'Which the court will no way allow after what's happened,' I spell out, but I can see that Dwayne has already got it. The case is listed in front of a district judge rather than a lay bench, presumably because of the horror of what might have been if the neighbour hadn't been on hand to intervene.

'Lawrence misses his brother and sister,' Dwayne goes on. 'Always talking about them.'

'That sounds incredibly difficult. Do you find it very upsetting when you see him?' This is not strictly my business, but I've said it now.

'Course I do. It's awful. I get tempted to start using again, every day.' He stares at me hard, clearly wondering whether I have any sort of clue as to what he's going through.

'But ... you're not going to, are you? Lawrence really needs you now.' I clear my throat. 'He's always needed you, don't get me wrong, but right now you're the only person who can – maybe – get him out of care.' I must be careful not to raise Dwayne's hopes. The local authority and the court will see him as unlikely to be capable of caring for Lawrence, because of his history. We're in for a major uphill struggle, to say the least.

'I know, I know. But I ain't got nowhere to live. And for the next three months I'm on a relapse prevention programme five hours a day.'

Dwayne's lack of housing is a major problem; but even if it weren't, there's no way the court will let him take on the care of Lawrence till he's been drug-free for a substantial period.

'What drugs were you using before you did the detox?'

Dwayne looks me in the eye. 'Cannabis, daily; and crack cocaine, at least every other day.'

'Nothing else?'

'That's bad enough, isn't it?' Dwayne shoots me an ironic smile. One of his front teeth is missing.

'Just checking.'

'What about the younger two?' I go on. 'Their dad'll be in prison for another three years at least.' Jez has instructed a solicitor, but there won't be a lot she can do, beyond ask questions.

'I'd happily take them too. They're brothers and sister, they should be together. Trouble is, I'm living with my mate, sleeping on his sofa. Can't have any of the kids there.'

'Not even Lawrence?'

'Nah. My mate smokes weed half the night, I don't want Lawrence around that.'

'Don't you get tempted to smoke with him?'

'It's difficult, but I'm trying to stay clean.'

'You on the housing list?'

'Yeah, in a low band. It's going to be years before I can start bidding.'

'Okay. First things first. I'll tell the local authority you want to be assessed to care for all three children and they'll have to do a parenting assessment. It'll be a series of meetings with the social worker, over a few weeks. And they're going to want a hair strand drug test. Are you up for that?'

'I'm clean. They can test me as much as they like.' The same tone of indignation, now mixed with pride. A slow smile spreads across his face. 'Social worker doesn't like me. She thinks I'm a good-for-nothing crackhead. Well, I was then, but I'm not now. Not anymore. I'm clean.'

'Great.' I smile back, glancing at Dwayne's dreads and wondering how long his hair is without the extensions. Average hair growth is one centimetre a month. To establish Dwayne's drug use over the preceding six months, the testing agency will need strands measuring at least six centimetres. 'I'm going to tell the court that until you went into detox you were using cannabis and crack cocaine,' I go on, 'because those will show up on the test and we'll be able to stress that you've been honest about it. Don't do anything to your hair till they've taken the sample.'

'Like what?' Dwayne stares at me in surprise. 'I'm not going to dye it, if that's what you're thinking!' He lets out a sudden roar of laughter.

'Well, what do I know ...' I begin, but then I too laugh. This man is likeable. And I feel he's sincere in his belief that he can hold it together for Lawrence.

It's on the tip of my tongue to point out that the local authority will want to know why he didn't alert them to the fact that Rosie was still doing a lot of heroin, while caring for the three children alone. They may well say Dwayne failed to protect Lawrence and therefore can't be trusted to care for him. But no, I think, we'll cross that bridge later on.

Dwayne repeats that if the local authority can get him a flat, he'll happily take the younger ones as well; but first he's really got to do the relapse prevention programme. Since he can't offer Lawrence a home immediately, I suggest he shouldn't actively oppose the application for an interim care order; but we need to make an application for him to have PR for Lawrence. I leave him to mull that over and go in search of the other parties.

I find the local authority team crammed into a small consulting room across the corridor. Their counsel's a tall, thin man called Nigel Hill, whom I've known for years. He greets me as I walk in, while the very young-looking blonde social worker shoots me a stony look. Her manager stands in a corner, back to the room, talking on the phone in a low voice.

I explain that I'm acting for Dwayne F and that he wants to be assessed to care for all three children. The young social worker turns towards Nigel with a thinly veiled look of disbelief and wrinkles up her nose.

'All three?' Nigel replies in his smooth BBC accent, studiously ignoring the social worker. 'That sounds rather ambitious. Isn't he living in temporary accommodation? And where's he at with the crack cocaine?'

I explain about Dwayne's recent detox, his commitment to the relapse prevention programme and his housing situation. 'He's not asking to take the children today,' I clarify. 'He wants to be assessed and he'd like more contact.' I gaze directly at the young social worker, who's now glaring at me across the table.

'He sees Lawrence once a fortnight,' she spits. 'The child's just had his mum vanish on him; he can't be expected to go to contact more often than that.'

I glance at Nigel to check he doesn't object to my speaking directly to his client. 'But why not?' I ask. 'Surely seeing his dad is the best possible thing. Somebody familiar. Somebody who loves him. My client would like the contact increased to twice a week. And he'd like to see the little ones, as well.'

Now the social worker regards me with fury. 'He's not their dad.'

I glance again at Nigel, who's looking faintly embarrassed by his client's attitude. 'He doesn't need to be their dad,' I reply coldly. 'He's their brother's father and a person who's well known to them. These children have just lost their mother and are living with strangers. It must be in their interests to see an adult they've known all their lives.'

I'm just wondering whether to point out that Dwayne was involved at times in a caring role, but the social worker cuts into my thoughts.

'If your client's got such a close relationship with the younger children,' she hisses, 'why didn't he tell us about Rosie's heroin habit?'

I turn to her with an icy stare. 'You'll have to ask him that,' I reply, 'when you assess him. I understood from your statement that the local authority was well aware of Rosie's habit; in which case why did they need Dwayne to tell them about it?'

The door opens and the children's guardian walks in, a slim young woman called Fiona Gratehead, whom I've heard of but never previously met. She's one of the latest group of newly appointed guardians for this area. I'm not much good at judging age, but I'd put her in her late twenties. She's accompanied by a short African man, her counsel.

Nigel updates them about our discussions and Fiona asks me where she can find my client. I ask for her view about the contact frequency, and she looks a bit flustered and says she'll give it some thought.

The next person to arrive is a middle-aged woman solicitor called Sally Reeves, who's representing Jez. She carries a patent leather bag with a gold chain and gives the impression of being rather bored with the case.

Nigel's sitting at the table drafting an order on his laptop. 'Viability assessments,' he calls out, trying to get our attention. 'Teresa, Sally, are your clients putting anybody forward?'

In every set of care proceedings the parents are asked to put forward names of any relatives or friends who could care for the children if the court deems the parents incapable of doing so. It's for the local authority to carry out 'viability' assessments of these people, to establish whether they may be suitable as kinship carers. If a viability assessment has a positive conclusion, the local authority will then be asked to do a more detailed assessment of the same person, over a period of about twelve weeks.[4]

I've already asked Dwayne if he wants to put anybody forward. His only relatives are his mother and sister. He gets on well with his sister, but she's got three children of her own and works full-time, so he doesn't feel he can ask her. As to his mother, their relationship has been strained for many years and he only speaks to her when he has to. And he's not convinced she'd be good for Lawrence.

Sally Reeves tells Nigel that Jez hasn't got anybody to put forward.

I'm listening with interest. It seems the case will boil down to a question of can Dwayne take on these kids or do they have to spend the rest of their childhoods separated from family. Which for Lawrence is likely to mean long-term foster care, because of his age and the strength of his attachments; but – now my stomach takes a lurch – for the younger two could mean adoption.

Just as I'm opening my mouth to enquire how the local authority see the children's future, Fiona Gratehead returns from meeting Dwayne and the court clerk puts her head round the door.

'Judge wants you in,' she tells us. 'I know you're still in discussions, but it's five past ten and if you don't come in now you're gonna get stuck behind his day case.'

Nobody wants that, so I dart across the corridor to fetch Dwayne and we file into court. We're in front of District Judge S, and Dwayne has to sit behind me, alone in the middle of the row, while Fiona sits at the far end. In my row there's Nigel Hill on the far left, then me, then Sally Reeves and, at the end, counsel for the children.

4

Initial Hearing

District Judge S is the most efficient of the district judges who sit at this court centre. He has neat salt and pepper hair and is probably in his mid-fifties. I watch as he strides across the podium with a purposeful air and slides into his high-backed red chair, gesturing to us all to take our seats.

'I've read your case summary,' he tells Nigel, 'and the social worker's statement. Very narrow escape these children have had.' He looks worried, but there's kindness in his eyes too. He scans all of our faces until his gaze comes to a rest on Dwayne. 'You must be Mr F. Thank you for attending court. We must all be extremely grateful to the neighbour who stepped in.'

Taken aback, I glance at Dwayne. He's also clearly surprised, but he looks District Judge S in the eye. 'Yeah,' he says slowly. 'Yeah, I am very grateful to her.'

'And the father of the younger two,' the district judge continues, 'is a serving prisoner, isn't he, and no link has been set up for him to attend today's hearing by video platform. Mr Hill, would you care to introduce the legal representatives?'

Nigel rattles through the introductions, going on to tell the district judge that the making of interim care orders for the children is unopposed and we've agreed a number of directions. In the traditional order of things, the mother's advocate speaks after the local authority has finished, followed by the advocate(s) for the father(s) and the advocate for the children. But as Nigel falls silent, I realise that, in the absence of the mother or anyone to represent her, I'm next.

'Miss Thornhill.' By the subtlest twitch of his eyebrows, District Judge S conveys that he's well disposed towards my client and ready to listen to what I have to say. I explain that, although Mr F doesn't oppose the making of an interim care order for Lawrence, he wishes to apply for parental responsibility for him and is putting himself forward to take on his full-time care. He's completed his detox, is about to start a relapse prevention programme and if he can sort out his housing he'll be asking the court to place Lawrence in his care as soon as he's finished the programme. And in the long run, he'd like to be considered to care for the younger two.

As I speak, District Judge S slowly nods. 'What does your client say about his current drug use?'

'He says he's drug-free. He was using cannabis and crack cocaine before the detox, but he got through it successfully and now he's clean.' I draw breath. 'We've included provision for hair strand testing in the order.' I pause to let this information sink in. 'In the meantime, Sir, Mr F is anxious to have his contact with Lawrence increased. Mr F has been a constant figure in Lawrence's life and feels his son really needs to see him more often than once a fortnight.' I look the district judge in the eye to ensure he's listening carefully. 'The child's in a placement on his own, separated from his siblings and missing his mother. And my client would also like to see the younger two.'

I swivel round in my seat towards Dwayne. It's my way of saying to the judge, 'Look at my client, see what a decent guy he is.' I often do this when I want to encourage a level of non-verbal communication between the judge and my client.

District Judge S turns to counsel for the children, who stands as I sit down. 'What does the guardian say about contact frequency?'

'She hasn't met the children yet, Sir,' counsel replies. 'She plans to see them in the next few days. Once she's done that she'll be able to form a view. We've made provision for her to file an initial analysis.' This is the document that the guardian has to file as soon as possible after the issue of proceedings.

'In that case we'll revisit the contact issue at the next hearing.' District Judge S turns back to Nigel. 'You can have twenty-four hours to finalise the order. Thank you all very much.' He stands up, dismissing us with an energetic nod.

When we get back to the consulting room, I tell Dwayne that the contact issue will largely depend on what the guardian says after she's met Lawrence. If she agrees he needs to see his dad more often, the local authority just *may* back down.

Dwayne throws me a look of cynicism. 'Not that social worker – she's got it in for me.'

'If she's got it in for you, we'll need to think about applying for you to be assessed by an independent social worker, someone who doesn't work for the local authority. But for now, you need to get stuck into the relapse prevention programme and stay in close contact with your solicitor.' Privately I'm wrestling with whether to warn Dwayne that the local authority may propose adoption for the younger two. No, I decide, that will cause him immense pain and he needs his strength right now, so we'll cross that bridge when we come to it. I tell Dwayne I'll look forward to seeing him at the next hearing.

But as I walk back to the station I consider how I could mount an argument against adoption. If Rosie fails to fight for her children, and if no other relative or friend comes forward, it will all depend on what Dwayne has to offer by the time of the final hearing. If the local authority remain opposed to him, they will have to convince the court that nothing short of adoption will meet the children's needs, a test often phrased as 'nothing else will do'.

This test derives from a line of case law that began in 2013. To place it in context, I must briefly jump back to 2000, when the then prime minister Tony Blair published a white paper announcing a policy of increasing the number of children adopted annually from the care system and speeding up the process.[1] The goal was for a 40 per cent increase in adoptions from care by 2004/05. There was to be an overhaul of the legislative framework, financial support for adopters, national standards and a national adoption register to help with the process of matching individual children with suitable adopters. The result was the Adoption and Children Act 2002, which also provided for the new legal status of special guardianship.

Whether or not it was wise, Blair's push to increase the use of adoption was successful, and growing numbers of children were adopted from care between 2000 and 2015.[2] The push was followed up by adoptee Michael Gove, who regards himself as a fine example of what adoption can achieve for a person's life chances. In 2011, while secretary of state for education, Gove announced plans to 'tackle delay in the adoption system' by a range of means.[3] These included speeding up the process of assessing prospective adopters and the removal of perceived obstacles in the process of matching children with them. Gove frequently spoke publicly about the merits of adoption and his influence probably accelerated a tendency on the part of local authorities to treat adoption as the preferred solution for younger children in their care, without always sufficiently considering the particular circumstances of the individual child. This somewhat careless approach led to growing concern on the part of senior judges, articulated in two landmark decisions in 2013.

The case of *Re B* concerned an application to place a three-year-old girl for adoption, which had been granted in the lower court.[4] When the parents appealed to the Supreme Court, the judges cited jurisprudence from the European Court of Human Rights that stressed that it's generally in the best interests of a child for her ties with family to be maintained except in cases where the family has proved particularly unfit, and, therefore, that family ties may only be severed in very exceptional circumstances:

> Everything must be done to preserve personal relations and, where appropriate, to 'rebuild' the family. It is not enough to show that a child could be placed in a more beneficial environment for his upbringing.[5]

Later in the judgment, it's stated that a care order with a care plan of adoption should only be made by a court where 'nothing else will do';[6] that it is a 'last resort',[7] to be made only in 'exceptional circumstances'[8] and can only be justified by 'overriding requirements pertaining to the child's welfare'.[9]

Three months later Sir James Munby, then president of the Family Division, gave judgment in the Court of Appeal in the case of *Re B-S*,[10] which again concerned adoption. He used this as an opportunity to speak out:

> We have real concerns, shared by other judges, about the recurrent inadequacy of the analysis and reasoning put forward in support of the case for adoption, both in the materials put before the court by local authorities and guardians and also in too many judgments. This is nothing new. But it is time to call a halt.[11]

He went on to state that in a care application where the plan is adoption, there must be evidence from both local authority and guardian addressing *all* the options that are realistically possible, containing an analysis for and against each option;[12] and that such evidence had been missing in a remarkable number of recently appealed cases.

Munby also said that the judge in an adoption case must not adopt a 'linear process' but instead must undertake a 'global, holistic, multi-faceted evaluation of the child's welfare', taking account of all the pros and cons of each option.[13] He stated that, although the child's interests are paramount, the court must not lose sight of the fact that those interests include being brought up by its natural family, unless welfare concerns make that impossible.[14]

These two cases were seen by lawyers acting for parents as very helpful statements of essential principles, ones that we could put to good use in our attempts to stem the tide of children being placed for adoption against their parents' wishes and, arguably, against their own interests.

I'm going through all this in my mind as I enter the station. The key issue for Dwayne will be whether he can demonstrate that what he has to offer the younger two children makes him a 'realistic option' for their long-term care, probably under a special guardianship order; it will then be for the trial judge to weigh up the pros and cons of care by Dwayne against the pros and cons of adoption. In reaching a decision in an adoption application, the judge's paramount consideration is the child's welfare throughout his or her life,[15] and he or she must pay attention to the adoption welfare checklist.[16]

5

By the Light of
the Moon

The cold air stings my cheeks as I follow my son across the field in the darkness. His headtorch spills a pool of harsh white light onto the baked earth path, causing the grassy slopes above and below to disappear into the night. I have to walk fast to keep up with him; his legs are now longer than mine and, under the pressure of GCSEs, his childhood habit of ambling slowly across fields has metamorphosed into an energetic, purposeful gait.

When we reach the kissing gate into the woods, he slips through and holds it open for me.

'All right, Mum? How's the case coming along?'

For a second I hesitate. Today's a Sunday and I've been at my desk since ten this morning, reading the papers and preparing cross-examination for a three-day final hearing that starts tomorrow. I'm feeling jaded, but the frosty air will pick me up.

'Don't ask, darling. It's a grim one … but I'm almost there.' I step through the gate and sling the loop of straw-bale string over the gatepost. 'How's the maths going?'

'Quite good, actually. I think I've cracked simultaneous equations.'

'Good on you, darling. You seem to be working very hard.'

'Not really, Mum. I slept till lunchtime.'

He was at a party till two in the morning, but he's been studying all afternoon and evening, with our cat curled tightly on his lap. This night-time sortie is the shared reward for our hard slog. We take the familiar track along the edge of the woods, in the shelter of the steep, forested hillside that rises to our right. Our booted feet crunch on beech leaves and we breathe in the winter night-time smells of damp and mould. There are muntjacs in here at night, and badgers, foxes, owls.

'Hey, Mum, look.' My son stops and points to a gleam of silvery white showing through the trees at the top of the hill. As we stand there in the stillness, the gleam becomes a crescent shape then a disc, casting a cool grey light over the spindly branches of the tallest trees. 'Isn't that cool. I think it's full.'

A loud rustling sound issues from the darkness far above us, followed by silence, then a crash, as if something's hurtling down through the undergrowth. Afraid for a second, I grab my son's arm.

'It's okay, Mum, it's just a fox.'

We walk on slowly and the sound stops as suddenly as it started.

'Gone down his hole,' my son announces in a tone of satisfaction. 'Back with Mrs Fox and the child foxes. I bet it's really cosy down there …'

'Bit damp, don't you think?'

'Not if you're covered in fur. And I bet they're all cuddled up together, Mum, Dad and all the babies.'

I love the way my son flips from cool teenager to playful young boy. 'Well, yes, that does sound nice.'

'Mum,' he says a moment later, back in his almost-adult persona, 'have you booked our tickets for the Pyrenees?'

'Not yet, but it's on my to-do list. Have you decided who you want to bring with us?'

For the last few years I've spent a couple of summer weeks walking in the French Pyrenees with various friends. By day we follow the red and white signage painted onto tree trunks and boulders, climbing to a high col most mornings and descending to a hamlet in the afternoon. At night we stay in refuges, sharing convivial three-course meals at trestle tables with whoever else happens to be in the same corner of the mountains. Physically it's exhausting, but I love the rugged landscape, and the rhythm of walking restores my weary mind and heart like nothing else.

Last summer, smelling adventure, my son asked to come with me and bring one of his school friends along. At fourteen the two lads were strong enough to carry backpacks and fit enough to climb a thousand vertical metres without complaining. They loved the mountains and the sense of freedom that comes with walking on, day after day. I put them in charge of watching the sky for signs of thunderstorms and scanning patches of dense undergrowth for brown bears.

My son names the friend he wants to bring with us this coming summer. 'He's asked his parents and they said it's fine. But you'd better email them.'

I smile in the darkness. To my son, it's a matter of a quick email exchange, not seeing that I have to convince the parents that their child will be safe with me in a mountain range in a foreign country. 'Okay,' I say, 'I'll call his mum next weekend.'

We're climbing now on a steep and narrow path that zig-zags up the hillside. My son's in front, but he holds his headtorch in his hand, illuminating the frosty ground at our feet. The air's cold on my cheeks and I pull my hat down over my ears.

'Which way now?' he asks as we reach the top of the hill. His breath comes out in a cloud of vapour.

'Along and down, it's getting late.' I need to pack my bag for court tomorrow and get to bed. My son will probably return to his laptop; he's a night bird and I've given up trying to change his habits.

We turn sharply to the right and follow the broad track along the top of the wood in the light of the moon. Branches crack below us, an owl hoots in the distance. At a fork we take the right-hand path and now we're descending steeply, back into the darkness of the lower-lying ground. In the far distance I see lights piercing the black, from the windows of the row of cottages where we live.

'When are we going, Mum?'

'Pyrenees?'

'Yeah.'

'Late July, about a week after school finishes.'

'What month is it now?' For some reason my son has never learned the order of the months.

'February. Almost your birthday.'

'Aww. I wish it was sooner we were going.'

I slip my arm through his. 'So do I, darling. I'd go next week if I could …'

6

The Psychologist's Evidence

Kylie G, a slight, frail-looking lass with a pale face, curly brown hair and green eyes, is the twenty-one-year-old mother of two little boys aged eighteen months and three. We met for the first time at nine o'clock this morning and in the course of our forty-five-minute conference I took quite a shine to her: she came across as vulnerable, sensitive and intelligent, with a powerful love for her kids.

Today is day one of the final hearing at which the children's fate will be decided. They've been in foster care for six months and the local authority are seeking a full care order and a placement order for each child,[1] the care plan being adoption. We're in front of His Honour Judge P, a kind man in his early sixties with old-school good manners and a knack for creating a calm atmosphere in his courtroom. Just as well, because counsel for the local authority is the grumpiest man at the local bar and counsel for the children is a sharp-tongued blonde woman who makes no secret of her contempt for parents.

Before leaving home this morning I checked I had a good supply of Panadol, anticipating a headache by lunchtime.

The key witness today is the consultant psychologist who assessed Kylie some months back. He's not a medic but likes to be referred to as 'Dr Moodlie'.

Where an expert such as a psychologist is instructed in care proceedings, it's generally the solicitor for the children who takes the formal lead. All parties contribute to the wording of the 'letter of instruction', which sets out what issues the expert is to address in his report; but in court the lawyer for the children gets to question him first.

At 9.45 am I ask Kylie to wait for me in the consulting room and walk across the concourse to the women's toilets. On the way I pass a bench where a lean man of middling age with bushy eyebrows and wire-rimmed spectacles sits very upright, his hands wrapped around a bundle of papers. As I pass, a cloud of tension wafts towards me. Oh dear, I think, that'll be Dr Moodlie.

I didn't warm to the man when I read his forty-page report on Kylie yesterday, in which he fully concurred with the local authority view that my client is incapable of providing good enough parenting to her boys. As I leave the toilets a few moments later I take a closer look at the figure on the bench, but his grim demeanour doesn't change my response: his jaw is clamped in a pessimistic line.

There's a shortage these days of adult psychologists willing to act as expert witnesses in care proceedings. I can't help wondering whether the decision to instruct this particular man, previously unknown to any of the lawyers in the case, was a wise one. We tend to go for experts we know.

At 10.15 we're summoned into court and I do my best to settle Kylie in the seat behind me. Her eyes are brimming with tears, her hands are shaking and I'm not convinced she'll make it through the morning. His Honour Judge P has noticed her distress; he leans forward in his seat, smiles a kind judicial smile and says how pleased he is that she has come to court today. Listening to the evidence will be hard, he tells her, and if it all gets too much all she has to do is whisper to Ms Thornhill that she needs a break. I swivel round towards Kylie as he speaks, reading a mixture of surprise, relief and embarrassment in her expression.

Counsel for the local authority gives the briefest of openings, reminding the court that he's set out all the key points in the written case summary he filed on Friday. As he sits down, counsel for the children rises to her feet and asks the clerk to fetch the witness. A few moments later the court door opens and the man with the bushy eyebrows walks towards the witness stand. The bundle of papers has disappeared and he's carrying a stiff leather briefcase, which he deposits uneasily on the floor beside his seat. His Honour Judge P greets him politely and asks whether he wishes to swear on the Bible or affirm; and does he prefer to sit or stand to give his evidence? Dr Moodlie says he'll affirm, and that he'd prefer to sit, please. As he sinks into the chair he lifts a hand to remove his spectacles but then changes his mind.

Counsel for the children asks Dr Moodlie to look at the court bundle in its ring binder on the witness stand and tells him where to find his assessment report, in Section E. Can he tell His Honour whether or not he still stands by his conclusion, namely that my client cannot safely care for her boys?

We wait in silence as Dr Moodlie struggles to lift wodges of paper and force them to slide over the metal hoops in the ring binder. Watching a nervous witness find their way around a court bundle would make a good, if cruel, spectator sport. Somewhat red in the face, at last Dr Moodlie announces he has located his report.

'And do you stand by your conclusion? Anything you wish to add?'

'Nothing to add,' he replies in a gruff tone of voice.

Next, Dr Moodlie is cross-examined at greater length by counsel for the local authority. The gist of his message remains the same: the young woman sitting behind me is a badly damaged individual and lacks the personal resources required to raise her sons.

'You don't use the term "personality disorder" in your report,' says counsel. 'Does she meet the criteria?'

'Well, she's young, so it's difficult to be certain. She displays traits of emotionally unstable borderline personality disorder, certainly.'

And now it's my turn. After a quick glance at Kylie, who has stopped shaking and is eyeing Dr Moodlie with a wounded expression, I get to my feet, pushing aside my feeling of dislike and forcing myself to smile at him. 'Good morning, Dr Moodlie,' I begin, throwing my voice across the courtroom towards the witness stand. 'I ask questions on behalf of the mother.'

The witness nods.

'At page E56 of the bundle,' I go on, 'you commend my client for engaging in the Triple P Parenting programme.[2] I assume you noted that Ms G participated in ALL ten sessions?'

Dr Moodlie grunts.

'A positive step, would you agree?'

He leans back in his chair, tips his head so that his nose is pointing up into the air, interlocks his fingers and sighs noisily. 'It's a start, certainly. But the key thing for Kylie is going to be the therapy.'

I bridle. 'Kylie' – my client may be young, but she's not his daughter. 'I'll come on to the question of therapy in a moment, Doctor Moodlie, but I'd like to stick with Triple P for the time being.' Rule number one when cross-examining professionals is to make sure that you, the advocate, remain in control; once you allow them to let rip with the points they're determined to make, you've lost the battle. 'Triple P is a challenging programme, is it not?'

Dr Moodlie shrugs his shoulders. For him, he seems to imply, Triple P would be a breeze.

'Many participants in Triple P drop out before the end of the course,' I continue. 'I assume you're aware of that?'

'Attendance patterns,' he replies in a tone of boredom, 'are not within my field of expertise. But yes, Kylie stuck it out to the end, or so it seems.'

'Or so it seems': a nice turn of phrase, implying that positive comments about my client may not be accurate. I ignore it. 'Her full attendance demonstrates a certain dogged determination, wouldn't you agree?'

He glares at me over the top of his spectacles and his tone becomes brusque. 'I draw no conclusions of that nature. She attended the sessions, that's all I can say.'

It's time to move on. 'I take it you've seen the updating documents filed after you wrote your report?'

He makes a curious hiccupping sound that seems to mean yes.

'Then you'll be aware that even the social worker acknowledges there have been no concerns about the condition of the flat in recent weeks? All clean and tidy when she visited on 3 January; no rubbish in the stairwell, no noise complaints from neighbours?'

'Which shows she can cope when the children are in foster care,' he replies slowly, not trying to hide his annoyance at having to repeat what he's already said in answer to questions from counsel for the local authority. 'It doesn't prove she'd be able to manage if she had them in her care.'

He's right, of course. The young woman seated behind me has had periods when she wasn't coping very well. At times the depression that haunts her has made it impossible for her to stay on top of things.

It was bad last May. Kylie brought the children to nursery late, sometimes with dribbles of breakfast on their clothing, sometimes hungry and asking for food. Both boys had headlice, which Kylie was slow to treat. The nursery workers saw the dark shadows under the young mother's eyes and noticed she'd lost so much weight that her clothes were hanging off her. Their referral to social services brought a young male social worker to Kylie's door and, unfortunately, on that particular morning she hadn't emptied the kitchen bin. Dirty nappies lay on the floor beside a child's safety cup full of rancid milk. Kylie herself was in pyjamas at 11 am, her unmade bed visible through a doorway.

I change tack. 'I take it you've read through the contact logs?'

Since their removal into foster care, Kylie has only been allowed to see her boys twice a week in a small room at the local children's centre, under the supervision of a family support worker, who writes a detailed log of each session. These show that Kylie has attended every contact offered (save for the one that clashed with her grandmother's funeral), and that her handling of the children has been warm and consistent. She's also had occasional contact via FaceTime, but the toddler won't engage and the three-year-old gets upset after a few minutes and says he wants to go home to Mummy.

'Yes, there's nothing in the logs that particularly worries me.' Dr Moodlie clears his throat. 'But as with the hygiene issue, it's one thing to turn up reliably for contact and quite another to have full-time care of two small children, seven days a week.'

Like 90 per cent of the mothers I represent, Kylie's a lone parent. She's of average intelligence, according to Dr Moodlie's cognitive tests, and my impression is that she desperately wants to do right by her boys. If the nursery hadn't made that referral, she might have been left to her own devices, to muddle through as best she could. But the social worker went back to his office and started to dig in the files, and soon alarm bells were ringing. Sixteen years ago Kylie herself came to the attention of the local authority when she and her two little sisters – all under six at the time – were taken into care after their mother was pushed down a flight of steps by the father of the youngest. A few weeks later the children were sent home to their mother, but from then on social services kept an eye on the family.

The background is set out in detail in the social worker's evidence. When Kylie reached eleven, her mother found a new partner who seemed a cut above her previous men; he was kind and gentle and helped with the children. The mother left Kylie and her sisters in his care when she worked the late shift at the local supermarket. After the younger two were in bed he led Kylie to the sofa and forced himself upon her, not once, but multiple times. Kylie's mother didn't believe what Kylie told her and at age fourteen, after three years of abuse, she fled to her grandmother, who called the police.

Kylie's allegation was taken seriously by the local force, but the alleged perpetrator went to ground before he could be interviewed, so there was no prosecution. Estranged from her mother, who insisted on standing by her absent man, Kylie lived with the grandmother for the remainder of her school years. These ended abruptly when she became pregnant, at seventeen, by an older boy she'd met in the park. Initially Kylie and the baby stayed with the grandmother, until, just before her second child was born, the local housing association gave Kylie a flat.

Another thing that set the alarm bells ringing concerned Darren, the twenty-five-year-old father of Kylie's older boy. The social worker learned that twice in the last year he'd been arrested on suspicion of sexual activity with underage boys. The first boy was fifteen, the second fourteen. There wasn't enough evidence to prosecute, but a social worker visited Kylie and warned her not to allow Darren to have unsupervised contact with his son. Despite this, the nursery say Darren has brought the child in, alone, on a number of recent occasions. From this the social worker concludes that Kylie, as a survivor of sexual abuse, lacks insight into the risk posed by her ex-partner and is therefore incapable of protecting either of her children from the risk of history repeating itself. It's something of an orthodoxy among child protection professionals that adult survivors of childhood sexual abuse lack insight into sexual exploitation risks to their own children. What the social worker doesn't seem to grasp is that as a young mother living in social isolation, it's almost inevitable that Kylie will occasionally accept help from unsuitable people.

Having trawled through the files, the social worker sought legal advice from his in-house lawyers as to whether pre-proceedings work should be started. Meanwhile, a week later he made another surprise visit to Kylie, at ten in the morning. Nobody answered when he knocked on the flat door, so he walked round to the front of the building and peered through the window of Kylie's ground-floor living room. The curtains were open and the baby lay on the floor, dressed only in a vest and chewing on a piece of cardboard. The three-year-old was squatting beside his brother, a packet of pills in his hand; Kylie was nowhere to be seen. As the social worker watched, the three-year-old managed to pop one of the pills out of its foil casing and slip it into his mouth. At that point, understandably, the panicked social worker thumped the window with the fist of one hand while calling the police with the other.

Before the police arrived, a dishevelled and anxious Kylie staggered to the flat door and let the social worker in, saying she'd overslept. She seemed genuinely horrified at the sight of her son holding the packet of paracetamol, but couldn't explain what it had been doing on the floor, nor could she recall how many pills had been in it when she went to bed the night before. She agreed that the child should be rushed to hospital for observation, not anticipating that later that day both children would be made the subject of an emergency protection order and placed in foster care. (The three-year-old later proved to be in rude health, with no symptoms of having swallowed more than the one pill.)

'It's fairly clear from the contact logs,' I resume, 'that this mother dotes on her boys – do you accept that?'

Dr Moodlie stares at me through lowered eyebrows. 'I don't disagree.' He shifts awkwardly in the chair and presses his spectacles against the bridge of his nose.

'Now, I want to ask you some questions about Ms G's mental health. We know she's on sertraline, 50mg, and is compliant with taking it.' Kylie's medical records were disclosed to the psychologist and he's set out in detail the antidepressant medication she's taken since the age of sixteen, the suicide attempt when she was seventeen (just before she got pregnant) and the minor overdose at nineteen that had her briefly hospitalised. 'You're recommending that she undergoes either schema-focused cognitive therapy (SFCT) or cognitive analytic therapy (CAT). How would she go about obtaining either of those?'

I know damn well, from bitter past experience with other clients, that it's most unlikely the NHS would provide either of these in the area where my client lives. To be offered even cognitive behavioural therapy (CBT) on a one-to-one basis, you have to have made two serious suicide attempts in the recent past. But I've no intention of making life easy for Dr Moodlie; he's been paid a handsome sum out of public funds to assess my client and write his report, so he can explain why he's recommended something that's not available.

'She needs to go and see her GP.'

'She's done that, Dr Moodlie, three months ago. She was told to self-refer to Happy Heads.' Happy Heads is an independent commercial venture to whom the NHS in Kylie's area sub-contracts the task of providing what it calls 'short-term psychological therapies' – meaning unclear.

'If you look at mother's statement, at C77,' I go on, 'you'll see that she self-referred to Happy Heads back in November, and is on a waiting list. She's been told it'll be at least another six months before any help is offered. In the meantime, it was suggested that she look at the company's website for tips on how to improve her mental health.'

I swing round briefly to check how Kylie's doing. For me this is both the most excruciating bit of the evidence for the client, where the poor woman has to witness professionals coldly discussing her mental health as if she were a malfunctioning dishwasher, and the part that makes me the most furious. How can a young woman whose depression developed after witnessing domestic abuse as a young child, followed by three years of repeated sexual abuse *and* abandonment by her mother, be expected to benefit from tips on a website?

Kylie's got her elbows resting on the desk, her face shielded from view by her hands. Her fingernails are chewed to stumps.

I turn back to the witness. 'You say at E77 that Ms G will need to do between twenty and twenty-four sessions of either SFCT or CAT, over a period of six months. It's hard to see how that would fit within the definition of "short-term psychological therapy", is it not?'

'I can't answer that. It depends on how Happy Heads defines "short-term".'

'Perhaps it will assist if I tell you that Ms G has already been offered a group that meets online, once a week for six weeks. That sort of intervention appears to be what's meant by "short-term".'

'I wasn't aware she'd been offered group-work. Has it started?'

'No, Dr Moodlie, Ms G didn't feel able to join a group where she'd be expected to discuss her difficulties with ten strangers. Hardly surprising, is it?'

I turn a stern, unsmiling gaze on the witness, before glancing across the courtroom to assess, fleetingly, whether His Honour Judge P gets the point I'm making. His eyes are downcast, as he scribbles by hand in a large hardback notebook. Good, I think, he's paying attention. And the sight of the pen in his hand sends a brief glow of affection through me; His Honour Judge P is seriously old school, with a reputation for old-fashioned compassion.

Dr Moodlie clears his throat. 'Group work's not what I had in mind.'

'I come back to my original question, Dr Moodlie. It's clearly urgent for Ms G to do the therapy if she's to have any prospect of resuming the children's care. Ideally she would have started it some months back, and it's vital that she starts it now. How should she go about obtaining the SFCT or CAT that you recommend?'

This is as close as I want to go at present in referring to the local authority care plan. The social worker says that Kylie's difficulties are too deep-seated and long-standing for her to address them in what the courts refer to as the 'timescale of the children', and the guardian agrees. On Dr Moodlie's reckoning, Kylie's therapy will take at least six months, and there's no certainty that it will effect the change in her mental health required for her to provide 'good enough' parenting. These are very young children, the social worker points out, currently settled in foster care, who at present would have a reasonable prospect of being able to form new attachments to adoptive parents.

Dr Moodlie stares at me coldly. 'I've answered that. The usual route is via the GP. If she's done that, and is on a waiting list, I've nothing further to suggest.'

'But Dr Moodlie, you're not even sure that when Ms G gets to the top of the waiting list she'll be offered the type of therapy you've recommended. Does the NHS in Ms G's locality provide SFCT or CAT, or does it not?'

I know he's going to say this is not a question he can answer; but surely it's something he should have considered before making his recommendation?

'You'd have to ask *them* that. I've specified the type of therapy she requires; I can't go beyond that. Service provision is not within my remit.'

'But you appreciate the urgency of the situation, from her point of view?' I smile now, trying to appeal to the human being hidden behind those tufty eyebrows.

'Mental health services are under a lot of pressure,' he replies blandly, then adds, as if he's had a blinding flash of inspiration,

'There are sure to be some SFCT practitioners operating privately in Kylie's area. It would be open to the court to fund the therapy, if it considers that it can be undertaken within the timescale of the children.'

Now he really has stepped outside of his field of expertise and it's my turn to sigh. 'Sadly it would not be open to the court to do that, Dr Moodlie. The court has no power to fund therapy for a parent.'

'Well, the court could order the local authority to fund it.'

'No, Dr Moodlie, again the court has no such power in law.'

The local authority could fund the therapy *without* being ordered to do so, of course. My instructing solicitor pleaded with them to fund it as soon as she saw Dr Moodlie's report back in October, knowing that the timescale of the children argument would be used against the client and pretty convinced that SFCT or CAT would not be available on the local NHS. She found a private practitioner of SFCT on the internet and established that they charged £95 per hour. She sent the therapist's CV to the local authority lawyer, arguing that Kylie was a very young mother, barely out of childhood herself, who had been through extremely adverse childhood experiences and yet who might be able to provide 'good enough' parenting if she were given adequate support. But the social work team had already made up their minds against her. Instead of seeking to persuade senior management that here was a deserving case, where a young family might be able to remain intact if the local authority dug into its pocket, the team's lawyer replied to my instructing solicitor with a curt refusal, referring to Kylie's lack of insight into the alleged risk posed by Darren, the incident with the paracetamol, and the budgetary cuts to which the local authority had been subjected in the past financial year.

And since the date of that email, nearly four months have gone by. Four precious months in which my client could have done more than half the required therapy while the children were in foster care, if funding had been available. Now, of course, it will be argued that it's 'too late'. Family Court judges are under huge pressure to avoid delay, even where the alternative is adoption by strangers. This is the fate towards which Kylie's little boys are inexorably heading.

'This situation's urgent, isn't it?' I put to Dr Moodlie. 'The clock's ticking loudly. These small children are growing up very fast – and you're aware of the care plan the local authority's putting forward.'

'I am.'

'You've said it's doubtful that Ms G can do the therapy and achieve the changes in her functioning in the children's timescales. But on the present evidence, the court can't be certain of that. Surely the only way to establish it is for the therapy to be provided?'

Dr Moodlie rubs his thumb along the side of his jaw. 'There are never any guarantees, with talking therapy. She might get better; or she might find it too difficult and be unable to engage.' He pauses. 'Either way it wouldn't be a good idea for her to have care of the children while she's doing the therapy. The therapist will have to go into some difficult areas and the whole process could prove quite destabilising.'

'So it should be done now,' I press, 'while the children are in foster care. Would you agree?'

For present purposes I'm ignoring the fact that the local authority has already identified adopters and intends to start introductions within two weeks of the court making final orders, which it will be asked to do at the end of the hearing. For even if, by some magical turn of events, some angelic body offered to fund the therapy today, I would be fighting a losing battle arguing that the children should remain in foster care while Kylie underwent it: the local authority and guardian would argue that the *timescale of the children* did not allow for further delay. More on this important concept later.

Behind me I hear a stifled sob as Kylie scrapes her chair back on the floor and makes for the courtroom door. Dr Moodlie glances at her and responds: 'Well, ideally she would have started the therapy back in October. If she had, we'd know by now whether she was engaging and the therapist would have some idea about the prognosis.'

I turn to the judge. 'I apologise, Your Honour, on behalf of my client. This personal material is acutely distressing for her.'

The judge flicks me the shadow of a sad smile. 'Do continue.'

Inwardly I feel some relief at Kylie's departure, as it's easier to let rip with my next question knowing that she's no longer listening. I would have much preferred it if someone from the offices of my instructing solicitor were available to support Kylie out in the corridor, but the days when legal aid paid for a clerk to 'sit behind counsel' are long gone.[3]

'Would you agree, Dr Moodlie,' I resume, 'that the situation this mother is faced with can be characterised as follows. She always made it clear that she was willing to engage in therapy. If the local authority had been willing to fund the therapy you recommended last October, or indeed if the NHS had been able to provide it, she might have been three to four months into it by now. Had the therapist felt she was engaging well and making progress, then it would have been very difficult for the local authority to argue that the children should remain separated from her on a permanent basis and placed for adoption; but since the local authority did *not* fund that therapy, there has been no change in mother's mental health – if anything she has become more depressed under the impact of the proceedings – and the local authority can and does argue that adoption is the only solution.'

Local authority counsel rises to his feet, so I sit down.

'Ms Thornhill is making a submission point,' he grumbles (quite fairly) to the judge, meaning I should save this point for my closing speech later in the week. 'The witness can't respond to that.'

The judge drops his pen and wearily puckers his forehead, turning his gaze on me. 'I think that has to be right; it's not an issue for this witness.'

I bob back to my feet. 'My apologies, Your Honour.' That's fine by me; I've made the point. I turn to the now tired-looking witness. 'Thank you, Dr Moodlie, no further questions.'

Local authority counsel knows that on day three he will have to try to convince His Honour Judge P that adoption is the *only* realistic solution for Kylie's boys, in other words that 'nothing else will do'. By the same token, I'll try to convince the judge that there *is* something else that ought to be tried. We're both driving towards our respective sides of the argument. Local authority counsel is laying the ground to argue that, since Kylie has not done the therapy, she's not currently fit to care for the boys and therefore nothing but adoption will do; I'm laying the ground to argue that there *is* a realistic alternative: the provision of therapy with the boys remaining temporarily in foster care. The two big weaknesses in my argument are (a) the lack of funding for therapy; and (b) that, even were funding available, it would entail delay. His Honour Judge P is likely to dismiss my proposal as *not* constituting a realistic option. If he doesn't do that, he'll almost certainly reject it on the ground that it would cause delay.

Driving home in the dark, I wrestle with feelings of failure, frustration and fury. Failure because I know we're going to lose this battle to get Kylie's children back and I feel impotent to help her; frustration and fury because, for the umpteenth time, I'm witnessing the charade of psychological evidence in the Family Court. What on earth is the point of a substantial sum of taxpayer's money being spent on instructing a psychologist – Dr Moodlie's report plus his day in court will result in a bill for several thousand pounds – when there's no money to fund the recommended therapy?

Many lawyers and some judges feel the same way that I do. One enlightened judge sometimes refuses to direct the instruction of a psychologist to assess a parent, on the basis that psychologists inevitably recommend therapy, which the local authority then refuses to fund. Skip the assessment, says this particular judge, the parent is *sure* to need therapy. If the parent's willing to do it, the local authority ought to spend the money. And don't hang around: offer the therapy from the day you issue the proceedings.

The problem, of course, is that judges have no power to *order* local authorities to fund therapy; and most senior managers, understandably worried about their budgets, refuse to do so. Not only that: most social workers have had no training in the world of psychotherapy and insist they need an assessment by a clinical psychologist to tell them what *type* of therapy is appropriate. This in itself is highly problematic, since most clinical psychologists have no experience of either receiving or delivering therapy, and the vast majority recommend a version of cognitive behavioural therapy for *every* parent they assess, as they're apparently not versed in the many alternatives available. CBT is effective for certain types of problem, such as addiction; but most of the clients I represent need more in-depth and longer-term psychotherapy.

'Who are you to pontificate about types of therapy?' the reader may well be thinking. 'You're a lawyer, not a psychologist.' A fair point, to which I say this: I've spent years in psychotherapy, for which I was able to pay privately. There's no way six – or even twenty-four – sessions of CBT would have enabled me to grapple with the damage my childhood did to me. I find it profoundly unacceptable that parents from impoverished backgrounds are fobbed off with an inadequate and tokenistic service, from commercially driven agencies such as Happy Heads, and risk losing their children when their mental health doesn't swiftly improve.

It's also profoundly stupid from a policy point of view.

Many of the mothers who come to the attention of the care courts hail from families where there is inter-generational trauma. In essence this is trauma that gets passed down from one generation to the next. It might manifest as sexual abuse, or as domestic abuse or poor parental mental health or substance abuse. With skilled psychotherapy, the trauma can be addressed; but if it's not addressed, then very likely its manifestations will continue. So from a child protection point of view, it would make more sense for the state to invest in the cost of psychotherapy for the women of these families who are of child-bearing age, rather than resort to removing their children.

For what we see again and again in the care courts is that mothers as young as Kylie, having lost their first-born children to adoption, go on to have more. A few years after the first set of proceedings they are back in court, with another baby, and the whole process begins again,[4] with its appalling costs both in human and economic terms.[5] The late district judge Nicholas Crichton saw that the only thing that would stop many young mothers having more children was to be allowed to keep and raise a child; and that this meant they *must* be given the intensive support they need to turn their lives around. In order to provide this he invented the Family Drug and Alcohol Court (FDAC), which I will talk about in the Epilogue.

The situation would be different, of course, if the NHS were able to provide high-quality therapy to parents who need it, and without a long wait. But the NHS, long starved of adequate resources and coming late to questions of mental health, has little to offer. To get long-term therapy on the NHS from a highly qualified and experienced psychotherapist, my understanding is that you have to be (a) actively suicidal, (b) sufficiently articulate and confident to push very hard to get what you need, (c) able to wait a very long time and (d) extraordinarily lucky. For the demographic groups whose parenting tends to come to the attention of social workers, the odds are stacked against them getting the service they need at the point where they need it – or, indeed, at all.[6]

7

The Timescale
of the Child

That the Family Court should operate with one eye firmly fixed on the passing days, weeks and months, so that children subject to proceedings are not left in limbo for any longer than is strictly necessary, is a principle with which no sensible person would disagree. In the years preceding the pandemic, however, the official obsession with speed in resolving care proceedings became an obstacle to clear thinking and in some cases an obstacle to children being returned to the care of their parents.

There was a history to this. In the early 2000s there had been a lot of criticism in the media about the length of time it was taking the courts to resolve care proceedings. Although the workings of the care courts were shrouded in secrecy, and although many care cases were resolved within a year, it was known that sometimes a case dragged on for two or even three years before a final decision was made. During that time period the child or children might endure a series of temporary placements, in none of which they could properly settle; or they might remain at home experiencing neglect and abuse. Research showed that in some cases children were sustaining emotional and behavioural damage as a result of delays in the child protection process.[1] Thus, broadly speaking, the media criticism was justified; but in my view the 'one size fits all' solution that was imposed created as many problems as it solved.

In 2003 the then president of the Family Division – the most senior family judge – introduced a guidance document referred to by lawyers as the 'Judicial Protocol'.[2] This imposed a limit of forty weeks (nine months) as the maximum duration in which each set of care proceedings must be resolved, unless there was very good reason to exceed it. Since this was 'guidance', not law, the courts had to try to comply but were not obliged to do so. At that time it was common in care cases for experts to be instructed – psychologists, psychiatrists and consultant paediatricians, for example – and some, though by no means all, of the delay was caused by the time it took them to investigate and report. The problem was compounded by a shortage of experts willing to accept instructions.

I was working as an in-house lawyer in a local authority child protection team at the time, an experience I'll describe in detail later on. Initially, my colleagues and I were shocked at the idea we now had to rush our cases through the courts in just nine months; but 'worse' was to come. In 2008, in response to research and continuing media criticism about delay, a younger generation of managerial-minded judges persuaded the then president of the Family Division to reduce the intended time frame for care proceedings still further: each case would now have to be resolved in just twenty-six weeks, or six months, from start to finish. The judges driving this change produced a fresh document to replace the Judicial Protocol, in which they set out a detailed framework intended to speed up the court process. The new document was entitled the 'Public Law Outline', soon absurdly abbreviated to the 'PLO'.

The increase in perceived speed was to be achieved by obliging local authority social work and legal departments to do a lot of work, such as the preparation of parenting assessments, the commissioning of psychological assessments, and tests for drug and alcohol abuse *before* issuing court proceedings, in the newly invented 'pre-proceedings process' referred to in Chapter 2. Previously this kind of work had been done *after* issuing proceedings, and under the direction of the court.

Imposing a requirement on local authorities to do 'pre-proceedings' work seriously burdened social workers. It did little, if anything, to reduce the period of high stress during which the family in question was under scrutiny and their children living with uncertainty about their future; but it improved the case duration statistics published by the Ministry of Justice. Competition ensued between different court centres in England and Wales, along the lines of 'our average care case takes 26.5 weeks, whereas yours takes 33 weeks! Ha ha, we're better than you.' While the resulting pressure may have had some positive impact on the rate at which local authorities tried to push their cases through the courts, it also helped to create an environment in which the needs of individual children drifted far from the minds of professionals, replaced by an obsession with the ability to demonstrate speed. The whip was cracked in each geographical court area by the presiding designated family judge (DFJ): it was as if his or her reputation and future promotional prospects now rested on the statistics for case duration in their area. If the welfare of the child had once been paramount in care proceedings, as declared in S1(1) of the Children Act 1989, this principle was now effectively jettisoned.

In 2014 the new, reduced time frame was given the force of law. The Children and Families Act 2014 amended the Children Act 1989 so as to *oblige* courts to drive cases through the courts in twenty-six weeks, with tight constraints on applications for extensions.[3] In the same burst of reforming zeal, the instruction of expert witnesses was now limited to cases where the parties could show that this was strictly 'necessary to assist the court to resolve the proceedings justly'.[4] The main reason given was that the routine use of experts such as psychologists was not warranted, given the presumed expertise of social workers and children's guardians; there is little doubt, however, that the underlying reason was the enormous cost of psychologists' reports and the political context of austerity.

As to whether social workers and children's guardians can fairly be expected to possess expertise in psychology, that is clearly open to doubt. After many years of practice the good ones undoubtedly have a lot of expertise, but that expertise is in social work.

There was once a time when the more complex cases were allocated to experienced social workers and guardians, with managerial support, but those days are long gone. By 2014 social workers and guardians were expected to shoulder enormous caseloads at an early stage in their careers, with minimal support, and most of them lacked both the expertise and the time to provide psychological input. Once qualified, social workers and guardians tended to be 'thrown in the deep end' and expected to cope, unsupported, with work which was sometimes way beyond their ability – as many would acknowledge. This state of affairs still pertained when I ceased practice in 2023.

From 2014 until the pandemic in 2020, the speed at which care proceedings were pushed through the newly established Family Court accelerated dramatically. The lay magistrates who preside over the lowest tier of the Family Court tended to adhere to the new twenty-six-week time frame rigidly; they appeared to want to show their local designated family judge[5] that they were doing as they'd been told, come hell or high water. Among the district judges operating in the middle tier of the court, too, there was considerable concern to be seen to comply.

Prior to 2014 the concept of 'planned and purposeful delay' had often been used to good effect in cases where work with a family might lead to rehabilitation of the children to the parents' care. This was now largely banished, replaced by unrelenting pressure on child protection professionals to bear in mind the *timescale of the child*. Packed into this little phrase is the assumption that it's almost never in the interests of children to be made to wait while their parents try to change, even when the alternative is stranger adoption. Thus from 2014 on, parents faced very tight timescales in which to show that they could get to grips with their drug or alcohol problem, or their chronic depression, or to separate from a violent or otherwise dangerous partner. This was particularly the case for any parent who, for whatever reason, had failed to engage in the pre-proceedings process.

Hence even in cases where, with the right support, sensitively delivered, a parent such as Kylie might have been able to resume care of her young children, the litany of the *timescale of the child* has often been used to justify an approach where rehabilitation isn't even attempted.[6] It goes without saying that while the requirement for speed is appropriate in some cases, it is not in all; children and families come in many different shapes and sizes, with many different strengths and problems; a 'one size fits all' approach inevitably leads to unjust and unhappy outcomes for some children.

Beyond that, it was incredibly unfortunate, not to say ill-judged, that the twenty-six-week framework was imposed at a time when the coalition government's austerity policy was already in full swing. By 2014 resources available to poorer families were greatly diminished from what they'd been even five years earlier – the axing of the Sure Start programme of children's centres is just one example – and children's services departments were under-funded and short-staffed. The result was that less and less good-quality social work was done with families by a workforce that was so stretched it could provide little more than crisis management. Where, in the past, mounting concern about a family might conceivably have led to a skilled social work intervention, now it was more likely to lead to the pre-proceedings process, followed by care proceedings rushed through the courts at high speed.

The twenty-six-week time frame was in force at the time Kylie's case was decided. It was pursued with vigour until spring 2020, when the pandemic intervened in all our lives. Covid-19 played havoc with the twenty-six-week rule, for it became much harder for local authorities to rapidly drive cases through the courts. Remote hearings had to be introduced overnight in a court system that, like many organs of government, was ill-prepared for a pandemic. Parents, social workers, police officers, judges and lawyers were struck down with the virus; court lists became clogged up with unresolved cases and the average length of a set of care proceedings increased from thirty weeks in 2017/18 to forty weeks in 2023/24.[7]

On day two of the hearing about Kylie's little boys, the morning is taken up with the evidence of the social worker. A tall young man who looks barely older than Kylie, he refuses to deviate from his line that the boys cannot wait for their mother's mental health to improve and that both are young enough to bond with adopters. I try my hardest to budge him, but fail.

In the afternoon it's Kylie's turn to go into the witness box. She's shaking as she stands up to walk across the courtroom and I feel guilty as I watch her, as if it's somehow my fault that she's facing this ordeal. For a second I try putting my twenty-one-year-old self in her place; I doubt I could have done what she's about to do. Counsel for the local authority is less aggressive with her than I was expecting, but Kylie speaks very quietly and gives monosyllabic answers, clearly intimidated. When she starts to cry, the judge stops counsel and suggests to her that she might benefit from a drink of water. I know he means well, but I've witnessed this offer to a grief-stricken mother too many times over the years. How can a few sips of water alleviate the excruciating pain of being told you're unfit to care for your children?

On the morning of day three it's time for the advocates to make our closing submissions. Counsel for the local authority makes quite a cruel submission, stressing that the incident with the paracetamol could have proved fatal. He repeats three times that the case is now in its twenty-eighth week and that 'these boys cannot wait any longer for permanence'.

When it's my turn, I point out that twenty-eight weeks is only two weeks over the twenty-six-week time frame. I remind the court that it can only authorise a care plan of adoption where 'nothing else will do'. In Kylie's case, I argue, there may be a realistic alternative but, due to the local authority's refusal to fund therapy, the evidence is not yet available. They should have offered this the moment they received Dr Moodlie's report four months ago; but it's not too late, they can still do so now. With therapy and a slightly longer time frame, she may be in a position to resume care of her sons.

The boys could remain in their present foster placement for the first three months of the therapy, I argue, after which, if mother was seen to be making progress, they could be gradually returned to her care. I plead with the judge to take the exceptional step of extending the court timetable and adjourning the making of his final decision to a later date. He should continue the interim care order and 'invite' the local authority to reconsider its care plan. (He lacks the power to *order* it to do so; but an 'invitation' from the court would weigh heavily with the local authority.)

The weakness in my argument, of course, is that my proposal would take the case well beyond twenty-six weeks and the local authority can't be ordered to fund therapy. The fact that the local authority has an adoptive placement lined up for the boys is not strictly relevant, but only a brave judge would overlook it. I've always thought of His Honour Judge P as decent and humane; but he isn't the type of person to stick his neck out. I interpret the uncomfortable expression on his face while I'm speaking as indicating that he wants to conclude the case now.

I finish my submission at ten past twelve, with Kylie sitting quietly behind me. Counsel for the guardian goes next, pointing out the flaws in my argument and declaring that the children simply cannot wait for their mother to sort herself out. When she's finished, His Honour Judge P looks up awkwardly and says he'll give his judgment at three o'clock this afternoon. Good, I tell myself, at least he's giving himself time to think it over. But in my heart I know the extra time is so that he can make his judgment appeal-proof.

Kylie and I make for the small, dark consulting room that has been our refuge for the last three days. She sinks into a chair and fixes her eyes on mine. 'What's he going to do?'

I place my laptop on the table. 'I don't know for sure, Kylie, but … I'm not very hopeful.' A look of despair descends on the features of the young woman in front of me. The dark circles under her eyes have grown larger over the last few days; she's told me she's not sleeping. 'I'll look very carefully at the judgment,' I go on. 'Sometimes judges make mistakes and then it's possible to appeal.' Shut up, I tell myself privately; don't give her false hope. This judge knows how to write an unassailable judgment. If it weren't for the incident with the paracetamol, I reflect for the umpteenth time, we might have been in a better position. That's what shifted the case from one of chronic low-level concern to one of serious risk.

Kylie sits hunched in her chair, her narrow shoulders brimming with tension, her cheeks grey. 'Are you going to have something to eat?' I ask gently, stooping to pull my lunchbox out of my bag.

'I can't eat,' she replies softly.

'But you should have something. Here, let me buy you a sandwich.' I take out my wallet and pass her a £5 note, telling myself it could be poverty rather than nerves that's getting in the way. 'Get some fresh air and a sandwich.'

She shakes her head. 'Thanks, T'reeza, but I can't till this is over. I'll eat later.'

The word 'later' strikes me as faintly reassuring. So Kylie can imagine life going on, past the devastating moment when the court announces its decision … although it's more likely that she simply hasn't grasped what's going to happen. Does she have any support to help her through the terrible hours and days that will follow the judgment?

'Kylie,' I begin in a faltering voice, 'do you have … someone to talk to? This evening? If it goes against you?'

The young woman's eyes fill with tears as she stares at the table top. 'Not anymore. I used to go up my nan's, but she's … gone.'

'Court rise!'

His Honour Judge P walks into court clutching a sheaf of handwritten papers. He's a thin man and this afternoon his stance seems less erect than usual. As he sits down in his red plush chair, his shoulders sag forwards, and I sense he's feeling a deep sense of unease about the task he's going to perform. When he glances at me, his customary smile is missing.

'I'm going to indicate my decision at the very outset,' he announces, looking up for a second and turning his face towards Kylie, 'to spare Ms G any more uncertainty.'

Many judges don't do this: they speak for an hour or more, setting out the law and giving their impression of each witness, before finally announcing where it has all been leading. Good man, I think. This is the best way to do it.

'With a very heavy heart,' His Honour Judge P goes on, 'I'm going to make full care orders and approve the care plans for adoption for these two little boys. I will also make placement orders, so that they can be placed with the adopters the local authority has in mind, without more ado.'

A loud gasp followed by a stifled sob issues from the row behind me. As I turn round, Kylie scrapes back her chair, grabs her bag and stumbles out of the courtroom. I rise slowly to my feet. This is now a very difficult situation. Kylie has me and only me to provide advocacy, legal advice and emotional support; but it's essential that I take a detailed note of the oral judgment that's about to be delivered.

His Honour Judge P looks at me, his eyes revealing acute discomfort (or so I read them). 'Do you want to follow her out, Ms Thornhill? Let me rise briefly. Will five minutes suffice?'

I thank him, wait while he leaves, then rush through the door into the lobby. Kylie's sitting on a bench, head in hands, her whole body shaking with sobs. I perch close beside her. I want to put my arms around her and hold her tight, but lawyers don't do things like that. So instead I put a hand lightly on her shoulder. 'I'm very, very sorry, Kylie,' I whisper.

She doesn't brush my hand away, but the sobbing continues, the unmistakable sound of acute grief and loss. We sit like this for three or four minutes, until I hear the court door open. The clerk stands in front of me, the picture of calm.

'Ms Thornhill?' he says softly. 'Judge is back in.'

I bend forwards with my mouth close to Kylie's ear and tell her I have to go back into court, to get a note of the judgment. 'It's very important,' I add. 'Please wait for me, we need to talk.' But as I stand up and walk towards the court door, Kylie also gets up. She throws me a look of agony mixed with rage – for at this moment I too am abandoning her – and runs towards the staircase. By the time I reach the courtroom, she's gone.

For the next hour I take a detailed note of His Honour Judge P's judgment. It's unfortunate that the mother has not had the therapy recommended, he says, but there's no certainty that it would have worked; and the little boys *cannot wait*. They've had six months in a temporary foster placement, and they need stability and security *now*. A decision to place children for adoption is always a draconian one, and can indeed only be made where 'nothing else will do'. The court is satisfied that this is the situation it's dealing with. Mother cannot care for the children at present, suitable therapy has not been made available to her and there is nobody in her extended family nor in those of the fathers who is able to take on the boys. The court must consider the situation as it is *now*.

The boys are young enough to bond with adopters. The local authority is to be commended for having found a family that can take them both, so they won't have to be separated. Mother clearly loves them. Photos of her can be shown to the children when they're older and start to ask questions. The adopters will be asked to send mother a letter once a year describing the children's progress, via the local authority letterbox scheme.

After His Honour Judge P leaves the courtroom, I approach the social worker's manager, a woman in her forties, and tell her I'm worried about Kylie. Can a welfare check be arranged?

The manager looks at me with an air of mild surprise. 'Obviously she's upset, but I think she'll be all right, don't you?'

I stare at her. 'I'm not at all sure,' I reply. 'You know her history as well as I do; she has no support, none at all.'

'Not even a friend she can talk to?'

I hesitate. 'I asked her at lunchtime who she could go to, tonight, and she said there was nobody.'

The manager picks up her handbag. 'Okay,' she says, 'I'll ask for a welfare check.'

At three o'clock the next morning I'm lying in bed wide awake, listening to the rain. A welfare check will involve a police officer knocking on Kylie's door at some point in the next forty-eight hours to check she's still alive. Nothing more. What has this young woman got left to hang on to? I ask myself. Is there anybody who's even *thinking* about her, right now, other than me? The questions provoke in me an all-consuming anxiety.[8]

When I get up, I've got to read a new set of papers. Before I do that, I'll email Kylie's solicitor and ask if she's heard anything from her; but by now, it could already be too late.

8

In the Woods

It's 8 am and I'm at the gate into the woods, meeting my friend Lynne and her lurcher. It's rained for the last three days, and rotting brown and purple beech leaves lie churned into the mud by passing boots.

I'm very tired this morning and my fears about Kylie have not vanished with daylight. 'I had a god-awful case this week,' I tell Lynne. 'So sad.'

She turns her head and looks at me.

'I'm worried the client's going to do something terrible; she was beside herself when we finished last night.'

'Lost her kids?'

'Yep, and it was all wrong, she should have got them back.' I mustn't say any more, but Lynne can tell from my tone of voice that the case has upset me. She says what she's said to me a hundred times before.

'I don't know how you do your job, Teresa. I couldn't cope with all that pain.'

I wrap my scarf more tightly round my neck. Lynne's words make me uncomfortable because we both know that *I* can't cope with the pain, either, and that sooner or later I have to get out.

'If I could earn a living doing something else, I would,' I tell her lamely, picking up a stick and throwing it for the dog, who hurtles after it down the track.

Like so many childcare lawyers I know, I'd love to do something less distressing; but over the years we've become very specialised, so that we can't, say, just switch to practise housing law or employment or immigration. Every few years I look into what it would take to change specialism, but after making enquiries and realising I'd have to go back to the beginning and build up a practice from scratch, I give up. I tell myself I'm too old to start again, and that better the devil I know ... And of course, perverse though it may sound, there are things about the job I'd miss, if I gave it up. I actually enjoy the client contact, even when it's harrowing. It feels real. It feels important.

Lynne has stopped walking and is gazing at me. 'They should give you supervision when a case really upsets you. You're being exposed to vicarious trauma.[1] You should get help to look at how it's affected you.'

I raise my eyebrows. At the bar you're expected to hold a really tight boundary between you and your client, so that at the end of a case you just give yourself a shake and walk away. And you're not really supposed to have feelings. It's the British public-school ethos: stiff upper lip and get on with the next case.[2]

'I know,' I reply, 'you're right. But at least I get paid enough to pay privately for support, if I want to. Social workers get paid much less and most of them don't get that kind of supervision, unless they have an exceptionally good manager.'

I spend the morning reading papers at home, ready for a con[3] in chambers this afternoon. There's still no reply from the solicitor who instructed me on Kylie's case. As I'm getting ready to leave for chambers, I receive a text from Michelle Gooden, the solicitor who represents Dwayne. Could I call her, please? She wants a word about a hearing at which she represented Dwayne earlier this week. So I finish scribbling a note to my son about what time to put the fish pie in the oven, sit down at my desk and call her.

Michelle picks up quickly. She's always under pressure, and we don't waste time on greetings. 'Ah,' she says, 'Dwayne. Bit of a drama Tuesday morning. Rosie – mother – came to court with a solicitor. She's back in town and talking about issuing an application[4] for a residential assessment with the younger two.'

Residential assessment units are independent organisations that assess troubled families in residential settings. Mostly the families are mothers with babies or very small children, but sometimes couples are assessed and occasionally the children are of school age. The unit provides the family with a large room or small flat and monitors the parenting very closely for six to twelve weeks. Then they file a detailed report, which will usually have a major influence on the court's decision-making about the child's future.

'What was Rosie like?'

'Loud, indignant, the local authority had no business snatching her children, she'd only popped round the corner for a couple of minutes when Lawrence set the J cloth alight ... But she looked really awful, thin as a rake, grey skin, bulging eyes.'

'Still using heavily?'

'Got to be.'

'So where's she been these last few weeks?'

'Christ knows. The neighbour who rescued the kids has given a statement to the police saying it wasn't the first time Mum had left them alone at night. And now, guess what, the poor neighbour's had a load of abuse on Facebook, calling her a child-snatcher.'

'Better if she'd left the kids to burn alive in the flat? Great. So what was the reaction to the residential assessment idea?'

'Local authority said, "No way". No residential unit will take her while she's using; and she hasn't explained why she vanished *and* the kids haven't seen her in all this time.'

'And the guardian?'

'Similar attitude. Rosie needs to stop using and do a detox before any unit will look at her. But even if she did that, what would a residential assessment tell us? The issue's what she might get up to if she had the kids back with her in the community. A residential assessment wouldn't tell us whether she'd leave them alone again. Pointless waste of public money.'

I can tell that Michelle shares the guardian's view; and I don't think they're wrong.

'Dwayne?'

'He was wobbling. I think he feels sorry for Rosie, so I sat on him. Local authority are already very worried that he didn't warn them how heavily she was using; it wouldn't do for him to be seen to be supporting her.'

'You told him to oppose?'

Michelle clears her throat. 'I told him if he couldn't oppose, then he should be neutral. But nobody was very interested in what he thought, they were too busy telling Rosie's solicitor what a stupid idea it was.'

'Who's her solicitor?'

'Brad Perkins. Some guy none of us had ever come across before. Forties. Probably a conveyancing lawyer trying his hand at childcare ...'

I smile to myself. I've always loved the blunt way Michelle puts things. 'Have you had Dwayne's hair strand test back?'

'Clear, just like he said.'

'Not even cannabis?'

'Squeaky clean; and he's well stuck into the relapse prevention work. But the social worker's still refusing to increase his contact.'

'He told me she had it in for him. Wasn't contact the main point of the hearing? Did the guardian give a view?'

'Guardian says Lawrence enjoys seeing his dad and should have contact once a week.'

'And the social worker still won't budge?'

Michelle hisses down the phone. 'That social worker's a nasty little so-and-so. Totally inexperienced, clueless in fact, and incapable of recognising a committed parent when she stumbles across one.' Michelle's a big fan of Dwayne. 'If she does his parenting assessment it'll be a hatchet job, so I want your views on whether we should try to instruct an independent social worker.'

An independent social worker (ISW) is someone with a background in child protection social work who's decided, for whatever reason, to go it alone, rather than working for a local authority or a charity. She or he accepts instructions to assess parents whose children are subject to care proceedings. The format for a parenting assessment is standardised, usually involving six to eight meetings between the social worker and the parent that generally take place at the parent's home, with the resulting report being anything from thirty to sixty pages.[5]

'I think it's worth a try,' I reply. 'Not sure if the court will buy it.'

Dwayne can only instruct an ISW to assess him if the court agrees. Michelle will need to issue an application setting out what Dwayne's asking for and why, and the court will consider it at the case management hearing in two weeks' time. Since an ISW is considered an expert, the judge can only agree to the instruction if he or she finds such an assessment is 'necessary to assist the court to resolve the proceedings justly'.[6] Principally, the court will want to know why the social worker can't do the job herself, so we'll need to have some evidence that she's already made up her mind against Dwayne.

'Do you have a particular ISW in mind?' I ask Michelle.

'Bonnie Richardson. She's by far the best. I use her whenever I can get her.'

I've had Bonnie on several cases and I agree with Michelle that she'd be perfect for this case. She's clear-sighted, compassionate and fair. And she's dual-heritage African Caribbean/white, which possibly means Dwayne will feel more comfortable being assessed by her.

'Have you checked she's available?' Bonnie's generally run off her feet.

'Yep, she can report in twelve weeks from receiving the letter of instruction.'

'Let's have a crack at it then, and combine it with an application for an increase in contact. We can use the social worker's refusal to increase contact as evidence she's not the right person to assess Dwayne.'

'That's what I was thinking. Okay, I'll issue the application today and just hope they list it on a day when you're free.'

We say goodbye and I run out of the house, forgetting to feed the cat, late now for my train. As I drive to the station I try to remember what's in my diary for the following week. I have an agreement with my clerks that I'm only in court three days out of five, so that I can get some time at home with my son. And yet I seem to be working flat out.

It takes me a long time to prepare for a contested hearing. For a final hearing in a care case, a court bundle often contains a thousand pages or more. Much of it is waffle and repetition; but unless you check each document, you risk missing some vital gem of information.

So in a week where I've got, say, a three-day final hearing, although I only get to spend three days in court, I need a good two days to do the prep. I can spend those at home, which means a walk in the woods at lunchtime and being in when my son gets back from school; but often the brief arrives on Friday evening for a hearing starting on Monday, and then I have to work all weekend.

I shouldn't complain. Barristers who work full-time – the vast majority – have to prep all weekend, *every* weekend, as well as every evening.

When I arrive at chambers I go into the clerks' room where our five clerks are hunched in front of their computer monitors, talking into headphones. I wave silently at their bent heads and take a quick look at my diary. Oh my God. For the next four weeks I've got back-to-back contested hearings, two of which are listed for four days, not three. I turn to Ash, the senior family clerk, a delightful man who always wears a grey satin waistcoat.

He catches my eye before I can open my mouth. 'I know,' he says, 'I'm really sorry, Teresa, but they won't all run, will they? Hartle and Benson lost their original counsel in one of the four-dayers, and I didn't think you'd want me to say no.' He grins. 'We'll make it up to you, don't worry. You can take some slack around Eastertime …'

I'm very fond of Ash, but Easter seems a long way off and the first four-dayer and one of the three-dayers are cases I know nothing about. Until I start to read the papers they will weigh like stones on my chest. For me, the unknown is always more anxiety-making than the known – a response reinforced by the ethos in legal circles that once a brief has been delivered, regardless of whether the barrister has had time to read it, she or he will be considered negligent if she fails to give any urgent advice that's required.

Happily, three of the four sets of papers haven't arrived, so that doesn't apply, *yet*. Even so, how I'm going to cram in all the prep alongside my son's birthday, which is coming up in two weeks, visits to my ageing parents and keeping our little household afloat, is beyond me.

I spend the next four weeks running from home to court – a different court centre in a different city each week – setting off at first light and travelling home in the dusk, to find my son unpacking yet another delivery from Tesco or Sainsbury's and asking me whether I want veggie burgers with baked potatoes or veggie sausages with rice. I'm past caring. Has he fed the cat? No. We watch *Channel 4 News* while we eat, until the latest twist in the Brexit drama sends me into such a furious rant that son gets up from the table and turns off the telly, complaining that he can't follow what's being said while I'm shouting at the screen. And then it's plates into the dishwasher as fast as possible, son goes back to his homework, and I take out my laptop and start my prep.

It's a particularly gruesome run of cases. The first week I'm for a little Ghanaian boy who's been removed from his parents after he told a teacher he was getting beaten with a wooden spoon if he didn't give his mother enough help in the kitchen. He was locked into his bedroom at night with no light and no means of getting to the toilet. The case goes part heard at the end of day three, because the time estimate was unrealistic, and the judge can't find another day that all the advocates can do for another six weeks. It's not good when this happens; momentum is lost and it's hard for the judge and lawyers to pick up the evidence where it was left off, not to mention the additional stress it causes to the family.

I'm planning to spend the rest of the week prepping next week's four-dayer, but Ash calls me as I'm leaving court and pleads with me to do a female genital mutilation (FGM) case the following day, something I've never done before. It'll mean a very late night reading the papers and looking up the law, but I like Ash and he's desperate, so I say yes. The case involves a Somali girl of twelve whose father is insisting she go abroad for a 'holiday' accompanied by her paternal grandmother, while the mother, who's in the process of divorcing the father, is convinced the real purpose is for the girl to be subjected to FGM.

The following week the four-dayer is a fact-finding hearing involving a little girl of three with an unexplained fracture of the left femur and bruising on both ears, which the medics think was caused by pinching. I'm for the grandmother, who lived next door to the parents and spent time alone caring for the girl in the time frame in which the injuries occurred.

A 'fact finding' is a hearing in which the court tries to establish how a child sustained an injury and who is responsible. During the preparation for the hearing, the local authority lawyer considers the history given by the family and decides which adults are in what's called the 'pool of possible perpetrators'. This will include any adult who was alone with the child in the time frame in which the injury occurred. Any person in the pool who is not a parent is then invited to 'intervene' in the proceedings, effectively becoming a party for the duration of the fact finding. So my client, the grandmother, is an intervenor.

I work hard on the case all weekend and by Monday morning think I'm on top of it, but when I arrive at court the parents produce a new piece of evidence that strengthens the case against the grandmother. When I discuss this with her, she loses her rag and threatens to sack me. That produces the toughest week in my professional life so far, which I'd prefer not to remember …

And then things get a little easier, but no less time-consuming. The second four-dayer is an alcohol case involving a lone mother with five children by four different fathers. She spends most of her time in the pub, drinking her benefit money and leaving the kids to fend for themselves. I'm for one of the fathers, a man who's played little role in his daughter's life and seems almost indifferent to the outcome of the case. Which on the one hand makes me cross, but, on the other, it's just as well, because I'm far from my best by now.

The following week a three-day case turns into five days. I'm for a Polish mother with serious mental health problems, exacerbated by the brutal assaults to which her husband subjects her on a weekly basis. My client's so vulnerable that I hardly dare discuss the case with her. The children are in foster care and it's clear they can't go home to her.

On the Friday lunchtime I call Ash and tell him I don't want to work the following Monday. He says it's fine, and I can have Tuesday off as well; then he's got a series of interim hearings for me on the Wednesday, Thursday and Friday.

I spend Saturday lying in bed with a headache, grateful that my son's with his dad. By the evening I'm feeling more human and I phone my friend Alastair who, like me, enjoys cold water swimming. I need an immersion, I tell him, to wash off the stress of the last few weeks. Right, he says, pack your wetsuit. On Sunday morning we meet at a motorway services where we abandon my car and drive in his van for an hour to the nearest beach. The water's so cold that my hands feel like they're burning, even through my neoprene gloves, but when I come out I'm a new woman.

9

Baby K

A few weeks later I've just got home on a Thursday evening and am starting to cook supper when Ash calls to say my diary's changed for tomorrow, Friday. One of my colleagues has gone part heard[1] on a fact finding so he wants me to cover a case of hers, representing a newborn baby through her guardian at an initial hearing. Ash has given the case I was meant to be doing to another colleague. The baby hearing is in a country town a long drive from where I live, the local authority are seeking removal and the mother's likely to contest, so it could be a long day.

After my son and I have eaten, I chuck a log on the woodburner, clear away our plates and turn to load the dishwasher. My son's already back at his desk on the far side of the kitchen, pulling on his headphones as he prepares to attack his physics homework. I envy his teenager's ability to concentrate late into the evening, when all I really feel like doing is lying on the sofa with the cat. Our beloved jet-black moggie is currently basking there in the heat of the stove, at full melting stretch. If I lie down beside him I'll drift off to sleep in seconds; but my papers for tomorrow morning must be read, and I've already left it dangerously late. I turn my back, sit down at the kitchen table and boot up the laptop.

BABY K

The brief tells me that Baby K, a girl, was born just after 2 pm today and doesn't yet have a name. Beyond this, the brief is very brief indeed. The guardian, Harriet Hart, has been in court all day on another matter and not yet read the papers; my instructing solicitor has no idea what her position will be. I turn to the application form and the social worker's statement, drafted some days ago, in which the baby is referred to as 'Unborn K'.

The mother, Chelsea K, is just eighteen years old. Chelsea spent approximately half of her childhood in local authority foster care, initially because the maternal grandmother (Chelsea's mother) had an alcohol problem and a violent partner (not Chelsea's dad); there were several incidences of unexplained bruising on Chelsea and unhygienic conditions in the social housing flat where they lived. After grandmother split up with the partner and stopped drinking, Chelsea went home, but she was thrown out again aged fifteen. By then grandmother had had two further children with two different men, both were on child protection plans and grandmother was thought to be drinking again. Chelsea went back into foster care, then at sixteen to sheltered lodgings. She had to leave this accommodation just after her eighteenth birthday, despite being six months pregnant, and since then she's been sofa-surfing, with occasional stays at grandmother's.

The social worker thinks Chelsea has a form of learning disability. They've had several long conversations about Chelsea's plans for the baby – where's she planning to give birth, where's she going to live, what she's bought in preparation – at the end of which Chelsea has been unable to repeat back to the social worker any of what they've discussed. The records show Chelsea went to mainstream school, but her attendance was strikingly poor and she left before taking any formal qualifications. Although the case has been in pre-proceedings for some weeks, Chelsea has yet to undergo a cognitive assessment.[2]

So that's the broad picture: a homeless, very young mother with a difficult childhood behind her, a suspected learning disability and little or no safe family support. Not a happy one, but in itself possibly not enough to establish the need for interim removal; much will depend on the mother's living arrangements and what support if any can be provided for her.

For interim threshold to be crossed, as I explained in Chapter 2, the local authority has to establish that *there are reasonable grounds for believing that the child is suffering or is likely to suffer significant harm and that the harm, or likelihood of harm, is attributable to the care given to the child or likely to be given to him if the order were not made, not being what it would be reasonable to expect a parent to give to him.*[3] With a newborn still in hospital, the 'is suffering' ground is unlikely to be made out;[4] the issue for Baby K is whether she's at risk of future harm.

In the section of the application form headed 'Grounds for the application', written prior to the birth, the local authority lawyer sums up the threshold criteria as follows:

Chelsea put Unborn K's health at risk by failing to book in for ante-natal care until she was eight months pregnant, despite a number of prompts from professionals.

Chelsea is currently homeless and appears to have no plan as to where she will live with Unborn K. She has suggested she could stay with maternal grandmother, but the local authority consider this would not be safe.

Chelsea is unsure of the identity of Unborn K's father. The individual she has named as the likely father is known to the local authority and suffers from severe mental health problems that sometimes erupt in violent behaviour.

Chelsea has been reluctant to answer questions about whether she is still seeing him. Unborn K would not be safe in his care and any contact he has with the child should be closely supervised.

There will have to be a DNA test[5] to establish whether this man is or is not the father.

Hmm. I can see why the local authority are worried about Baby K, but immediately I search for a pretext to pick holes in their threshold. A competent lawyer always looks critically at the case put forward by the local authority, searching for what may be missing or overstated.

I remind myself that, at this initial stage of the proceedings, the local authority only has to establish *interim* threshold, which sets a lower bar than that required for a final order to be made. Probably the court will find that interim threshold *is* crossed, which will give it the power to make either an interim care or an interim supervision order; but it will not be *obliged* to make one of these orders.

Before making any order, the court has to take into account both the 'welfare principle', which requires that the child's welfare shall be the court's paramount consideration[6] *and* the 'no order' principle, which says that the court shall not make any order 'unless it considers that doing so would be better for the child than making no order at all'.[7]

In order to meet these requirements, the court has to consider the whole picture, and, most crucially, what the child's care and living arrangements will be if it makes the order sought as opposed to what the child's care and living arrangements will be if it makes no order. The court should also consider the possibility of declining to make an interim care order and instead making an interim supervision order. An interim supervision order leaves the child in the care of the parent, subject to low level supervision.

Without wanting to cause the reader confusion, I should also explain that a court may make an interim care order in the context of a care plan that the child will remain at home with the parent; or a care plan that the child will live in a residential assessment unit with the parent. In other words, the making of an interim care order does not always entail removal from the parent.

Where the local authority *do* want to remove the child from the parent, as in this case, they can only do so if they can meet a test known by lawyers as 'the test for interim removal'. This test is a creature of case law and not something you can find in The Children Act 1989. It has been considered many times by the higher courts.

At the point in time I'm writing about, around 2018, the most recent judicial statement of the test for interim removal was that removal can only be authorized if the child faces *'an imminent risk of really serious harm'* in parental care.[8] The harm may be physical, emotional, psychological or sexual, or indeed a combination of all or any of these. So again, for Baby K, the issue will depend on where the mother proposes to live, what support if any she can muster, and whether she'll have the good sense to closely supervise any contact between the baby and the man she's named as the putative father.

As I mull on the case, it strikes me that with her various vulnerabilities, this is a mother who should be offered a parent and child foster placement,[9] or a residential assessment, before any decision is made as to whether the baby should be removed from her care. She's homeless through no fault of her own, and given her dismal childhood it's very likely she will need some modelling as to how to safely care for a tiny baby. I'm surprised that there's no discussion of either placement option in the social worker's statement; she simply wants to place the baby, alone, in foster care. I wonder who's representing Chelsea tomorrow.

At six thirty the next morning I fill a flask with tea, scribble a note for my son and set off cross-country on a series of winding A roads. It's a beautiful drive, with fields of winter wheat and clumps of bare trees at the top of every rise. But mostly I'm thinking about tiny Baby K and wondering what's going to happen to her by the end of today.

By nine I've made it to the remarkably new building that houses the court and am sitting in a cramped consulting room without a window, waiting for the guardian to arrive. As I unscrew the lid of my flask, the local authority solicitor puts his head round the door, a balding man in his early fifties who tells me he tries to do his own hearings because 'it's better than sitting in the office all day!' I smile and ask if there's any new information.

'Not really. Still no name for the baby. I've got her birth weight: six pounds two ounces' – he purses his lips – 'bit on the light side, not too bad. Hospital say she's fit and well, ready for discharge this afternoon.'

'Is the mother here?'

'On her way to court, by taxi. We wouldn't expect her to take the bus.' His expression is slightly smug, as if the provision of a taxi constitutes an act of true generosity.

'Have enquiries been made about a parent and child foster placement?'

Now he looks worried. 'Not that I know of. Why, is that what the guardian wants?'

'I haven't spoken to her yet, but the court will want to know what other options you've considered.'

'Well, yes, I don't think we'd support a parent and child foster placement, but I'll take instructions.'

And with that he's gone.

I doodle on the cover of my counsel's notebook. It's unfortunate that the hospital consider Baby K ready for discharge. Without wanting to wish harm on a newborn, it might have been better if the poor mite had had some very minor ailment requiring her to remain in hospital for observation. Then the local authority might not have been in such a hurry to get the matter into court, and mother could perhaps have stayed with her. She might even have been able to breastfeed. But no, Baby K is 'fit and well', the over-stretched and under-resourced hospital require the mother's bed, and this efficient local authority lawyer has got the matter into court at lightning speed.

Baby cases often make me feel slightly sick. I think it's the sense of powerlessness that goes with being a small cog in a dysfunctional system, when the stakes, for the child involved, are so very high. As a newborn, Baby K is about as vulnerable as it's possible for a human being to be. No doubt everybody's doing their best to protect her, but at present, I assume, she's lying alone in a glass cot in a busy maternity ward, while her mother heads for court. Not the best way to spend your first morning outside the womb.

There's a lot of research indicating that the first few hours, days and weeks of a baby's life are crucial to the formation of her sense of self. Gentle care, love and attention are the key needs, and if those needs are not met, there can be lifelong consequences in the growing child's ability to form attachments.[10] That's why newborn baby cases give me this queasy feeling in my stomach. It's as if we professionals have our calloused hands on the baby's soul. None of us mean to do the child harm, but do we really comprehend the full potential significance of our actions?

Recent case law acknowledges the importance of the early days and weeks to the formation of a bond between mother and child, and the courts have gradually become more reluctant to order separation of a newborn from the mother. In a case decided by the Court of Appeal about a year after the occasion I'm describing, Peter Jackson LJ said:

The removal of a child from a parent is an interference with their right to respect for family life under Article 8. Removal at an interim stage is a particularly sharp interference, which is compounded in the case of a baby when removal will affect the formation and development of the parent–child bond.

Accordingly, in all cases an order for separation under an interim care order will only be justified where it is both necessary and proportionate. [...]

A plan for immediate separation is therefore only to be sanctioned by the court where the child's physical safety or psychological or emotional welfare demands it and where the length and likely consequences of the separation are a proportionate response to the risks that would arise if it did not occur.

The high standard of justification that must be shown by a local authority seeking an order for separation requires it to inform the court of all available resources that might remove the need for separation.[11]

This is a fine decision and has been much cited by lawyers acting for parents. Prior to the decision, good practice already dictated that a local authority seeking separation should provide details of resources that might remove the need for it, but it was very useful to have this spelled out by the Court of Appeal.

There are, however, no restrictions on the *processes* to which mother and baby may be subjected immediately post-birth, even though a court may ultimately refuse to order separation. For example, I'm not at all happy that, right now, instead of holding her baby in her arms, perhaps breastfeeding, this young mother is sitting in a taxi speeding away from her. It may take all day for the court to decide whether or not to accede to the local authority's removal application, a crucial first day of life during which baby K will be bottle-fed in a busy environment by a series of different nurses.

I get up and stretch. Harriet Hart is still not here, so I'll risk leaving my laptop unattended and make a dash for the toilet across the corridor. A few moments later, when I'm washing my hands, a distraught young woman in tracksuit bottoms and a T-shirt emerges from the cubicle next to the one I've just used. Her face is drained of colour and her unbrushed hair forms a chaotic cloud around her head. When she staggers towards the sink, I can tell she's in pain. A smear of reddish brown extends down the back of her leg from her crotch.

'You all right?' I ask.

She turns her head and stares at me, giving the impression of someone in a state of shock. 'Not really, no,' she blurts out. 'Still bleeding.'

Then the penny drops. 'Are you … Chelsea K?'

Nodding, she takes a step towards the paper-towel dispenser, staggers and a moment later she's on the floor. Horrified, I squat down beside her.

'Did you hurt yourself?'

Chelsea heaves herself into a sitting position, back propped against the wall. 'Not really. I'm so weak. And everything hurts.' She wraps her hands around the lower part of her abdomen and tilts forwards.

'You poor woman, of course it does. You only gave birth a few hours ago, didn't you? Have you eaten anything?'

I feel an acute sense of shame: what kind of system is it that drags a teenage mother to court in this condition? If she were my daughter, I'd be outraged on her behalf. She should be lying in bed gazing at her baby.

Chelsea shakes her head. 'I can't eat, not with all this going on. And I didn't sleep at all, it was so noisy in that place.'

'Can I get you a cup of tea?'

'I'll be all right, I've got a bottle of water somewhere.'

'Have you met your lawyer?' Then I realise I haven't explained who I am. 'I'm the lawyer for your baby,' I say uncomfortably, watching Chelsea's face. If it were me who'd just given birth, I'd be tempted to tell this woman in a black suit to f*** off, my baby doesn't need a lawyer, thanks very much, she needs her mother. But Chelsea looks at me placidly.

'My lawyer's in that little room,' she says slowly, 'across the corridor. Mona somebody.'

'Muna al Rashid? I'll go and fetch her.' Muna's somebody I like and respect.

I leave Chelsea sitting on the floor and a couple of moments later find Muna on the concourse, pacing up and down in a dark grey suit. She's a good-looking woman in her late thirties and one of the best care lawyers I know. I tell her what I've just witnessed.

'Oh for goodness' sake!' she cries. 'That poor girl, she doesn't know what's hit her. Why did they have to rush this into court, *today*? It's brutal.'

'I guess the hospital want the bed.'

'Sure they do, but how about a parent and child foster placement?'

'I couldn't agree more.'

Muna's face lights up. 'So is that the guardian's position?'

'Oh I'm not saying that, I haven't met her yet.' I throw Muna a meaningful look. 'Good luck.'

When I open the door of the consulting room Harriet Hart is hanging her jacket over the back of her chair and booting up her laptop. She's a stocky young woman with a confident air, and I realise she must be another one of this year's cohort of newly recruited guardians. I introduce myself and she smiles at me with such warmth that I'm moved to tell her what I've just witnessed in the women's toilets.

Harriet shakes her head. 'That's not on,' she says in a Scottish accent. 'Poor wee girl. She's only eighteen, isn't she?'

We speak for a few minutes, and to my relief Harriet makes it clear that she wants me to push the local authority very hard over why they say they need to separate mother and baby; and why they didn't do a cognitive assessment during pre-proceedings; and why they aren't suggesting a mother and baby foster placement. She may be new in the job, but she's clearly the kind of guardian I enjoy representing.

While we're talking, the legal adviser, a middle-aged man with a beard and greying hair, knocks on the door and says the magistrates want us in court. I explain that all parties need time to take instructions and then we'll need a round-table discussion to see whether we can resolve this without a contested hearing. The adviser looks unhappy. He understands all that, but Mr Chairman always insists on a 10 am start.

So at three minutes to ten we gather up our laptops, cables and bags, and make our way into the modern, timber-panelled courtroom. It's an attractive room, suffused with light from windows near the ceiling, but I wonder how the government can justify building stylish new courtrooms when services to families are being cut back to the bone.[12] I sit down at the end of the row and study the bench: a middle-aged male chair with a lined face and angry eyes, and two anxious-looking female wingers. Hmm, I think, this is going to be challenging. Glancing at the row of seats behind me, I see that Chelsea is shivering in her flimsy T-shirt.

The local authority solicitor addresses the chairman in a tone of exaggerated politeness, turning his wrist to look at his watch and emphasising that his team are ready, right now, to start a contested hearing. When he finishes speaking, Muna al Rashid explains, in an icy tone, that while the local authority may think they're ready, they've failed in their paper evidence to address the issue of the mother's apparent learning disability and have omitted to provide the court with any details of what arrangements could be made for mother and baby that would not entail separation. On the evidence before the court at present, it's arguable that interim threshold is not met. If the court decides it is met, then the court will need information about all the options that could be made available to keep mother and baby together before it can consider what order to make.

Glaring at Muna, Mr Chairman picks up his papers and demands to know why this information is missing.

'That's a question for the local authority, Sir,' she replies tartly. 'This is their application, not the mother's.'

At this point I decide to butt in. I tell Mr Chairman slowly and clearly that it's imperative that the parties are given time to sit down together and discuss the case in some detail, before the hearing can proceed. There's always a possibility that agreement can be reached, an outcome that would avoid the need for a lengthy hearing. I would very much like to add that the mother is not in a fit state to spend the day sitting on a courtroom chair, and that she should be allowed to return to her infant daughter at the earliest opportunity; but it's not my place to say that and I manage to keep my trap shut.

After the bench has begrudgingly agreed to give us forty-five minutes, we leave the courtroom and reassemble in a slightly more spacious consulting room, with a frosted glass window. The local authority solicitor is initially defensive in response to Muna's and my insistence that enquiries must be made as to the availability of a parent and child foster placement; but after Muna points out that surely he wouldn't want the case to find its way to the Court of Appeal, he sends the social worker away to phone her manager.

And so the morning goes by, with phone calls and hurried discussions and interludes where we are called back into court, only to explain to an increasingly irate Mr Chairman that we're still not ready to proceed. He tells us repeatedly that he and his wingers will not sit one minute past 4.30 pm. At 1 pm the local authority solicitor informs us that his client department have identified a mother and baby foster placement, but the service manager says it's not a suitable environment for a mother with a learning disability. Harriet demands to be given more information, and while we're waiting she begins a search, on her tablet, for a residential assessment unit that could take the mother. Residential units with expertise in working with learning disabled parents are few and far between, but this guardian is not one to give up easily.

At 2 pm, despite the fact that the mother is now feeling too unwell to come into court, the chairman insists that we start the hearing. Muna seems confident she has detailed instructions and agrees to proceed in her client's absence. Not having any money for transport back to the hospital, Chelsea remains in the building, presumably alone in a consulting room. I just hope someone has provided her with something to eat and a stack of sanitary pads.

The local authority solicitor tenders the social worker, and for the next hour Muna subjects her to an intense cross-examination. Why didn't she arrange a cognitive assessment for the mother as part of the pre-proceedings process? Wasn't it obvious she'd need a parenting assessment tailored to her learning needs? If so, why wasn't this arranged? And why didn't the social worker escort Chelsea to the Housing Department to make an application for her own accommodation? Given that the social worker thought this young mother-to-be had a cognitive issue, surely that was the least she could have done to help her? And wasn't it obvious that Chelsea would need support in setting up a home and learning to care for a small baby? In which case, why didn't she investigate the possibility of a parent and child foster placement? Or, failing that, a residential assessment?

The social worker appears only a few years older than Chelsea and, as it becomes apparent that she's way out of her depth, I begin to feel a little sorry for her. I'm staring at the chairman, trying to figure out what he's making of all this, when a much older woman slips into the back of the courtroom, tiptoes to the side of the local authority solicitor, squats down and whispers in his ear. A moment later the solicitor looks nervously at Muna, clears his throat and begs the chairman's leave to interrupt. He has new information, he explains, and would ask that the court rise for ten minutes.

Making little effort to conceal his fury, the chairman glares at the solicitor and says he can have seven minutes. He picks up a biro and waves it at the digital clock on the wall, which shows the time as 15:10. 'The court won't sit one minute past four thirty', he growls at us. 'And we need an hour to draft our decision and reasons.'

To make it easier for the local authority to have whatever hurried discussions are required, Muna, Harriet and I leave the courtroom.

Personally, I'm exhausted, although up to now I've played almost no part in the hearing. Harriet wants to know what we can do if the bench place the baby in foster care. 'It's all wrong,' she keeps telling me, 'we'll have to appeal.' Late on a Friday afternoon, that means an urgent telephone call to the clerk to the circuit judge for the area and an application to the court we're in for a stay.[13] Which, judging by the attitude of the chairman, he'll refuse. I'm discussing this with Harriet when Muna sidles up. 'Don't worry,' she says calmly, 'I've got my clerk on the line already, forewarning the clerk to His Honour Judge … that there may be an out-of-hours application coming his way.'

Two minutes later, the local authority solicitor bursts out into the lobby. 'We've found a parent and child foster placement that can take them,' he announces, rather as if that was what his clients had been batting for all along. 'No need to continue the hearing. We'd like an interim care order, mother and baby can go to the placement this evening, and we can come back in a week for a case management hearing.' He grins at us all. 'Or even two weeks, there shouldn't be any urgency.'

'I should think so!' Harriet exclaims under her breath. 'What a farce!' And then out loud, directed towards the solicitor, 'Now can this poor young woman please be taken back to the hospital and reunited with her baby?'

10

The Guardian in Purple

It's 11.30 on Monday morning and my two-day case has collapsed, leaving me delightfully free. I'm putting off phoning my clerks because I know that when I do, they'll immediately find other cases to plug the gap. After slowly pulling on my trainers in the robing room, I decide to take the stairs to the ground floor. From the top of the last flight, I spot a familiar figure on the concourse below. Niamh O'Loughlin is a guardian I've always admired for her fierce independence. Of all the guardians working in this court area, she's the last one to go along with the local authority's views for the sake of an easy life. She says what she thinks and, however much hostility she encounters from social workers and their lawyers, she stands firm.

When I reach the lobby, Niamh's standing by a pillar sending a text message, a bulging canvas briefcase resting against her ankles. She's wearing a purple dress that shows off her slim figure and her sharply cut grey-blonde bob.

'Hiya, Niamh,' I call as I reach her, 'how's things?'

'Teresa,' she replies in her Dublin accent, 'I didn't see you there. I'm steaming, since you ask. Judge Z has just refused me a psychological assessment of a suicidal fourteen-year-old. He says it's not "necessary", the social worker is perfectly capable of assessing her needs.'

'And is she?'

'He – no way!' She murmurs a name, well known to both of us, and fixes me with her large green eyes. 'We all know he'd struggle to work out the needs of a puppy; how's he going to get to grips with a fourteen-year-old who's been self-harming since she was seven and been through four failed foster placements?'

'Oh dear, Niamh. Where's the girl placed now?'

'In her third residential placement, threatening to set her hair alight, smashing the windows of staff cars and punching a pregnant care worker in the stomach.'

'You going to appeal?'

'Possibly. I need to talk it over with my counsel, but he had to rush off to another hearing.' She frowns, then forces a smile. 'How are you?'

'I'm fine,' I reply. 'Quick cup of tea?' For once I have time to spare, and there's a café next door.

'Lord, I've a million things to do this afternoon, I shouldn't really. But yes, twenty minutes, that'd be grand.' She smiles again, picking up her briefcase.

As we approach the revolving door of the building, we see it's chucking down with rain outside. Niamh puts up her umbrella – purple to match her dress – and we run the twenty metres to the café.

'What've you got on this afternoon?' I ask as we sit down at the back with mugs of tea.

'My PLR.'

'Your *what*? Child protection's riddled with acronyms, but this is a new one on me.

'Practice learning review. It's CAFCASS's idea of supervision, a fine waste of time.'

I find the idea of Niamh needing supervision a bit odd. 'How does that go?'

She wrinkles up her nose. 'It's a numbers exercise. The manager goes through one of your cases and you have to answer questions about it.'

'Like what?'

'Like, is the case going to exceed the twenty-six-week limit; how many times have you met the parents, that sort of thing. It's not real supervision at all, it's compliance management: that's all CAFCASS are interested in.' She picks up her tea. 'And in addition, you have to be observed twice a year by a manager while doing the job; giving evidence in court, for instance, or visiting a child or talking with a parent.'

'But you're so experienced!'

'I've been in social work forty years, but to CAFCASS my experience counts for nothing. The only thing they care about is my data and principally how many cases I've completed within twenty-six weeks.' Her arching eyebrows leave me in no doubt as to her opinion of CAFCASS.

'But it's not within your control to make a case finish in twenty-six weeks!'

'CAFCASS criticise you if just one of your cases goes over.'

Now that we're sitting opposite each other I notice how tired she looks, despite the careful eye make-up. 'Yesterday,' she goes on, 'I closed a case. It was a really good outcome; I persuaded the local authority to allow the child to go home to live with her dad. I wrote a note about it on the file, but nobody will read it. With CAFCASS a good outcome counts for nothing. All our managers care about is their statistics!' She wrinkles up her nose in disgust. 'As a guardian you're supposed to be the voice of the child, but CAFCASS don't care about that. If *you* care, you're completely alone.'

I'm not really surprised by any of this. Twenty-five years ago the typical guardian was a very experienced social worker who had wearied of working in a local authority environment and summoned the guts to go it alone as a self-employed 'guardian ad litem' (the old terminology). Many of the women and handful of men who made this choice, such as Niamh, were the brightest and most independent-minded of their cohort of social workers; people who felt it was healthy for local authority interventions in families to be independently scrutinised from the point of view of the child's needs and wishes and welfare. As guardians they were self-employed and could take on as much or as little work as suited them – although I never met a guardian who didn't work extremely hard.

After CAFCASS was set up by the government in 2001, some guardians continued to be self-employed and others chose to become salaried officers of the new organisation. Gradually, however, self-employed guardians were phased out, and those who decided to remain had to swallow the bitter pill of operating within CAFCASS's increasingly restrictive framework. Their work was monitored more closely than before and reports now had to be written on a standardised template and checked by managers before being filed with the court. The overall impact was to dumb down the role of guardians and reduce the attraction of the job for able, independent-minded people. At the same time, the size of guardians' caseloads increased exponentially.

'CAFCASS has deliberately devalued the role of the guardian,' Niamh goes on. 'These days we're so run off our feet, we can barely keep up. Twenty years ago I used to have a caseload of twelve families and I saw some of the children either weekly or fortnightly.'

'And now?'

'Now I've got twenty-four cases. In a case involving a baby, I might see them three times over the whole twenty-six weeks of the proceedings.'

This fits with what I see in court on a daily basis. Over the years, guardians' reports have become increasingly skimpy and superficial, reflecting a much shallower knowledge of the child and her circumstances than in the past. If I need to challenge a guardian's evidence in cross-examination, I'll always ask how many times she's met the child; and generally the answer, often given in a defensive tone, is 'twice' or 'three times'. A good guardian knows that, for most cases, this is wholly inadequate; but they simply don't have time to visit more frequently.

The café door blows open, letting in a smattering of raindrops.

'My God,' says Niamh, shaking her head. 'Terrible weather for early June!'

'Climate change,' I grimace. 'Who decides you have to hold twenty-four cases?'

'The managers.'

'And who are they, these managers – are they trained social workers?'

Niamh sighs. 'A long way back in their careers, most of them were social workers. CAFCASS is a top-heavy organisation, with far too many managers. They're paid ridiculous, outrageous salaries.'

'Unlike guardians?'

'We get paid *even less* than social work managers, despite all our years of experience.'

I love the energy with which Niamh communicates. I've seen her give evidence in court several times and she speaks with more conviction than any other guardian I know. 'Mind you,' I rejoin, 'a lot of the guardians I come across these days have nothing like your level of experience. Some of them look like they're fresh out of college. The guardian I was in court with this morning was twenty-five at most.'

Niamh raises her eyebrows. 'These days you only have to have worked for three years in children's social work to become a guardian.'

'Why do they recruit people who are so green?'

She looks me in the eye and purses her lips. 'They see them as malleable. People with just three years post-qualification experience aren't going to rock the boat, are they? CAFCASS doesn't like guardians like me who stick their necks out. Nor do local authorities …'

She's right, in a way. Many social workers in our area groan if they learn that Niamh has been appointed in their set of proceedings. Local authority lawyers too. But lawyers who act for parents delight in her willingness to question and challenge. She's often our best hope of preventing a child's removal into care.

'A lot of us admire the dogged way you say what you think is right for the child.'

For a moment her eyes light up. We're both thinking of Jordan, a little boy whom the local authority wanted to place for adoption after his learning-disabled mother had a mental health crisis. The paternal grandmother wanted to take on the child's care, but the local authority said she was unsuitable due to historic concerns about her care of her own children. Niamh disagreed, arguing that in twenty years the grandmother had matured, and that Jordan's relationships with her and his mother were so close that he would struggle to settle in an adoptive family. I only played a bit role in that case, representing Jordan's largely absent father, but I was delighted when the judge accepted Niamh was right. He rejected the local authority care plan and made a special guardianship order placing Jordan with the grandmother.

'I've heard that CAFCASS have a recruitment problem,' I go on.

'Sure, they do. CAFCASS have driven a lot of experienced people away, as they've become more corporate in their approach. We're not respected or valued for the skills that the job requires. Older guardians are leaving. In some areas of the country, CAFCASS can't recruit at all and have to resort to "golden hellos" or use agency workers.'

As Niamh speaks, Harriet Hart pops into my mind. She gave the impression of being highly competent, despite being thirty-five at most. But, sadly, she wasn't typical of the newly recruited guardians I come across these days. I wonder how long she'll last in the job.

The café door blows open again, letting in another blast of rain. I glance at my watch: 12.15. I ought to go, and so ought

Niamh, but I'm enjoying this conversation. 'Don't you think, Niamh, there's a huge problem with social work recruitment and training?' I've a bee in my bonnet about this; I firmly believe that many of the wrong people are recruited as social workers. I'd like to see a more rigorous training process and better pay to help recruit people of a higher calibre.

'Oh, absolutely. When I trained in the 1980s, social work was seen as a soft option; but the reality is, you have to be pretty bright to do the job properly. You've got to be able to absorb complex information quickly, for one thing, especially in court work; and you've got to be able to hold your own with all manner of people.' She pauses. 'But social work's not the job it once was. There's nothing creative about it anymore. It's become so corporate and so risk-averse.'

'Do you think there should be a minimum age for people to become social workers?'

'I certainly think they need life experience; they shouldn't go into the job straight from university … And, as we know, some people go into social work to fix their own problems, which is highly problematic because in the current training there's not much emphasis on self-awareness.'

'Was there ever?'

'When I trained in 1981, there was a psychotherapeutic approach and we were encouraged to reflect on our own issues. We were expected to be aware of what kinds of thing we'd come across in the work that might trigger us. Then I worked abroad in the 1990s, in a social work team where there was a big emphasis on reflective practice, and we got proper supervision. But when I came back to the UK in the early noughties, reflective practice was a thing of the past. In the local authority I joined, we got supervision of a sort, but the emphasis was on getting the work done.

'As for recruitment, of course it's problematic. Some people are attracted to social work for the power it gives them. They make it a battleground between them and the parents. And some have a very punitive attitude and impose their own middle-class values on working-class parents. Some social workers load up their court statements with negatives, to help them build a case against a family.'

She drains the last of her tea. 'But cuts in childcare legal departments don't help. In the past a lawyer would have checked what a social worker wrote, and that doesn't happen much now.'

I totally agree. The waffly, imprecise manner in which many social work statements are drafted is another of my bugbears, although, to be fair, if I were under the level of pressure experienced by many social workers, I too might not write very clearly.

Niamh puts on her jacket as if preparing to leave, but she's still talking. 'The other thing I see as a major flaw in the system is the lack of long-term research on families who've been through court. There's no accurate picture of how effective social work and Family Court interventions are.'

'Who do you think should do it?'

'CAFCASS would be in a good position to carry out research. Even with adoption, there's very little long-term research on the cohort of children who were adopted since 2000.'

Niamh's looking at her watch now. We say a hurried goodbye and head out in opposite directions into the rain.

11

Final Hearing

It's a warm Saturday afternoon in July and I'm sitting at my desk at home, preparing for a conference with Dwayne on Monday afternoon, a week ahead of his son's final hearing. My lad's with his dad and, after a quick trip to the supermarket this morning and a stroll in the woods, I've set aside the rest of today and tomorrow to prep the case. I'm feeling gloomy, not so much from having to work all weekend but more from anticipating an outcome that will distress Dwayne and devastate young Lawrence.

I succeeded, some months back, in persuading the court that Bonnie Richardson should do Dwayne's parenting assessment. She was ordered to do one of Rosie too, but Rosie only attended three out of eight sessions, whereas sensible Dwayne attended all of his.

It's clear from the tone of Bonnie's fifty-page report that Dwayne made a largely positive impression on her. He was open about his traumatic childhood and how it drove him into drug abuse; she recognises his devotion to Lawrence and his ability to reflect on the damage that his son's experiences in Rosie's care caused him. In one of their meetings, Bonnie pressed Dwayne on why he didn't act more protectively towards Lawrence when he could see that Rosie was slipping further and further into heroin addiction; Dwayne became distraught while trying to answer this, saying he'd been nervous about what the local authority might do if he made a referral, but that now he bitterly regretted his inaction.

Bonnie took Dwayne through all the standard topics covered in parenting assessments – children's routines, healthy eating, setting boundaries around behaviour, support with school attendance, housekeeping and budgeting – and concludes that Dwayne has sufficient knowledge and experience to provide good enough care for Lawrence. In her report she adds that, with suitable support and housing, he could probably cope with the younger two as well. But there's a serious risk that, under the pressure of life as a lone parent, Dwayne will relapse.

Bonnie points to Dwayne's long history with drugs and the fact that, this time round, he's only been clean for five months. She accepts that he's doing very well, with negative hair strand results and negative urine tests from the agency carrying out the relapse prevention work; but in her view five months is just too short a time to give confidence that he's well and truly out of the woods. Then she adds, almost as an aside, that he hasn't done any therapy to address the emotional legacy of his abusive childhood and that, until he does the work, he'll remain vulnerable to addiction.

If Dwayne *had* done therapy *and* been drug-free for a year, Bonnie goes on, that would be a different matter. Then the court could have some confidence that he wouldn't relapse, and she'd very likely be recommending that he take on the care of Lawrence with the possibility of the younger two joining them at a later date. But, as things stand, she can't recommend that the court place *any* of the children in his care. The proceedings have already been running five months, and if you add on the seven months till Dwayne will, hopefully, have been drug-free for a year, that will be 'way outside' the children's timescales.

I groan as I read this. I had naively hoped that Bonnie, with her child-focused attitude and her pragmatism, would say that this was a case where that old-fashioned thing, 'planned and purposeful delay', was warranted. That the children, especially Lawrence, would have so much to gain from the chance to live with Dwayne and so much to lose if a decision were made that they could not, that an extension of the timetable was justified, to allow Dwayne more time to consolidate his abstinence. But no, Bonnie is doggedly toeing the official, inflexible line on the timescale of the child. I feel bitterly disappointed.

In the conference on Monday afternoon I discuss the report with Dwayne. He's already read it several times and is feeling intensely frustrated with the situation he's in. With the help of his drug support agency he's managed to move from his friend's home to a room in a 'dry' house for recovering addicts. He's been told by the local authority housing department that if Lawrence is placed in his care under a court order, he'll be offered a two-bedroom flat.[1] He's never done any therapy, beyond a few counselling sessions during the relapse prevention programme, but he's willing to give it a go – except that his benefit money won't stretch that far.

Dwayne tells me he finds abstinence easier when he's busy, so since we last met he's taken on some voluntary work driving a delivery van for a charity that provides second-hand furniture to families on low incomes. He's attended all the contact with Lawrence he's been offered – the social worker was eventually persuaded by the guardian to increase the frequency to once a week – and I've read in the contact logs that the supervisor recognises there's a warm relationship between father and son.

When I bring up the subject of Bonnie's report on Rosie, Dwayne looks me in the eye and tells me he couldn't bring himself to read it. I can see that he's moved from feeling sorry for her to feeling furious. After the day when she attended court unexpectedly, Rosie hung around just long enough to meet with the ISW three times and see the children in supervised contact twice. One evening on the communal staircase she confronted the neighbour who'd made the police statement, demanding that she retract it. The neighbour called the police, but Rosie left the building before they arrived, getting into a Transit van driven by a man the neighbour didn't recognise. Since then Rosie has only contacted her solicitor intermittently and refuses to pick up her phone whenever Bonnie or another professional tries to call her.

I tell Dwayne that Bonnie's conclusions about Rosie are clear: she's in the grip of heroin addiction, living a chaotic life, and has no insight whatsoever into the impact on her vulnerable small children of her drug use and her disappearances.

Despite the weight of evidence against him, Dwayne is clear he still wants to contest the case. I explain that we can't challenge the threshold criteria – it's a fact that he was homeless and using crack cocaine till six weeks before the proceedings were issued, and a fact that he didn't warn the local authority about Rosie's escalating heroin use – so we must focus on challenging the care plans.[2] These are long-term foster care for Lawrence, with only minimal contact – six times a year – with Dwayne; and stranger adoption[3] for the little ones. To make matters worse, Lawrence will have to move, because his current foster carer only takes short-term placements. The local authority are searching for suitable long-term foster carers.

Just as we're finishing the conference, Michelle receives an email with the guardian's 'final analysis' attached. We all skim-read it, and see that on her last visit to Lawrence, earlier this week, he told her that 'until Mummy comes home' he wants to live with Daddy and his brother and sister; and if he can't, then he'd like all three of them to live with Gemma, his current foster carer. Despite this, the guardian supports the local authority's plans. Her only minor disagreement with them is as to the frequency of contact between Lawrence and Dwayne; the guardian feels that six times a year (once in each school holiday) is not quite enough. She'd like eight times a year. Bonnie Richardson says twelve times, or once a month.

A week later, at nine o'clock on Monday morning, I'm sitting in a small consulting room opposite Court 17, waiting for Dwayne.

We're listed in front of Her Honour Judge D, having lost District Judge S somewhere in the trail of interim hearings during the last few months. Her Honour Judge D is a relative newcomer in our court centre from a recent recruitment drive in which, it seems, the Judicial Appointments Commission went out of its way to appoint more women.

I get up from my seat and stand at the open doorway of the claustrophobic little room, wondering what has held Dwayne up – it's not like him to be late. At the end of the lobby the lift doors glide open and the local authority team tumble out. I recognise the social worker, her manager and Amanda Hughenden, a barrister from my own chambers who's representing them this week and has a young male pupil in tow; but several strangers form part of the group as it marches across the lobby towards me in a bizarre formation that sends a shiver of dread through my stomach. One of the people I don't recognise is probably a student social worker, attending for 'courtroom experience'; another will be the local authority solicitor and the third ... who knows.

I hate the way local authorities permit their staff to attend court en masse, insensitive to how intimidating this is for a lone parent like Dwayne, who must face them with only his lawyer at his side. Even I feel intimidated, after all these years in the job. I understand that student social workers need to get some idea of what goes on in a courtroom; but do the team manager and the local authority solicitor and the person I can't identify really need to be here?

Whether or not it's deliberate, when a phalanx of professionals turns up on behalf of the local authority, the parents feel as if they're outnumbered and outgunned. When the Children Act 1989 came into force, much was made of the claim that, in England and Wales, care proceedings were 'not adversarial'; but nothing could be further from the truth. If I challenged the team manager's presence, I'd be told that the social worker is young and inexperienced and requires her manager's support at this, the first occasion when she's had to give evidence. I'm sure she does value his support, but what about equality of arms? And where's the support for Dwayne, who's also giving evidence for the first time? If he had a supportive family, his parents could sit on a bench outside the courtroom, waiting to speak with him in the breaks; but if he had a supportive family, chances are he wouldn't be here at all.

Amanda Hughenden calls out a greeting and I smile politely as she leads her people into the room beside me, where several of them will be obliged to stand. There's one small table and a handful of chairs per room, and the partitions are like cardboard; unless I move, I'll hear Amanda giving confidential advice to her team and they'll hear me giving confidential advice to Dwayne. Cursing silently, I pack my laptop into its case and move to the far end of the lobby, where, thank God, I find another empty room.

I've just sat down again when Dwayne appears in the doorway, gaunt as ever but dressed, unusually, in a dark suit. He's a tall man and his trousers are slightly too short, revealing a pair of badly scuffed trainers; but that doesn't matter because the judge will only see him from the waist up. His dreadlocks are held back from his shoulders with an elastic band.

I get to my feet to greet him and ask how he's feeling.

He shrugs his shoulders. 'Not good. I know what's going to happen. Just can't figure out what I'm going to say to Lawrence.'

I shake my head. I too am very worried about how Lawrence is going to take the inevitable outcome of this hearing.

But I'm relieved to hear the realism in Dwayne's words. Michelle and I told him in the conference that our chances of persuading the court to go against both the local authority and the guardian were close to zero; I wasn't sure at the time whether he'd taken it in.

I pull out a chair for Dwayne and return to mine. 'So, you've had a bit of time to think things over. What do you want to do, Dwayne? Do you still want me to challenge the care plan of long-term foster care for Lawrence, or should I tell the court you accept it and focus on the contact issue?'

Dwayne looks at me uneasily. 'I don't accept it, T'reeza; I just know what the judge is going to do. You and Michelle told me, didn't you?' He sighs, places his hands palm down on the table and drums with his long, slim fingers. His anguish fills the space between us. 'I think I've got to contest the care plan, otherwise what am I going say to Lawrence? He's little now but he's going to grow up and ask lots of questions. I don't want to have to tell him that I didn't fight for him.'

'No,' I say, 'of course not. So how about this? We can't dispute threshold, so I'll focus on what should happen now. I'll put it to the key witnesses that the care plan for Lawrence is a recipe for disaster. I'll point out all the problems with it; and then I'll go on to deal with the contact issue, looking at it from the point of view that the court has ignored what I've said and decided to accept the plan of long-term foster care.'

Dwayne nods. 'Sounds all right. You play it the way you think best, T'reeza. Will I definitely have to go in the box?'

'I really think it's best that you do. You'll come across very well. Be sure to face the judge when you're answering questions, keep your voice up and look her in the eye. I don't know this judge but I haven't heard anything bad about her.'

Although the court is meant to sit at 10 am, there's always a lot of what lawyers call 'housekeeping' on the first day of a final hearing. The mother is represented by counsel, but he's quite inexperienced and doesn't have any up-to-date instructions, so we legal reps have a long discussion about whether or not he should withdraw. It's five to eleven when finally we go into court and ask the judge to decide.

Her Honour Judge D turns out to be a small, plump woman with round red cheeks, auburn hair and a disarmingly warm smile. Great, I think, this may not be as bad as I was expecting. Counsel for mother raises his concerns and she tells him she'd like him to remain in court, at least for today, despite having no instructions. 'You never know,' Her Honour says, 'mother might turn up half way through the day. Where's she living?'

Counsel says his instructing solicitor doesn't know. She was staying in a caravan outside the town where they have their offices when she first consulted them, but that was four months ago and they haven't heard from her for three months.

'Very well,' the judge replies. 'I think the best thing we can do is to get started.' She turns to counsel for the children, a bulky, avuncular man called Jerry Hodge. Although the proposal to instruct Bonnie Richardson came from Dwayne, once the court agreed to it, it became a joint instruction by all parties, with the solicitor for the child as the lead solicitor. That means it's for Jerry to call the witness and examine her in chief.

The court clerk fetches Bonnie Richardson from the lobby and ushers her to the witness stand. She's a tall, good-looking woman of about fifty, dressed in a pale pink suit. I note the dark shadows beneath her eyes, tell-tale signs of a woman who works far too hard; but who in this crazy world of child protection isn't permanently exhausted? The judge asks whether Bonnie wishes to swear on the Bible or affirm, and when she says, 'Swear on the Bible', the clerk brings her the holy book and tells her to raise it in her right hand and repeat his words.

'I swear by Almighty God.' Bonnie Richardson's rich, musical voice rings out across the large courtroom. 'That the evidence I shall give' – another pause – 'shall be the truth, the whole truth, and nothing but the truth.'

I let my attention wander as counsel takes Ms Richardson through her report, the updating court papers she's read since she wrote it and whether anything she's read has altered her conclusions.

'No,' she replies with confidence. 'My conclusions stand.'

Counsel for mother should go next, but given his lack of instructions he has no questions to put.

I stand up, smile and explain that I'm asking questions on behalf of Dwayne F. Ms Richardson makes eye contact but doesn't return my smile. That's okay, this isn't a social event. I paraphrase the nice things she's said about my client's parenting skills and ask her if I've stated her views correctly.

'You have.'

'Your major reservations about my client taking on the care of Lawrence appear to be twofold: the fact he's not had therapy to address his childhood experiences and the relatively short period of time that he's been drug-free?'

'Correct.' She pauses. 'Mr F had a very difficult childhood and really needs to work through what happened. I'm sure his childhood trauma is fuelling his drug use.'

'Er, *was* fuelling it, I assume you mean? You're aware he's been drug-free for the last five months?'

'Sorry, yes, that's right.'

I'm trying to scribble a note of Bonnie's words at the same time as asking questions, a task I find well-nigh impossible. 'It would have been open to the local authority to fund therapy for Mr F over the last few months we've been in proceedings, would it not?' I continue.

Ms Richardson looks taken aback. 'It's always open to a local authority to do that,' she replies, 'if the parent wants to engage.'

'But in this case it's not been offered, has it?'

'I've no idea.'

'Did you ask Mr F whether he was willing to go into therapy?'

'I mentioned it in passing. He said he couldn't afford to pay. He's on benefits.'

I've made the point, so I move on. 'I'm sure you're aware that if Lawrence doesn't move into his father's care, there's no alternative option for him within the extended family? Nothing on the paternal side, nothing on the maternal side; and no friends have come forward.'

'I've seen that in the social worker's final statement.'

'And that the local authority care plan is long-term foster care, while the two younger siblings are placed for adoption.'

'Yes.'

'I appreciate that these are the local authority's plans, not yours; but to some extent they follow inexorably from your conclusions that neither parent can safely parent any of the children.' I pause, trying to make eye contact: I want Bonnie Richardson to fully own the consequences of her position. 'Would you agree that Lawrence, who is just six and seven months, has sustained a great deal of loss in his young life?'

'He's lost his mum, which must have been very difficult for him.'

'Indeed. But it's not only his mum. He's lost his younger brother and sister, for whom it appears he carries deep feelings of responsibility – would you agree?'

Ms Richardson looks at me and hesitates. 'I wasn't asked to assess the children; but yes, from what I've read he was in a caring role towards his younger siblings when they were living with Mum.'

'And from the night of the fire,' I go on, 'Lawrence has been placed separately from his brother and sister. So he's already faced a double, or rather a triple loss, hasn't he?'

'I believe there's been some sibling contact over the last few months.'

'Once a fortnight, the children have met up with their carers at a soft-play centre for an hour. Not a lot of contact for young children who've spent their entire lives in the same household up to that point, would you agree?'

Bonnie doesn't hesitate. 'No, not a lot.'

'So in this context, isn't it particularly important for Lawrence to remain in close contact with his father?'

'He needs to see his father, yes.'

'Surely he needs more than just to "see him", Ms Richardson? Lawrence has told the guardian very clearly he wants to *live with* his dad – I assume you've seen that?'

'He's too young to understand the risks.'

'He is very young; but let's look at what he's facing. This is a child who, if the local authority plan is endorsed by the court, will shortly have to bid farewell to his little sister and brother – two of the people he loves most in the world *and for whose well-being he feels responsible* – for the remainder of his and their childhoods. He *might* see them again, once or twice a year, if adopters are found who will support contact; but it's just as likely he won't see them until after all three have turned eighteen – would you agree?'

'It all depends on the adopters.'

'Exactly. But you and I know that it's relatively rare for adopters to support sibling contact.'

The witness looks as if she's not sure what I'm asking, so I go on: 'What I'm putting to you, Ms Richardson, is that the local authority care plan will entail this little boy, even if he's lucky and the adopters see the importance of sibling contact, going through an experience of repeated losses. Do you accept that?'

Ms Richardson is beginning to look uncomfortable. She turns her face away and looks at the judge. 'He will experience loss, yes,' she says quietly.

'And those losses could be somewhat mitigated, could they not, if Lawrence were allowed to live with his dad?'

Now she stares straight ahead of her, saying nothing. Then she turns back to me and says, 'The risks are too high.'

'It's not only the loss of his immediate family that he'll have to deal with under the local authority care plan, is it?' I plough on. 'I expect you've seen that he's going to have to move placements. The foster placement he's in at the moment is a short-term one. So he's going to have to change placement *and* change school.'

Now Ms Richardson looks surprised. 'I didn't appreciate he had to change placements. Where does it say that?'

'It's set out in the addendum to the social worker's final statement; perhaps that didn't reach you?'

She frowns. 'No, it didn't.'

The two-page addendum statement has not found its way into the witness bundle that's propped open in front of Ms Richardson on the witness stand, but Jerry Hodge kindly passes his copy to the clerk, who jumps up and carries it over to her. I wait while she reads it, before resuming. 'Bearing in mind the need for a change of placement if Lawrence goes into long-term foster care, and the grief this little boy is going to experience, compounding the grief he's already experiencing in relation to his mother; bearing all that in mind, do you want to reconsider your conclusion?'

I'm aware that the judge has swivelled in her large red chair and appears to be listening intently, small hands raised above her laptop, ready to take down the witness's answer to this all-important question.

After a long pause, in the course of which I glance at Dwayne and see deep vertical frown marks on his forehead, she delivers her verdict. 'No. I would like to say yes, but I think that without the therapy and without a longer period of abstinence, the risks are *just too high.*' Pause. 'If Lawrence went to live with Dad, and Dad started to use crack again so that Lawrence had to be removed, that would be even more devastating for Lawrence than what he will face if he's moved to a long-term foster placement.'

My moment of wild, irrational hope only lasted a split second. I make a note as I take a breath and glance again at Dwayne. 'I'll move on,' I say, struggling to conceal the disappointment I'm feeling. 'Let me ask you about contact between

Lawrence and his father, should he remain in foster care. You've said it should be once a month, twelve times a year in all.'

'Once a month is the minimum, in my view.' Ms Richardson holds her head on one side. 'And if in a year's time, Dad's done some work on himself and is still drug-free, then he could apply to discharge the care order. I'm not against Dad, he has a great deal to offer Lawrence; but right now it's too soon, and the risk of failure is too high.'

I know this is the absolute best I'm going to get out of her, so I utter a polite 'Thank you, no further questions' and sit down.

12

A Country Home with Horses

After the lunch adjournment, it's the social worker's turn to give evidence – the same young woman I've encountered at previous hearings. To my jaded eye she looks absurdly young to be making life-changing decisions about small children, but I note a new confidence in the way she holds herself. Her straight blonde hair hangs to her shoulders and she's wearing a lot of make-up. When it's my turn to ask questions she sticks her chin in the air and glares straight at me, daring me to challenge her textbook care plans. I feel I'd be wasting my breath if I went over the losses her plans entail for Lawrence, so I focus on the possibility he might be able to return to his father's care in six to twelve months' time.

'But that's not the local authority plan,' she tells me in a tone of indignation. 'We've identified a long-term placement out in the country, and Lawrence needs to understand that it's going to be his permanent home. If father can't accept that, we may have to reduce contact even further.'

I feel a surge of fury as she delivers this crushing blow. I want to glance at Dwayne but decide it's better not to. As I take a deep breath to calm myself, the judge leans forwards in her chair.

'There's nothing in your addendum about a specific placement,' she begins. 'Tell me about the one you've found. Is it a single carer or a couple?'

With a look of mild panic, the social worker turns her chin towards the judge. 'It's an older couple, Your Honour. They've already got a teenage girl in placement. A big house in the middle of fields ... oh, and they've got horses. Lawrence could learn to ride.'

Now I do glance at Dwayne, in disgust. I've heard this tale a number of times before; how the foster home the local authority can provide is infinitely superior to anything the impoverished parent would ever in their wildest dreams be able to deliver.

The judge frowns, and tells me to continue. I hope she's as irritated by the social worker as I am.

'So your plan is that young Lawrence, a dual-heritage child of six, who's spent his entire life in the inner city, should leave behind every person he's ever known to start a new life in an unfamiliar rural world?'

It's my turn to glare. I recall only too sharply the culture shock I went through when I moved out of the city into the country, and I'm white and middle-aged.

'He'll adjust,' she says breezily. 'It's pure luck that this placement has come up. The female foster carer doesn't work so she'll drive him to and from school.'

'Which school?' the judge presses her. 'The one he's at now?'

'Oh no, that's much too far. He'll go to school in the next village.'

'Do they have a place for him?'

The social worker looks uncomfortable. 'Not yet, Your Honour. I mean ... I'm still looking into it.'

Frowning, the judge turns her eyes on me, indicating I should resume my questions.

'The most you can possibly say is that Lawrence *may* adjust to a new life,' I correct the social worker. 'Surely you can see that if you move him out of the city you'll be expecting an awful lot of this little boy?' I fancy I glimpse the judge momentarily raising her eyebrows heavenwards, which gives me a fresh glimmer of hope. 'Now,' I go on, 'let's look at the alternative to your plan for Lawrence. I take it his current carer could continue to look after him for a few more months, perhaps a year, if she was asked to do so?'

The social worker says nothing. 'Well?' I press her. 'What's your answer?'

'I've no idea,' she retorts. 'I haven't asked her. Our plan is for permanence in a long-term placement.'

'Yes, we're all aware of what your plan is, but the court has to evaluate it. Possibly it's not the best plan for this child, no disrespect intended.'

For a split second the judge meets my eye, and I sense she's trying to warn me to go gently with this young, inexperienced worker. So I soften my tone. 'You heard Ms Richardson suggest that if Mr F did some therapy and remained drug-free for a full year, then it might be possible for Lawrence to return to his care. We all know it's best for children to grow up in their own families where possible, don't we?'

'It's not possible,' she replies. 'The risks are much too high.'

'They may be too high *at present*; but if Mr F underwent therapy to deal with his own childhood experiences, and was allowed sufficient time to consolidate his drug-free lifestyle, Ms Richardson has said the risks might diminish to an acceptable level.' I put down my pen, fold my arms and stare at the witness. 'Have you considered funding therapy for Mr F?'

'It's not our plan for Mr F to care for Lawrence. He can go to his GP if he wants therapy.'

'But you know as well as I do, there would be a lengthy delay before Mr F got any therapeutic help via the NHS,' I reply, 'whereas it's open to your authority to fund it privately, right now.' I draw breath. 'Have you discussed the idea with your manager?'

'No, I haven't, because rehabilitation is not our plan. We'd never fund therapy for a parent who wasn't going to be caring for a child.'

'Even where the therapy might enable them to do so?'

'It's not our plan. I don't know what you're getting at. The plan is for Lawrence to grow up in long-term foster care.'

I glance at the judge.

'Time to move on, I think, Ms Thornhill.'

Dwayne is visibly nervous when he arrives at court next morning, ready to give his evidence. The judge does her best to put him at his ease, smiling warmly and telling him that if he prefers he can sit to answer questions. Dwayne chooses to remain standing. It's a brave move, but possibly unwise. He shifts from foot to foot, giving the impression that he's uncomfortable with his considerable height.

After he's affirmed, I invite Dwayne to describe Lawrence. For a second he looks at me in surprise. I turn my head towards the judge in a very deliberate gesture, trying to remind him that it's her he's got to communicate with, not me.

'Well,' he begins, 'he's a normal little boy. Funny, affectionate, likes his footy. Loves his brother and sister, oh boy does he love them.' Dwayne's eyes light up as he speaks and I notice the judge begin to smile.

'You're aware the local authority are wanting to place the brother and sister for adoption,' I go on. 'What impact would that have on Lawrence?'

Dwayne takes a deep breath, stretches out his neck and gazes momentarily at the ceiling, as if gathering strength from on high. When he opens his mouth to speak, his eyes are closed. 'He'll be devastated. He's already missing his mum really badly; if he thinks he's lost his little brother and sister – and me – that'll be like ...' – he searches for the right word – '... like his whole world's fallen apart.'

I'm pretending to write down Dwayne's words, but there's no need. It's as if someone has opened a window and a blast of cold air has been let into the courtroom. This is reality, I think to myself. Dwayne is forcing this bunch of professionals to face up to the pain this little boy is about to suffer.

I wait a few seconds for Dwayne's words to sink in. The judge has her head down and is typing furiously. Then I continue. 'If you were given the opportunity to do some therapy, Mr F, would you take it?'

'Yeah, I would.'

'And if Lawrence could stay in the foster placement he's in now, while you did it, would you agree to that?'

Dwayne half closes his eyes. 'I don't see why he couldn't live with me while I did it,' he replies. 'I could see the therapist while he's at school.'

'But there's also the drug issue,' I go on. 'The ISW says you need to be drug-free for a year before you take on the care of Lawrence.'

Dwayne looks at me. 'I don't agree with her, to be honest; but yeah, if that's what it takes, I'd agree to Lawrence staying where he is for a year ... But I don't want him moved, having to change school and all that, no way.'

I tell him there'll be more questions from the other barristers, then sink back into my seat. I wish Dwayne hadn't said he didn't agree with Bonnie Richardson; but at least he said he'd agree to Lawrence staying put while he did the therapy. Not that I'm under any illusion that any of this is going to happen. Even if the judge is sympathetic to Dwayne, as I sense she probably is, her powers are very limited. She's unable to order the local authority to change their care plan, just as she can't order them to fund his therapy.

The judge's first task in this hearing is to evaluate the risk that the local authority say Lawrence would face if he were returned to his father's care. Once she's done that, she has to consider, by reference to the welfare checklist set out in S1(3) of the Children Act 1989, what is the best solution for him and what order to make, if any. The welfare checklist includes the child's wishes and feelings, his emotional and physical needs, any harm he has suffered, the ability of his parents and any other relevant adult to meet his needs, and the powers available to the court.[1]

If the judge decides that, despite any risk she has identified, Lawrence would be best off living with his dad, she could refuse the application for a care order and instead make a child arrangements order[2] for Lawrence to live with Dwayne, together with a supervision order.[3]

It's possible, of course, that the judge's preference would be to make an order for Lawrence to remain in foster care on a temporary basis while his dad does therapy and maintains abstinence for a full year; but there's no such thing in law as a time-limited care order. Once a care order is made, it lasts until the child is eighteen – barring a successful discharge application.

While I'm musing on the possibilities, I look up again at Her Honour. There's a remarkable warmth in her face and I like her. But, I reflect, the poor woman is newly appointed and would have to be improbably bold to send Lawrence to live with Dwayne against the recommendations of an ISW, a social worker and a children's guardian. And even if she were that bold, it's likely that one of them would appeal against her decision.

Just as we're leaving court, Her Honour tells us that an application for an emergency protection order has been put into her list for two o'clock, because there's no other judge available. We could hang around and see how long it takes; or, since the only remaining witness is the guardian, we can go away and return at ten o'clock tomorrow morning. After the guardian's evidence the judge will hear closing submissions; and then she'll give her judgment at 2 pm on Thursday. Nobody wants to hang around for several hours, so we opt to adjourn till Wednesday.

That evening, after loading the dishwasher, I re-read my notes of Dwayne's evidence and think about my submission. It won't take anybody by surprise; I'm going to bang on about the likely emotional damage to young Lawrence arising from losing Mum, Dad and siblings at the age of six; and in relation to the younger two, I'm going to argue against the care plan of adoption, claiming that this is not a case where 'nothing else will do'. With the provision of therapy for Dwayne and the acceptance of 'planned and purposeful delay', in six months' time there could be a real option for all three children to reside with my client. I'm well aware my argument has its weaknesses. Dwayne might struggle to engage in therapy, even if the local authority were to fund it. The court is supposed to look at the situation as it pertains *now*, at the time of the final hearing, not at the situation that might pertain six months into the future; and even with therapy and abstinence from drugs, Dwayne's ability to cope as a lone parent is untested. Initially he'd have three unsettled children on his hands, all with wounds from being abandoned by their mother and from the months of uncertainty in foster care.

I get up from the kitchen table and pace the length of the room. My son's at his desk, headphones sealing him into his own private world of maths and rap. If I were Dwayne, I muse, would I be able to cope with those three little ones, all on my own? Dwayne would be re-housed if the children came to him, but probably in one of the grimmest areas of the city, and Lawrence would have to change school, yet again.

Moments like this are a constant in my working life, since so often in care proceedings *there's no good solution*. Much as I dislike the social worker, I can see why she's come up with the plan she has. For the younger two, who are probably small enough to adjust to an adoptive family, it may well be the best thing. It's the impact on Lawrence that deeply troubles me.

*   *   *

The following morning, the evidence of Fiona Gratehead, the guardian, takes less than an hour. She accepts that mistakes have been made and that it would have been better had Dwayne been offered therapy. He should be granted PR for Lawrence, but she can see no realistic alternative to the local authority's care plan. Adoption will be the best thing for the younger two, and the fact that it may prove distressing for Lawrence should not be taken into account by the court in reaching decisions for each of them. The only respect in which she's shifted her view is as to the frequency of contact between Lawrence and his father. She now agrees with Bonnie Richardson that father and son need to meet once a month.

After a ten-minute break, the judge listens politely to all our submissions. Her expression has become more inscrutable as the week wears on and I'm no longer convinced of her sympathy towards my client. I wonder how new she is to sitting and how many final hearings she's dealt with so far. If she's very new in the job, she's likely to be extremely cautious. At ten past one she sends us off, saying she'll email us her judgment at noon the following day and deliver it verbally in court at 2 pm.

At noon on Thursday I'm sitting at a desk in chambers, eating a sandwich and waiting for the judgment. At 12.03 the email arrives, so I open the attachment and scroll to the last of its twenty-two pages.

> I therefore make a care order in respect of Lawrence; and care and placement orders in respect of his younger half sister and brother, who will be placed for adoption. Mr F is granted parental responsibility in respect of Lawrence.

'Oh my God!' I mutter. So she's bought the local authority plan wholesale, just as I feared she would. Lawrence is to lose his siblings, and the younger two are being sent off to grow up among strangers. Loving, thoughtful strangers, let's hope, who'll provide them with a good childhood; but the crucial link with their birth family is to be severed.

My colleague, sitting at a desk on the far side of the room, looks up.

'Bad result?' he enquires politely.

'Bitterly disappointing,' I reply. 'Client's going to be devastated.'

PART TWO

LOCAL AUTHORITY LAWYER

13

The View from the Mountains

Outside the little stone hut there's a rudimentary bench, the perfect spot to eat our breakfast. I swing my backpack to the ground, perch aside the plank of wood and zip up my jacket. It's a pristine August morning but up here at 2,050 metres the air's surprisingly cold. A hundred metres below me, my son and his school friend amble slowly up the steep, grassy track from the hamlet where we spent the night. I glance at my watch: only seven thirty. The sun's already high in the sky and the mountain chain to the east forms jagged shapes on the horizon, edged with a ribbon of white light.

Today's going to be the longest, toughest day of our ten-day walk, and I'm relieved the boys got up in time to make an early start. My worry now is whether we're carrying enough food to satisfy their ravenous teenage tummies. Yesterday, in Bagnères-de-Luchon, I bought an extra large *pain de campagne* to supplement today's supplies, but by the time we stopped for the night they'd eaten the whole thing.

I swivel round on my perch, face into the sun and let its delicate early rays warm my eyelids. The little hut sits in the middle of pasture land and I breathe in the sweet smell of rich, well-watered summer grasses. After the struggles of the first few days when the weight of my pack and the weakness of my lawyer's legs held me back, I now feel fit and strong, ready to walk for weeks on end. I'm trying to block out the knowledge that, in just three days from now, we'll be wending our way to a village with a railway station and starting the long journey back to Paris, where we'll board the Eurostar for London. It seems such a waste of everything we've achieved: fitness; the ability to rough it and, in my case, the adjustment of my ear to the twanging accents of Languedoc French.

If it weren't for school, I tell myself, I would chuck in work and spend the remainder of the year's good weather pushing eastwards on this Pyrenean journey.

Behind me I sense movement; the thud of boots on stone and a jolt as two muscly youngsters join me on the plank of wood.

'Orright, Mum?' My son pulls out his water bottle and flips up the spout. 'Anybody in the hut?'

His friend gets up and gives the weathered timber door a push. 'Nope,' he tells us as it swings open. 'Just a few empty sacks and a bale of hay.'

The friend's a black belt in taekwondo. As my son starts to rummage in my backpack for food, his friend sits down on the grass in his orange shorts and does the splits. Just like that, as if it's no big deal.

I gasp in admiration.

'Where's the salami?' my son demands.

'I've hidden it,' I reply. 'We're in France, not Germany. No meat for breakfast.'

'What's instead?' Son glares at me.

'Nuts, cheese …'

Son divvies up the first of our three remaining baguettes, and I dole out a fistful of almonds and a lump of goat's cheese to each of them. 'Ten minutes,' I tell them, 'then we must move.' We've got another three hundred metres of rocky ascent to reach the Spanish border, then an easy stretch where we follow it for a few kilometres, and then – the most demanding part – a

1,300-metre descent through near vertical beechwoods to the refuge where we're spending the night.

As fifteen-year-olds, compared to my fifty-something, the boys could out-walk me if they wanted to. But as we set off, they fall into conversation about Miss C, the English teacher everyone adores, and whether she was as drunk as she appeared when they bumped into her at a recent festival. Soon I'm a hundred metres ahead of them, slogging my way up a rugged incline, stopping to catch my breath, looking back at the minuscule buildings in the valley where we slept. By the time I reach the top, the boys are out of sight and I prop myself on a rock, scanning the grassland that stretches out in front of me.

The wind has dropped and there's warmth in the sun. I unzip my jacket, stuff it into my backpack and set off slowly. I shouldn't walk too far ahead of the kids, but on the other hand it's good to have some space to myself.

Kylie G's in my thoughts this morning; I see her pale features and the dark shadows under her eyes. I never heard back from the solicitor who instructed me, despite emailing her several times. I'll never forget the moment when Kylie ran across the concourse and down the stairs during the judgment. I want to believe that by now she may have picked herself up and started to move on, but it's beyond me. In her shoes, I couldn't do that; my son is everything to me.

I've stopped noticing the springy turf my feet are treading. I'm back in England and the sense of guilt that has haunted me all spring and summer descends like a cloud, accompanied by a voice that says I could, and should, have done more to help Kylie. I don't know what, exactly; but things might have worked out differently if I'd been a better advocate; if I'd provided more emotional support; if I'd found some shred of a ground to appeal the court's decision. Or if I'd overstepped professional boundaries and gone to find her after the hearing? The idea of doing that went through my mind more than once;

part of me believes it's what I should have done. Found her, held her while she wept, listened, supported her.

I stumble into a hollow in the turf, look up and force myself to focus on the view. Ahead of me to the east the line of peaks stretches to infinity, blue-ish in the morning light. Maybe Kylie's okay, I tell myself; but how's that possible? She had no support – no trustworthy parent, no close friend, the beloved grandmother gone. The legacy of abuse probably played a part in her isolation; but so many of the mums I represent are struggling to raise children without a sense of community around them.

Up here it feels like I'm on top of the world. A hundred metres to my right, black bollards mark the border. Beyond, the land falls away and when I turn to the south, I can see into four or five intricate dark-green valleys. Back to the west, the boys are two black specs moving towards me.

Warm sunshine caresses my cheeks, but my mood's growing sombre. I picture six-year-old Lawrence and wonder how he's doing in that rural placement. Is he having fun, learning to ride? Or is he yearning for his mum and dad, and worrying about his little sister and brother? I move on slowly, running through in my mind the clients I've represented this year who lost, or failed to be reunited with, their children. The list is long, the sense of failure persistent, even in the cases where I know I said and did everything that could be said and done. There were other cases, of course, where some might say I didn't do my best. There was a case early in the New Year when I was recovering from 'flu and felt exhausted throughout the hearing; and one or two in which, if I'm honest, I didn't fully believe in the client. A lawyer is a human being; some cases fire you up more than others.

This time next week I'll be back in chambers, preparing whatever hearings my clerks have crammed into my diary. Damn, I think, I really don't want to go back to work so soon … In fact I don't *want* to go back at all. I'm not sure I've got the stamina to weather another three years of constant anxiety, the headaches, the exhaustion, the isolation, and then the gnawing sense when it all goes wrong that I'm to blame.

In three years' time there'll be a natural cut-off point, for then my son will leave school, and at that point I've long determined I must change career. Friends often remind me that after school comes university and the need for financial support gets greater, not less. Well yes, I usually say, I'm not going to abandon him, but perhaps I could earn my crust doing something different? They look doubtful. Like what? Anything, really. A job in John Lewis would do me. Selling expensive coffee machines to people with easy lives ... Or then again I could turn our cottage over to Airbnb; I could let out every room and sleep in the shed at the bottom of the garden ...

At half nine I'm sitting on the ground, back propped against the fourth bollard, contemplating a narrow stony path that starts a few metres in front of me and zig-zags down into a steep-sided valley. Two short bars of paint on a rock, one red, one white, tell me this is our route. Given that I can't quit lawyering right now, I muse, perhaps I should look for a part-time job like the one I did when my son was little, working in-house for a local authority. It posed its dilemmas, but it wasn't as stressful as the bar.

I take a swig from my water bottle. Several hundred metres below, a dozen creamy dots spread in an arc across a lush green pasture; I can just hear the tinkling of their bells. Further down still I spy a grey stone hut – the summer quarters of a shepherd – and the meandering silver line of a stream.

The boys are getting closer, still deep in conversation. Chocolate, I think, unzipping the secret inner pocket in my backpack.

'Hiya,' my son's friend calls out. 'That Spain down there?'

'Got to be.'

'Looks just like France, doesn't it?' Grinning in his baseball cap, he flops down beside me on the grass and accepts the squares of chocolate I offer.

Ten seconds later my son arrives, but instead of taking his ration he grabs my backpack and thrusts his hand inside.

'Oi!' I shout, 'get out of there!' But it's too late. Gangling in his red fleece and baggy knee-length shorts, he seizes the bar of chocolate and dances off to a rocky perch, cramming several squares into his mouth at once.

'Brat!' I shout. 'Ungrateful child! You'll regret doing that in eight hours' time, when you're exhausted and starving and there's none left.' I glower at him while he sniggers. I pretend not to notice that his friend is giggling too.

'She always calls me "child" when she's pissed off with me,' he explains. 'Don't you, mother dearest?'

Child saunters towards me, dangles the now almost empty Lindt carton over my head and drops it into my backpack. But I'm still frowning and his face falls a little. 'Come on, Mum, don't get all stressy, we're on holiday, remember! We're supposed to be having fun.'

'Yes,' I say, shoving the carton into its not-so-secret pocket and struggling to my feet. 'We are having fun, but I'm not in the best of moods.'

'What's up? Are we walking too slowly for you?' He flings a long arm in the direction of the stony path. 'We can trot down this, if you like.'

'No darling, it's not that. It's the thought of going back to work next week, if you must know.' I glance at him, uncomfortable now, aware he won't want me talking like this in front of his friend.

Child wipes the chocolate from his mouth. 'Her work stresses her out, big time,' he explains to his friend. 'Don't become a child abuse lawyer, right? It's the worst job on the planet.'

We're all on our feet now, buckling waist straps and chest straps, ready to set off. 'I'm wondering if I should pack in the bar,' I tell my son. 'Go back into local authority work. Less travelling, so I'd be around more at home. Less money, but I wouldn't get so stressed.'

I thought he'd like the idea, but a look of abject horror is spreading across his face. He steps in front of me, blocking my path. 'Mu-um,' he almost shouts, 'you *hated* it when you did that job before. It drove you nuts! Don't do *that* again, *ple-e-ease!!* ...'

14

Anxiety Levels Rise

Now, dear reader, I'm going to take a flying leap back in time to 1992, the year I first worked for a local authority, long before my son was born. I want to talk about my experiences working as an 'in-house' childcare lawyer and the way the working environment for in-house lawyers deteriorated over time. To me, this explains some of what can go wrong in care proceedings.

In 1992 I'd only been at the bar a handful of years, but already I was weary of being at the beck and call of clerks who sent me here there and everywhere at the drop of a hat – as clerks are supposed to do. My clerks were lovely people, but I found the unpredictability very difficult. I felt drained, I wanted to write, and a part-time job in a local authority appealed because it would mean I had two days a week to do just that, every single week.

So I moved out of London and took a job in the legal department of a metropolitan local authority, in the team that dealt with child protection. Like my solicitor colleagues, I was to provide legal advice and representation to the social services department, which operated from a number of offices in different areas of the city. It was a large and friendly team, run by another ex-Londoner who cared passionately about the families we were dealing with. He was from a working-class background and understood very well the type of pressures the parents were under.

Compared with how things would develop in the 2000s, our working lives as local authority lawyers were relatively easy in the early 1990s. We had spacious offices, with only two or three lawyers to a room and a dedicated team of support staff and typists. We dictated our correspondence into Dictaphones; email and 'self-servicing' had not yet arrived. I distinctly recall the leisurely manner in which we checked the finished letters for typos, signed them and placed the sealed envelopes in the 'OUT' tray for the typists to send to the post room. A carbon copy of each letter went on the case file, and if the filing became too voluminous we could pass that task to the support staff, too.

Little attention was paid in those days to the requirements of confidentiality. The case files were made of flimsy cardboard, bearing the surname of the child in large letters. We kept these in stacks on the floor beneath our desks, in full view of the office cleaners.

As to the work itself, there was nearly always time to think a child's situation through before giving advice. Our client department tried to involve us at an early stage, which meant we could help to steer cases in a positive direction. If there was a sufficiently high level of concern to call a case conference about a child, we were invited to attend. This involved sitting round a table at the local social services office with the parents, their solicitor and key professionals – social worker, teacher, GP, family support worker, sometimes the health visitor – while the concerns were discussed and a vote taken as to whether the child should be placed on the child protection register.[1]

Sometimes there were remarkable divergences of opinion between different professionals. The school might say, for example, that the parents were doing their best in a very difficult domestic situation, that the children were settled in school and that putting them on the register was not justified; while others felt that the risks to the children were unacceptably high and that they must be placed on it, or even be made the subject of care proceedings.

For us as lawyers, while attendance at case conferences was time-consuming, it could be very useful. By the end of a couple of hours we had a feel for the case and for the human beings involved in it. We also had some sense of which professionals would be the key witnesses if in the future we were instructed to issue care proceedings, and how they would come over in the witness box. And we could now anticipate which professionals the parents might try to call to give evidence in their defence, and how *they* would come over.

In other cases, where the concerns were already acute, our first step would be to hold a meeting with the social worker and their manager. The invention of the 'pre-proceedings process' was way off in the future; in the early 1990s it was a question of, first, whether threshold was crossed; and, if it was, then 'Do we issue right away, or do we wait to see if further social work with the family will produce results?'

Even in those days, thirty years ago, social workers carried large caseloads, but they had more time to do real social work – building relationships with families and children – than they'd have by the mid-2000s. This face-to-face time was to be whittled away over the following period of years by requirements to do more and more paperwork, and to rigidly follow prescribed procedures, which resulted in social workers spending little time with families and a lot of time sitting at computers – a situation that continues today.[2]

Going back to our meeting with the social workers, if the decision was made to issue, the lawyer who had given the advice would draft the application, prepare a document setting out the threshold criteria and check the social worker's initial statement.

Many of the cases, then as now, involved families headed by lone mothers. A typical threshold document listed the mother's failings, which were allegedly causing the children significant harm, without any mention of the father. I don't know why we didn't routinely point out that the father – or fathers, as was often the case – was causing the children significant emotional harm by his absence from their lives; instead we bought into the cultural ethos that parenting was primarily the responsibility of mothers.

Issuing the proceedings was a cosy process that involved telephoning the court office and chatting on first-name terms with clerks who saw local authority lawyers as upstanding rescuers of children, rather than as parties to a contested process in which the social worker, rather than the parent, might conceivably be at fault. This gave us an advantage from the off; if we wanted the initial hearing listed on a particular day, for example, when the counsel we wanted to use was available, the clerks would do what they could to oblige. No such advantage was available to parents, who at this stage might not even be aware that their children were about to become the subject of proceedings.

Once we had a court date, we had to get the papers served on the parents, usually by engaging a process server who would visit them at home and try to hand the papers over personally.

We then had a choice whether to represent our social worker clients ourselves, or to brief counsel. I tended to represent my social workers, at least in the early years when I was anxious not to lose my court skills. But over time I found it more difficult to stand up in court opposite barristers who spent all day, every day, doing advocacy. As a local authority lawyer I was seen by the local bar as a lesser form of legal life and, gradually, I lost my courtroom confidence.

One thing I recall as challenging us local authority lawyers in the early 1990s was the volume of case law produced by the higher courts. The Children Act 1989 had come into force on

14 October 1991 and from then on, as with any piece of new legislation, questions arose as to the intended meaning of particular sections, and clauses in sections, and even individual words. Most of these were resolved in appeals to the High Court, Court of Appeal and House of Lords (the forerunner of the Supreme Court); but until a final judgment was given, it could be difficult for lawyers to give clear advice.

One such question was what was the point in time at which the threshold criteria had to be met, in a given case: in other words, at what point in time must the child be *suffering* or *likely to suffer* significant harm, for threshold to be crossed. Was this when the child first came to the attention of social workers? Or when she was accommodated under S20, if indeed she was? Or when the proceedings were issued? Or at the date of the final hearing? Eventually, in 1993, the Court of Appeal decided that the so-called 'relevant time' was the point when the 'process of protection' commenced, provided the process had continued until the date of issue.[3] The process of protection commences when action is taken to protect the child from the situation in which she is suffering or at risk of suffering significant harm, such as when the child is taken into care under S20. In a case where the child remains in the care of the parent at the date of issue of the proceedings, on the other hand, that's the date when threshold must be crossed.

I left my local authority job and went back to the bar from the mid-1990s until my son was born. My next period of work as a local authority lawyer began when he went to nursery school in the early 2000s. This time round I joined an all-women team of child protection lawyers with an exceptionally able and sympathetic immediate manager, in a new, urban local authority. Many in the team had young children and we understood the need to cover for each other when things went wrong at home. Our contracts provided for carers' leave as well as sick leave – that much was good. But the workload was increasing, the working conditions were deteriorating and the wider context in which we did the work was becoming increasingly fraught.

In February 2000 an eight-year-old Ivorian girl, Victoria Climbié, had died in London from severe injuries and ill-treatment sustained at the hands of her great-aunt and the woman's boyfriend, with whom she had been living. In the ten months prior to her death, Victoria had come to the attention of no fewer than four different social services departments, two hospitals, numerous housing officers, police, churches and charities; yet there had been no attempt to remove her from her carers (and no court proceedings). A shocking catalogue of communication failings and errors of judgment was identified in the subsequent public inquiry, chaired by Lord Laming, which reported in 2003.[4] This led to the updating of the key government guidance on child protection, *Working Together* (see Chapter 2), in 2006.

Publicity surrounding a child's death at the hands of their carers always sends a cold shiver down the spine of local authority lawyers. As the people to whom social workers turn for legal advice when they have serious worries about a child, local authority lawyers bear a high level of responsibility. They can only advise on the basis of the information the social worker supplies, which, in emergency situations, is invariably incomplete. Speaking on the phone to an anxious social worker or their team manager, the lawyer has to weigh up what she's told, any documents she has read, the factual questions that remain unanswered, and the possible consequences both of action and inaction. The underlying issue for the lawyer is whether, on the available evidence, it appears that the threshold criteria are met; but even if it does, there are also considerations to be discussed with the social work team such as the likely emotional impact on the child of rushing into court and obtaining an order for interim removal. In the early 2000s, new applications for care orders were mostly heard by lay benches, and it could be dangerously easy for a local authority to obtain an interim care order authorising removal, even on the basis of weak or questionable evidence. Even if a judge subsequently refused to extend the order, with the result that the child went home, a lot of damage might have been done to the child's emotional well-being.

On the other hand, where a lawyer wrongly advises that threshold is *not* met, this may result in a social work decision to back off, in circumstances where intervention could have saved the child's life. The ultimate decision to issue – or not issue – care proceedings, however, is taken by the social worker and their manager, not by the lawyer.

In the case of Victoria Climbié, although a number of professionals expressed concern about her, it appears that this never resulted in legal advice being sought as to whether she could be removed from the care of the great-aunt. No lawyer was criticised in Lord Laming's report, the main recommendations of which led to the establishment of the Every Child Matters programme[5] under the then Labour government and the creation of the office of children's commissioner.

Laming described numerous junctures at which action could and should have been taken by social workers to protect Victoria. His report served as a terrifying reminder to social workers and child protection lawyers of the need to be super-vigilant in cases of suspected physical abuse. Strictly speaking, lawyers are not responsible for errors made by social workers; but in the aftermath of Climbié we spent a lot of time drafting written legal advice in which we set out the investigations that must be made and the need for great caution.

Over the next few years, ever-increasing workloads, a decision that attendance at case conferences was too time-consuming and must stop, cuts in the provision of support staff, the introduction of automation and frequent office moves all added to the pressures on the team of in-house lawyers I'd joined. The senior managers who dictated our working environment appeared to have little if any comprehension of the nature of our work and the level of concentration it required, nor for the requirements of confidentiality. Our immediate manager did her best to advocate on our behalf, but her pleas were mostly ignored.

Each time we were made to move offices, the new space allocated to us was smaller than the previous one, despite the fact that the team was expanding. In the wake of the 2008 banking crisis, management was wrestling with budgetary cuts but chose to spend a lot of money on independent 'consultants' with zero understanding of child protection, who were brought in to dictate how the legal department should be run.

Eventually, crammed into over-crowded open-plan offices with high levels of noise, we spent our days glued to our computer screens. We now had to do our own typing, photocopying and filing, while support staff no longer fielded our incoming phone calls. The budget for continuing professional development was slashed, so we were no longer sent on courses to keep us up to date with the ever-evolving case law. In theory we should have read the dozens of new care and adoption cases being decided by the Court of Appeal, but there was never any time. My colleagues and I became de-skilled as lawyers, while at the same time being obliged to work harder and faster and to absorb more work-related stress than we had previously.

And then came the case of Baby Peter Connelly, murdered by his mother and step-father in 2007 in the London Borough of Haringey. Peter was just seventeen months old when he died. By then he had suffered more than fifty injuries, despite being seen sixty times by social workers, doctors and police over an eight-month period. Unlike in the case of Victoria Climbié, local authority lawyers *were* implicated in this tragedy. Two months prior to Peter's death, a legal planning meeting was sought by his social worker, but seven weeks passed before it took place, partly due to the inefficiency of the legal department. When the meeting eventually occurred, the lawyer, who was relatively inexperienced, had not seen the medical report on the child's most recent injuries and felt unable to advise on threshold. The social worker and team manager were reluctant for care proceedings to be issued and, even had the advice been given that threshold was met – which it clearly was – the ultimate decision whether or not to issue would have been theirs. Nevertheless, there was a clear failing in the legal service provision. Nine days later, Peter was dead.

The publicity surrounding the case and the two serious case reviews[6] that followed resulted in a greatly heightened level of anxiety among both social workers and local authority lawyers, which was felt across England and Wales. Although there was no change in the law following the case, it became easier for local authority lawyers to persuade courts to make interim care orders with care plans of removal in cases of suspected physical abuse, a state of affairs that would continue for several years to come.

One or two years after the Baby Peter case, senior management decided to introduce tech to the legal department, which they thought would enable the staff to do more work in less time. I don't know whether they considered the negative impact it was likely to have on the child protection team in particular, on our capacity to build relationships with our clients and make humane and sensitive judgments, all key elements of good-quality child protection legal work; if they did, they must have concluded it was a price worth paying.

Our old-fashioned cardboard files were replaced by a computerised case management system, and by 2011 we were doing everything on the computer, relying on a string of passwords. From the point of view of confidentiality, it was a big improvement. But from other points of view, the impact was less positive. Almost all contact with the client department was now by email; we sometimes conducted a whole set of proceedings without meeting the social worker face to face.

In a separate development, we no longer went to court. Senior management directed us to use counsel for all but the simplest hearings, with a stipulation that we must brief the most junior ones available, to save costs. This had a further de-skilling effect on those of us who liked advocacy; but, more concerningly, it meant that often we didn't meet the people involved in our cases: neither the parents, nor the social worker and team manager, nor the children's guardian; and we couldn't look at the face of the judge and read how they were reacting to the application we'd put before them. Instead, we were forced to rely on attendance notes from counsel, written – and read – at high speed.

From now on we spent our days locked to our computer screens. The job had lost its human element, and it was growing much harder to do it well.

In parallel to these developments, under the coalition government's austerity programme, services of benefit to children living in poverty, such as Sure Start and many youth work facilities, were dismantled.[7] At the same time, local authority cuts meant that the human resources available within social services departments were greatly reduced, so that social workers were obliged to spend their time fire-fighting emergency situations, rather than undertaking positive work to support families and enable children to remain at home. By 2011 our client social services department was chronically short-staffed, under-supported and demoralised, while individual caseloads grew ever larger.

And then, when our social workers needed us to be available to advise them more than ever, a new money-saving directive arrived from on high with regard to the use of counsel. In reversal of previous instructions, from now on we *had* to do all our own court hearings and would need special permission to use counsel. Given the size of our workloads, this was totally unrealistic; and many of the team felt they'd lost any advocacy skills they had previously possessed.

The constant stream of unhelpful demands from senior management left me musing, on bad days, that the dysfunctionality of the families in our cases was mirrored by the dysfunctional nature of the local authority's legal department.

15

Duty

It's a spring morning. I've dropped my son at school and am sitting at my desk in the room I share with my two favourite colleagues, Fran and Wendy, and two locums who joined the team recently. Fran, Wendy and I used to have a room to ourselves, but senior management decided that a three-person office breached some policy or other so they had the partition wall removed and made the room bigger. It's harder to concentrate than it was, but the mutual support remains very good.

My stomach's in a knot this morning because I'm on duty. This means that, on top of doing my own work, I must give emergency legal advice to any social worker requiring it in any of the five social work offices dotted around the city. Being on duty can be very demanding, so as a team we take it in turns and nobody has to do it more than twice in a month. The trick is to arrange your slots for days when your other work is relatively quiet; but that's almost impossible to control.

Normally when I arrive at work I have a brief chat with Fran, check my diary and make a list of essential tasks to get through in the course of the day. But today, as I open my mouth to say hello, there's an instant ambush in the form of a handwritten note lying in wait on my keyboard.

CALL RICHARD MOSS AT EBURY HILL
14 YEAR OLD FROM LONDON
GANG CULTURE
GUNS

Damn, I think as I sit down, boot up my laptop and log into my phone. A minute later Wilma's on the line. She's one of the few remaining members of our support staff and beloved by the team.

'It's Richard Moss again, he says he needs to speak to you *now*.'

Richard's a social work team manager we hear from a lot, but none of us like him because he has a pushy manner and is always trying to cut corners. I glance at Fran, who mouths 'Richard?' and wrinkles up her nose.

'Okay,' I say, grimacing. 'Thanks, Wilma, please put him through.'

'Morning,' booms Richard's voice down the line. 'Just a quick one, Teresa. Fourteen-year-old lad, Mum's in London Borough of Tower Hamlets but he's here in – (he names an area of the city notorious for drug-dealing), arrived about five days ago. Tower Hamlets say he's been out of school for a year, smoking crack cocaine, likely to be carrying a knife.' He sighs noisily. 'We're pretty sure he's been sucked into county lines and we want to get him back to London as soon as possible. Back to Mum.'

'What makes you think he's doing county lines?' With my free hand I grab a notepad and a pen; every phone call has to be recorded.

'Tower Hamlets say he was on the fringes of it down in London. And he's come here and gone straight into a gang. He was seen last night going into a crack house with a bunch of men.'

'What kind of men?'

'All adults, some in their twenties, all known to the police. Couple of them carry guns. One on the sex offenders register.

All known users of crack cocaine.' I get the sense Richard's getting impatient with my questions. 'Look,' he goes on, 'as soon as we can pick him up, we're going to drive him back to London. Just wanted to run it past you.'

Uh-oh, I think, this isn't a genuine request for advice, it's an attempt to get legal cover for something Richard knows he shouldn't do. He wants me to say, 'Yes, fine, drive him back to Tower Hamlets,' so that he can record it on his file as 'Legal advice sought, plan approved'.

'You can't do that, Richard,' I tell him. 'Section 47. He's been found in your area, which means you're under a duty to make enquiries so you can decide whether you need to take action to safeguard or promote his welfare ...'[1]

'Which we've done,' he cuts across me. '*And* we've been in touch with Tower Hamlets.'

'Who said what?' I deliberately adopt a more abrupt tone; it's the only communication style Richard understands.

'They wanted us to make the enquiries, and we've done it. Our conclusion is that the lad would be better off back in London.'

'How did you reach that conclusion?' I ask coldly. 'It doesn't sound like he's well off in London. Is he living with his mum?'

'Not exactly ...' Richard sounds uncomfortable. 'He's on the move most of the time, as far as we can tell.'

'So you can't take him "back to Mum", can you? I mean, you can, but it's obvious he won't stay there. So there's no basis for saying he's better off in London, Richard, is there? You have to take action to *safeguard and protect* him.'

While I rummage in my desk drawer for my copy of the Children Act, I make a mental list. Presumably the lad's at risk of harm to his health from drug use, harm to his sexual development from child sexual exploitation, harm to his social development from getting dragged into criminal activities, harm to his intellectual development through not going to school and, at the worst, physical harm through gun violence.

'The type of action envisaged by Section 47,' I tell Richard, 'is things like *making an application to the court* ... It sounds to me like you may have grounds to apply for an interim care order. Maybe even an EPO.'

I know very well this isn't what Richard wants to hear. His team are overloaded and he's looking for a way *not* to take on this extra case. It's understandable but it's an attempt to avoid his legal responsibilities. And it seems blindingly obvious the lad's at risk of significant harm.

Richard's tone is growing sharp. 'That's for Tower Hamlets to do. I'm not getting involved in care proceedings with a kid who's just blown in on the wind.' Another noisy sigh. 'Right-o, Teresa, thanks for the advice. Think we'll just have to agree to differ. Gotta go now 'cos one of my team's calling on my mobile. Think he may have found the lad.'

'Let me know what happens, please.' I hear a click and the line goes dead.

Wendy grins at me from her desk. 'Richard Moss,' she pronounces in a tone of disdain. 'He rang me about the same lad when I was on duty yesterday, and I gave him the same advice as you. He thought he might do better by shopping around ...'

'Ha, well, I'm glad we both said the same thing.'

I call up the attendance note template on the screen and start to type, so that if Richard calls again tomorrow there'll be a clear record of what I told him. After a few minutes I stop and check my inbox. Shit, it's as I thought – thirty-seven emails waiting for my response. My cases are busy at the moment. But if I don't finish the attendance note I may forget some of the detail. I'm halfway through when a new email arrives, marked 'URGENT, FAO Duty'.

It's from Pauline, a social worker at the hospital on the outskirts of town. She's a level-headed, sensible woman and I like her a lot. She's written it in note form:

Baby D, female, five weeks old. Brought in by babysitter
at 6 am in state of collapse. Contusion over left temple:
suspected bleed on brain. Now being stabilised in ICU.
Steps being taken to locate mother. Please advise urgently.

A jolt of fear goes through me. This one's as serious as it gets
and I need to respond quickly. I abandon the attendance note
and start to write a reply, but my phone's ringing and Pauline's
number flashes up on the display.

'Pauline,' I say as calmly as I can.

'Mother's just arrived, reeking of alcohol.'

'They let her into ICU?'

'No way, they won't let her in in that condition. But she's
shouting and yelling that it's *her* baby girl and she's come to
take her home.'

'What does she say about how the injury happened?'

'We can't get any sense out of her, she's off her face. Oh, and
she's got quite nasty bruising on her neck. Been in a fight, by
the look of her ...'

'And the babysitter? What did she say?'

'That one minute the baby was fine, sleeping in her Moses
basket, and the next time she went to check on her, her lips
were turning blue and she'd gone all floppy.'

'What's she like, the sitter?'

'Very upset, appropriately so. Seems very ... genuine, if you
know what I mean. She's a neighbour, and the mother asked
her to watch the baby so she could go out for a drink to cele-
brate her birthday with the baby's father.'

'The father's with her?'

'Nope, no sign of him. And the babysitter says she's never
met him.'

'Have you called the police?'

'They're on their way now.'

I glance across the room at Wendy and Fran, who are whis-
pering with one of the locums by the door. They can tell that

I'm dealing with something challenging and are doing their best not to disturb me. Wendy glances at me, mimes lifting a cup of tea to her lips and raises her eyebrows questioningly. But I shake my head. I'm too full of adrenalin to think about tea.

'Okay, Pauline, I'll start drafting an application for an EPO. But if mother sobers up and you can persuade her to sign consent to Section 20, then we may not need it. Although perhaps the situation's too risky.'

'I want a court order. The woman could come back tonight and demand to take her baby.'

Pauline's right, and I realise my suggestion was daft. When it looks as if a tiny baby's been assaulted, court proceedings are the only sensible way forward.

'Yes,' I say, 'I get it. Give me the baby's name and date of birth and I'll start the application.'

'Agata D, 2 February 2011. Parents are Polish, not married and don't live together.'

'Parents' names and addresses?'

I scribble down the information and Pauline promises to update me mid-morning. Jesus, I mutter under my breath as I put the phone down. Poor little creature, I hope she survives. Or, more to the point, I hope she survives without brain damage. I dial the court office to tell them I'll be issuing an application for an EPO, and while I'm waiting for someone to pick up I open a new folder for the case on our case management system and start to complete the C110A, the application form. It's a badly thought-out ten-page document with silly questions like the date of birth of the social worker, but I've filled it in so many times that I know which bits to ignore.

After about five minutes a clerk in the court office picks up the phone, and I outline what's happened and tell him I need an urgent hearing. Okay, he says, fax it over and I'll put it in front of Her Honour Judge X. But I must have it by noon at the latest, she's got a busy list. I glance at my watch: 10.25. That's fine, I tell him, I'll get it to you well before then.

It takes me thirty-five minutes to do the bulk of the form. I'm just thinking what to put under 'Grounds for the application', when Richard Moss calls again. Assuming he's decided to accept my advice, I pick up the phone. 'What's up? I ask in a friendly voice.

'You're not going to believe this,' he tells me, his tone a blend of anger and despair. 'The lad's been picked up by the police for allegedly raping a thirteen-year-old girl in an alleyway outside a nightclub.'

'Last night?'

'Three o'clock this morning.'

'Is he likely to get bail?'

'Not if I've got anything to do with it. He'll be facing very serious charges, won't he, sex with an underage girl[2] *and* rape. He's in the youth court this afternoon. I'm hoping the bench will remand him into secure accommodation.'

Anything, I think to myself, so that you don't have to add him to your caseload. If the boy goes into secure via the criminal route, then it's the Young Offenders Team, not the front-line child protection people, who have to deal with him.

'Yes, Richard,' I say coldly, 'but what if the court *don't* remand him into secure? What if they consider the evidence to be very thin and give him bail? What are you going to do *then*?' A stinging sensation is starting to creep up the back of my neck, the place where all my stress-related headaches begin.

On the other end of the phone Richard groans. 'If they let him go, I'm going to do what I was always going to do. I've got our student social worker lined up to drive him to London after work tonight and drop him off somewhere central.'

I wince. Then I grab a scrap of paper and note down his words, verbatim. I'll have to go to the service manager about this, the person above Richard in the social services hierarchy. But first I absolutely must issue the EPO on the baby.

In another fifteen minutes I finish drafting the EPO application and send it to the printer, a giant, all-singing, all-dancing machine shared by everyone who works on this floor and housed in a room down the corridor. The Ministry of Justice hasn't yet reached the level of techy sophistication where applications can be emailed to the court office, so instead I have to print it, sign it and fax it. Relieved to stand up at last, I lock my screen and walk towards the print room, plastic ID card in hand. This card, which bears the staff member's name and photograph, allows us to pass through locked doors in the building and to collect the documents we've sent to the printer. Many members of staff wear their cards round their necks, on a thing called a lanyard, but doing that makes me feel like a hospital in-patient, so I prefer to leave mine on my desk till I need it.

Usually there's a line of people spewing in and out of the print room but not today. Uneasy, I open the door. Scrawled on a sheet of A4 and sellotaped to the massive machine are the following words:

OUT OF ORDER. ENGINEER CALLED

Shit shit shit. Slamming the door, I run up the stairs to the next floor, where the copier's working, but there are eight people waiting and the man at the machine is printing two copies of a 300-page report. If I don't get this application to the court office soon, the matter won't get listed today. I prop myself against the wall and stare, angrily, at the people in front of me. It's hard to believe that the stuff they want to print is as urgent as an application to protect a badly injured five-week-old baby; but the ethos of senior management is that everybody who works in the legal department must have access to an equal share of our inadequate facilities, regardless of need. If I tried to jump the queue, chances are the news would ricochet around the building, and I'd be hauled over the coals and given a warning.

So instead I decide to call the court office to reassure them that the application's on its way. I take out my mobile and dial the number, but at the other end the phone just rings and rings. They're desperately short-staffed, but still, it adds to my sense of annoyance. How can any of us operate a decent service without the resources we need?

I give up, put my phone in my pocket and shuffle forwards in the queue; but a couple of seconds later it starts to vibrate with an incoming call. This time I don't recognise the number.

'Is this the duty solicitor?' The woman on the line sounds distraught.

'Yes,' I reply, 'that's me. But I'm not in my office, I'm standing in a queue for the printer.'

'Hi, then I'll just give you the bare outline. I'm Emily in the intake team at …' She names her office and continues. 'I've had a referral concerning a little girl, aged six, in Year 2 at primary school.' Her tone is steadier now. 'Parents are separated and she spends half the week with Dad, the other half with Mum. Last night she was with Dad.'

I guess what's coming.

'Her teacher thought there was something wrong when she came in this morning, child was very quiet, which isn't normal for her, so she took her aside and asked if everything was okay. Straight out, child says Daddy licked her fu-fu when he got her out of the bath last night, and she didn't like it. I know the teacher shouldn't have questioned her, but she did. She asked if he'd done it before and the child said yes, he does it every time she stays with him.' Emily pauses for a second. 'The reason I'm ringing, apart from the obvious, is that Dad's picking her up from school at 3 pm. We need an EPO.'

I turn and glance at the people queuing behind me, all of whom have alert, concerned expressions as if they've overheard every word. I feel horribly uncomfortable. 'Why can't the mother pick her up?' I ask softly. 'Have you spoken to her?'

'The mother's not answering her phone. She works away a lot of the time, in different places, and we don't know where she is.'

By now I'm at the front of the queue and my head's spinning. I hold my card against the printer's little scanner and press start. 'Emily, give me five minutes and I'll call you back.' I wait while the machine spews out the application form for the baby, grab it from the print tray, glance again at the line of waiting people and run back down the stairs. In the room where our support staff work, Wilma's sitting at her desk typing at her usual breakneck speed, but she glances up and smiles. I know she can tell, from that one glance, that I'm under pressure. I grab a pen off her desk, scrawl my signature onto the form and ask her to please fax it to the court office, marked 'Very urgent'.

A second later I'm back at my desk. Our two new roommates are both on the phone and Wendy's typing away like a lunatic, but Fran looks up from the document she's reading and picks up a mug. 'Tea now?' she mouths, and I give a thumbs-up. There comes a point in a morning like this when I resort to caffeine to help with the pain shooting up my neck into my head. She stands patiently beside my desk while I search in my drawer for my mug. 'Got counsel lined up for the EPO?' she asks gently.

'Oh my God, no I haven't!' It's completely slipped my mind to call chambers.

'You nut,' is the response. 'You'd better ask Wilma. What time's it listed for?'

'Not been told yet, and Wilma's only just faxing the application now.' How could I forget to book counsel? When it's an EPO we don't have to do the advocacy ourselves, for the simple reason that if we did we'd not be in the office to cover duty.

'I'd offer to do it,' Fran goes on, 'but I'm not wearing the right clothes …' I hand her my mug and a teabag, and she makes for the door, svelte in her jeans and trainers. Then I run back to Wilma and ask her to drop what she's typing and call the clerks in the local chambers in search of counsel. Wilma gives me an exasperated look but says she'll do what she can.

So now I'm back at my desk, popping a couple of Panadol Extra (the ones that contain caffeine, my favourites), eyeing the steaming mug of tea and dialling Emily's number. I've never come across her before but, thus far, I'm impressed.

'I've spoken to the mother,' she tells me. 'She didn't sound that surprised, said she's always had worries about her ex.'

'So why's she sending her child to stay with him overnight?' I fail to hide the annoyance I feel towards this mother.

'No idea. But it's worse than that. I told her she had to come home *right now* and collect her little girl from school, but she said no, she can't do that, she's away with her boyfriend for the next two nights. She said she'll speak to her ex next time she sees him.'

'Bloody hell, Emily. We'll have to apply for an EPO and take the child into care. Did you tell her that's what would happen if she didn't come home?'

'Oh yes, I spelled it all out. And I asked whether the grand-parents could care for the child, but grandma lives in Portugal and grandad works nights. I've asked the Family Placements Team to look for an emergency foster placement.'

'Tell her we're going to court this afternoon.' Glancing at my computer screen, I spot the arrival of an email from Pauline at the hospital. 'I'll draft the application and get it issued,' I go on, 'please email me the family's details.' I don't like making a deci-sion to issue in such a hurry, but if mother changes her mind and magically appears, I reflect as I put down the phone, the court could make a child arrangements order for the child to live with her full-time and for Dad to have no contact pending an investigation.

Exhausted now, I take a swig of tea and open Pauline's email. The baby's mother is being abusive to the nursing staff and the police are threatening to do her for a public order offence. The baby's condition is deteriorating. What time should Pauline be at court? I tell her 1 pm, but I don't yet have the name of coun-sel. If I told her the truth, that I don't yet *have* counsel, that might stress her out, I tell myself, and she's got enough on her plate.

Next I swallow more tea and start to draft the application for the EPO on the six-year-old. As I'm filling in the details, I remember that I'm supposed to file a parenting assessment, a final statement and three care plans by 4 pm today on one of my regular cases, which is nearing final hearing. The social worker's a young man who writes abrupt emails without any greetings or niceties, such as 'Filing date?' or 'Child's gone missing', not seeming to appreciate that we lawyers are not his close colleagues. Whether he's capable of writing what I call a 'straight sentence' remains to be seen: some social workers, especially those who've had less formal academic training, struggle to express themselves on paper. Chances are, if I looked through my inbox I'd find the documents there, waiting for me to check. But there's no way I have time to do that, so I push the thought to the back of my mind and get on with the EPO. And as soon as it's issued I must send that email to Richard Moss's service manager, which will probably produce a furious eruption from Richard, but if I don't send it and something happens to the kid from London, that will be even worse … I wonder whether the student social worker is insured for driving children he's not working with to London in his car.

When I get to the section of the application form where I'm supposed to set out the local authority's plan for the child, I stop typing and call Emily again. She doesn't answer so I leave a message: have you got the emergency foster placement?

It seems draconian to whisk the little girl into care, but if the mother won't return and there are no other available relatives, the social worker has no choice. It's one of those situations where the child will sustain harm, come what may: either she returns to Dad for, potentially, more sexual abuse; or she endures an abrupt move into care. If she goes into care, chances are she'll feel that it's all her fault, for telling her teacher what her dad's been up to. If only the mother would wake up to reality and rush to court, but there's no reason to think she will.

I've just finished the application and sent it to the printer when Wilma puts her head round the door.

'Sarah Galloway,' she says. 'New pupil at Barton Street Chambers.'

Oh Christ. I wouldn't choose to send a pupil on a baby-with-head-injury EPO; but at least the case is covered. There's rarely a choice of barrister for last-minute emergency applications. 'Thanks Wilma,' I try to smile. 'Much appreciated ... Oh, and I'm going to need another barrister, believe it or not. We've got a second EPO this afternoon.'

'Want me to phone Barton Street again?' Wilma looks tired, but then we're all tired in this job, all of the time.

'Yes, please. It's a sexual abuse case. Somebody with a bit more experience, if possible?'

'Time?'

'No idea. Say 2 pm, but they'll need to be available all afternoon, it could get listed at 3. Or 4 ...'

Wilma leaves and I run along the corridor once again, clutching my plastic card, up the stairs and back into the printer queue. Thankfully it's a bit shorter now, just five people in front of me. Ten minutes later, application form in hand, I'm back in the support staff office. I sign the form, fill in the fax cover sheet and lift the lid on the machine.

But this time I'm not in luck.

'It's fucking jammed,' shouts a voice from the back of the room. Georgia, a delightfully foul-mouthed woman who's worked in this office since she left school, stands up and walks towards me. She's plump, with dyed purple hair. 'I've reported it,' she goes on, 'but they can't send anyone till this afternoon.'

This is too much for me and I let out a string of expletives.

Several heads are raised briefly from their screens and I mutter an apology, while Georgia giggles and pats me on the arm. 'Take it down there yourself,' she suggests, 'Go on, a walk'll do you good, T'reeza, you've had a shitty morning.'

She's right, of course; Georgia's always right. And luckily I'm wearing trainers, so I can jog. Slightly embarrassed about my outburst, I smile sweetly and ask her for a large brown envelope.

By 1.45 I've delivered the application to the court office and am back at my desk. I do feel slightly better, and dear Fran has bought me a very fat sandwich from the café on the corner, which just may help soothe my aching head. But I haven't done a brief for either of the counsel I'm sending to court this afternoon. I spoke to Sarah Galloway on my mobile while I was queueing at the court office, and she seemed to get the picture. The barrister Wilma found for the sexual abuse case is a man in his sixties, who normally deals with family finance – read, he probably has no clue about care proceedings. I look up his email address and send him some garbled instructions, with the little information I have to hand.

And then I notice that the office has gone remarkably quiet. Fran's in supervision in another room with our manager, Wendy and one of the locums must be out getting lunch, and the other one never speaks. *And* my phone's stopped ringing. I unwrap the sandwich and sink my teeth into fresh granary bread, egg, cucumber, tomato, cress. 'Drained' is the word that best describes how I'm feeling, as if I've just run a marathon. But nothing's gone horribly wrong, I remind myself; my headache's under control and now I can look at that final statement and the care plans, and anything else that's waiting in my inbox.

Except that first, dammit, I must start today's time sheet, which I should have started at 8.30 this morning. Every minute of our working time has to be recorded, in six-minute units, on a paper spreadsheet. There are codes for each different activity, such as 'MIN' for admin, LAV for giving legal advice and DFT for drafting documents. The time sheets have to be submitted, on pain of death, at the end of each month. The purpose, we're told, is so that the legal department can charge the social services department for our work – a new internal accounting system, aimed at saving money – which has probably, somewhat dangerously, made social workers more reluctant to contact us for advice than in the past. From the lawyer's point of view, timesheets serve to increase our stress levels, because if we don't demonstrate we're spending 80 per cent of our time doing legal work as opposed to admin, our productivity will be questioned. Given that we don't have secretaries and we work in noisy rooms with endless interruptions, I often feel that in reality I spend 80 per cent of my time doing admin as against 20 per cent doing legal work; but I've learned to conceal this.

So I dig in the bottom of my desk drawer and pull out a blank timesheet. Today, since I've mainly worked on three cases, I can fill it in with big blocks. Ten times six minutes equals one hour. I've spent at least two hours on the baby EPO and another two hours on the six-year-old girl. Richard Moss's fourteen-year-old? I'll call that one hour. Ha, that gets rid of five hours out of my eight-hour day, all under the codes LAV and DFT. I experience a passing frisson of satisfaction.

Now I can turn to the final statement. I get it up on the screen, enlarge the print and skim the first few pages. Just as I feared, it's a mess. There are sentences without verbs, singulars and plurals mixed up in random fashion, typos galore and places where I have no idea what the social worker's trying to say. We're not supposed to waste our legal brains editing statements, that's the social work manager's job; but there's no way I'm sending the document to court in its current form. I start to make amendments, using track changes. By the time I get to page 5 I've run out of patience; fifteen minutes have gone by, and I've had to make crossings out and insertions in every paragraph. And I know what the social worker will say if I take him to task: he hasn't got time to check what he's written. Neither has his manager. Well, funnily enough, neither have I.

Team managers are supposed to check their social workers' documents before they're sent to us for filing with the court, but a lot of managers simply hurl the document at legal, assuming we'll do the checking for them. And often, when I'm less busy than today, and because I have a thing about badly written prose, I *do* edit statements. I have to enter it on my time sheet as another activity, such as PCB – 'preparing court bundles'. It would be more accurate to put UMPCS ('unpacking the meaning of poorly constructed sentences') or EESV ('ensuring every sentence has a verb'), but such codes don't exist. Today, however, I really don't have time for any editing, so I send the statement back to the social worker, telling him to start at page 6 and go through the document till it's fit to file. I'm on the point of copying in the manager, but that would really piss off the worker, so I desist.

Phew, I think, I've got an excuse *not* to file those documents today. I email the court and parties, explaining that the documents will be filed tomorrow, with my apologies. Then I check my diary, see that I've missed a training session this morning on something called 'manual handling', which all local authority staff are required to attend; it's to do with shifting boxes and I'm not remotely sorry I forgot about it. Back to the glut of emails in my inbox, which now number a glorious eighty-seven. Half a dozen are from senior management and I flick through them first, thinking they'll all be things I can delete. But no, there's a whole bunch of new commandments that have to be taken on board.

As of next week, all TOIL (time off in lieu) must be taken by the end of the month in which it was accrued. Great. So if I work extra hours in the last week of any month, perhaps due to an emergency on one of my cases, it's tough. Next, childcare lawyers must submit their stats by noon on Friday. Stats are an analysis of how many new sets of proceedings you took on in the current period, how many you completed and what type of order was made at the end of each one. It's a headache to garner all the information and I'm damned if I'm doing that this week. Then, an announcement that makes me groan out loud: there's another move of office on the way, probably in June but possibly not till August. Great, I think, they would choose to do it just when half the team are away on summer holidays; ten of us will have to pack the boxes for a staff of twenty. Why don't we kick up more of a fuss? But I know the answer: my colleagues are lovely people and too long-suffering for their own good. Very few are in the union.

I abandon the management emails and sort through some documents I need to read for a legal planning meeting tomorrow. It would be better for my dry, tired eyes if I printed them out and read them on paper, but I can't face another wait in the queue for the printer. I'm halfway through a social work chronology when the phone rings. I can tell from the number flashing up on the screen that it's Stacey Green, the social worker in my trickiest case, the one with the self-harming teenage girl. Stacey's newly qualified and doesn't get on with her manager.

'Hello,' I say as brightly as I can.

'All right?' she replies, and immediately I pick up a wobble in her voice.

'Fine, and you?' I try to sound brusque. I know something's up, but it's not my job to provide her with emotional support – that's for her manager. I hear her take a breath, as if to gain control of her voice.

'Rubbish, since you ask. We're down to three workers in our team and I've just been told I have to pick up all the cases Sharon didn't deal with before she left. Four of them, on top of my existing caseload.'

'Oh blimey. Tell Adrian you can't do it, it's too much.' Adrian's the manager. The words come out before I can stop myself. It's not for me to help Stacey fight her corner, and I should have kept my trap shut. But she's young and inexperienced, and I think Adrian's out of order, trying to load all that onto her.

'It wasn't Adrian,' she goes on, 'we haven't seen him for weeks. He went on holiday and now he's off sick. It's the woman who's covering for him. I told her I can't take four more cases, but she said I've got to.'

I sigh noisily. This is the kind of thing that drives people out of social work, before they've even got established. 'Well, I'm really sorry to hear it, Stacey, I think they're asking far too much of you.' I glance at my colleagues, who are all now back at their desks; I shouldn't be expressing such strong opinions. But they're all head down, absorbed in their work. 'So what about Lydia Hussein,' I go on, referring to the case where I'm acting for Stacey. Any news?'

Lydia's fourteen, of mixed Pakistani and Welsh parentage, and her mother hanged herself in the family home when Lydia was four. She's been in and out of care since she was eight and is now self-harming so frequently that no foster placement will take her. The plan is to move her to bespoke provision where her considerable mental health needs can be met; but, as with all seriously troubled teenagers, finding a suitable placement is well nigh impossible.

'That's why I'm calling,' Stacey replies. 'I think I've cracked it.'

'You have?'

'North Wales, some little place I've never heard of. The Sea View Trust. Does that mean anything to you?'

'Never heard of it either, but go on. What are they offering?'

'It's in a lovely area,' she says, 'all green and hilly, near the sea'.

'You've visited?'

'Not yet, but I will, if management agree the funding. It's not cheap.'

Residential placements for children who need to be placed alone can cost hundreds of thousands of pounds a year. Even if the placement proves suitable for Lydia, Stacey's in for a battle with the powers that be. But I'm wondering about the distance. Lydia's very attached to her younger siblings and has been seeing them once a fortnight in her current provision. I doubt they could visit her that frequently if she's placed so far away.

'Have you discussed it with Lydia?'

'Not yet. I need management to agree it first.'

Hmm. 'It's a long way away, Stacey,' I say as gently as I can. 'How would you arrange the sibling contact?'

Silence.

'I know Lydia doesn't want to see her dad,' I go on, 'but the little ones are very important to her.'

'Yeah, but this is the only placement we've been offered.' Stacey's starting to sound defensive. 'It's got education on site, and she'll be on a four-to-one.' A four-to-one means there will be four staff available at all times to supervise Lydia and intervene when she tries to self-harm.

'When did you last see her?' I ask, trying to sound casual but dreading the response.

Stacey hesitates. 'At the handover meeting, when the case was allocated to me.'

'What?' I say bluntly. 'You haven't seen her since then?' Stacey has had this case at least four months.

'I've been flat-out busy. And she won't want to talk to me if I do go and see her. She hates social workers.'

I take a deep breath. 'I know you're overloaded, Stacey, I do understand that.' It's not going to help if Stacey feels I'm criticising her, especially given the attitude of her manager; but what's the guardian going to think when she learns that Lydia hasn't had a social work visit in *four months*? We're back in court next week.

'If,' I say slowly, 'you get approval for the placement, you'll need to draft a statement setting out what it has to offer, with the brochure attached as an exhibit.' I pause. 'I'll need it by first thing Monday, so I can serve it on the court and parties in advance of the hearing. But you'd better spell out that you haven't been to see it yourself, you haven't visited Lydia and you haven't discussed the placement with her.'

I'm constantly having to advise social workers how to deal with criticism. Generally my approach is 'fess up quickly and apologise', because an honest acceptance of failure can help reduce the force of other professionals' anger. In this case, however, Stacey deserves the roasting she's going to get for not visiting Lydia.

We say goodbye and, feeling very weary, I transfer my hand-written notes of the conversation into a typed attendance note. I'm sorry for Stacey, but even more sorry for poor Lydia. Then I go back to the social work chronology I need to read for tomorrow's meeting, but my ability to concentrate is shot to pieces. I'm reading a sentence for the third time when Georgia walks in, waving a handwritten phone message.

'Your phone's off the hook,' she says bluntly, dropping the message on the desk in front of me. 'I tried to buzz you three times. Stephen Ball needs urgent advice.'

I glance at my phone's receiver and, sure enough, it's at a wonky angle. How clever of me, I think to myself, no wonder I've had peace for twenty minutes. I push it down firmly till it clicks and smile guiltily at Georgia.

She grins. 'You're gonna love this one. Looks like another EPO.' Georgia has worked in this team for such a long time that she could give sound legal advice all by herself, despite her job title of admin officer.

I glance at the message, from a man who works in an intake team in the poorest district of the city.

'Mum in front office, screaming and shouting and waving her arms about. Child, 3, playing on the floor, oblivious, like he's seen it all before. She's off the wall. We can't let her take him home. Please advise.'

I stare up at Georgia. 'What the fuck's going on today?'

She shrugs her shoulders and makes for the door, saying, 'It's normal, innit? I've had three EPOs in a day before now.'

I pick up the phone once more and dial Stephen's number.

16

The Locum

Some years later, queueing for the Eurostar in Paris on our way home from the Pyrenees, I reflect that my son is right. Working for local authorities drove me nuts and I shouldn't go back to it, unless I really have to. The queue's not moving so I heave my backpack onto the ground and glance round at the boys. My son's squatting down, fixing his walking poles to the loops on his pack; his friend's lolling against a pillar, chatting on the phone with his girlfriend. Both lads look absurdly fit, with cheeks aglow from the sun and calf muscles bulging. Two and a half hours from now we'll be in London, changing trains for our rural destination. For them it's several weeks' more holiday; for me it's back to chambers.

I carry on at the bar for the next six months. It's no less exhausting and emotionally draining than before, but I convince myself there are compensations. The work's interesting and the money's good. I'm away from home far too often, given that my son's an only child approaching his GCSEs; but his dad helps out, sometimes staying overnight so that I can book a cheap hotel in whichever city I'm working in. I'm often lonely and the work's hard, but I cope.

Towards the end of that winter, however, my elderly and beloved mum has a fall and becomes unwell. Chambers lets me go and I spend two weeks caring for her alongside my sister, until, just days after her ninety-fifth birthday, Mum dies.

This is a big and painful loss. I could do with some quiet months to absorb what's happened, but at the bar any respite granted is always brief. I'm expected to pick myself up and carry on, like a soldier on the front line in a war. I keep going for a miserable eight months, until it becomes obvious to me that I'd do better to quit. I want to grieve and to rest, I don't mind living on less money and I've had enough of the unrelenting pressure.

I spend a quiet, sad summer at home, followed by another trip to the Pyrenees. The following autumn, with my son now studying for his A levels and funds running low, I decide I'd better risk a part-time job in a local authority. This time I'll work through an agency; being a locum means it's easier to quit if the setting, or the workload, prove intolerable.

By now local authorities are having trouble recruiting child protection lawyers. As with social work, nobody wants to do the job. The typical childcare legal team has a small core of permanent staff consisting mainly of women with young children; the rest are locums. The agency I join swiftly finds me a post in a nearby city, working just two days a week in the office, and one from home.

I dress carefully for my first day at work, not sure what to expect. If I look like a barrister, my new colleagues may think I'm stuck up; but if I'm too scruffy, the managers could feel I'm unprofessional. So I aim for clean and tidy, but no suit and no black. All I've been told is that I'm taking over a caseload from a woman who's gone off sick, and that the social work team she advises is exceptionally busy.

I walk from the station to the stained concrete tower that houses the offices of Z City Council. Stepping through automatic doors, I find myself in a lobby humming with harassed-looking people who crisscross the floor while talking on their mobiles. The receptionist tells me she'll call my new manager and I stand around feeling like a child joining a new school halfway through the year, till a young Black woman walks across the lobby towards me. She's smiling broadly, as if someone's just told her a joke.

'Hi,' she says, 'I'm Sonia, pleased to meet you. We're going up to the fifth floor.'

The warmth in her eyes sets me at my ease and I ask her what sort of team it is that I'm about to join. Still smiling, she glances at me sideways.

'A madhouse! But don't worry, you'll be fine. They're a nice enough bunch.'

'What sort of madhouse?'

'Oh, you know, very busy, chaotic, lots of staff off sick … but I'm leaving on Friday! Whooppee! I'm going back to college to do my Masters.'

She's so obviously on a high that I instantly wish it was me quitting to go back to university. But when we enter the lift, Sonia's expression becomes more serious. 'You're taking over Charlotte's work,' she says. 'She been off three weeks with stress. They thought we could cover her cases within the team, but they were all in such a mess – oops, I didn't say that, right? – that we've had to get another locum. You. On top of the six locums we've got already.'

'Blimey, that's a lot of locums.'

Sonia looks me in the eye. 'They can't recruit. I told you, it's a madhouse … But I'm out of here on Friday! Yay!!' She punches the air with her fist and my heart starts to sink as the lift propels us upwards.

When the office doors swing open, it sinks a little further. In front of me, fifty or sixty grey Formica desks are jammed together in rows, under the harshest strip-lighting I've ever seen. It resembles a typing pool or a factory. Most of the desks are occupied by weary-looking women who sit motionless, shoulders hunched, right hand on mouse, eyes glued to screen.

Sonia shows me to a chair with a broken arm towards the end of the middle row. 'You can sit here today,' she tells me. 'It's hot desking – first come, first served. Best to get in early.'

I nod silently. Now I passionately wish it were me leaving on Friday. But part of the deal when you're a locum is to act tough and not complain. You're a hired gun, here to do a job then go away. Not really my style, but I must try to play the role.

A tall woman in a red trouser suit is walking towards us waving a sheet of paper. 'T'reeza?' she greets me with a brisk smile. 'I'm Janine. I'm gonna show you how the case management system works. IT haven't done your log-in yet, so for today you can use mine.'

We sit down side by side and for the next hour Janine rattles through the basics of the system. Tech has never been my strong point, and within five minutes I'm lost. It's years since I had to use a system like this.

'Don't worry,' Janine keeps saying, 'you'll pick it up. It's simple, really, much better than the system we had before. I really like it.'

I force a bright smile. Then I tell her she's lost me, and could we please go back to the beginning and start again?

We've just finished when the manager walks up, a haggard-looking woman with spiky grey hair, in a black dress that has seen better days. She moves very slowly, and one glance tells me the poor woman badly needs a holiday. She introduces herself and replaces Janine in the seat beside me.

'Right,' she says, searching my face as if to help her predict whether I'm capable of saving her team from ruin. 'We're going through a rough patch at the moment, staff falling like nine pins.' She manages a weak smile. 'I'm very glad you could start straight away.'

Then she produces a sheet of paper with a list of Charlotte's cases. I glance at it briefly, alarmed to see there are at least fourteen, all of which I'm expected to keep on top of in just three days a week.

'A lot of these are nearing final hearing,' the manager tells me. 'But Charlotte was still waiting for the final evidence.' She frowns and sniffs. 'Bit of a problem with some of our social work teams, you'll find; they're not the best at filing their stuff on time …'

Christ, I think; if the final evidence was overdue *before* Charlotte went off sick, three weeks ago, then it's drastically overdue now. Since the introduction of the Public Law Outline, the courts have become extremely strict about parties filing their evidence on time, because any delay threatens to mess up the twenty-six-week time frame. In the court area where I was last in chambers, if a party was even one day late, they had to make a formal application to the court for permission to file late.

I sense my new manager is harmless, just desperate for help, so I decide to broach the subject with her.

'Doesn't your local court raise the roof if you file late?'

She tips her head to one side and purses her lips. 'District Judge N has been known to reduce one of our solicitors to tears for late filing; but she's the only really nasty judge we have. Our designated family judge, His Honour Judge C, will huff and puff a little bit but you know he doesn't mean it. I wouldn't say we get a lot of stick for late filing …'

I'm astonished, bordering on indignant. How can it be that in relatively tiny countries like England and Wales, the law can be interpreted so very differently in different court areas?

'And do you manage' – I consider how to put this delicately – 'to comply with the twenty-six weeks … on the whole?'

Manager gives me a bit of a funny look, as if I've put my finger on a raw nerve. 'Not in the cases where we file very late, no we don't,' she tells me bluntly. 'You'll see that Charlotte's got half a dozen final hearings coming up, with counsel booked to represent us, and it's possible that some of these will have to be re-timetabled. But please *try* to get them back on track if you *can*, I'd appreciate it.'

She hands me the case list, pushes back her chair and stands up. 'Good luck, and let me know how you get on. I sit over there if you need me.' And with a wave towards the far side of the room, she drifts away, leaving me to sort out the excruciating mess.

I spend most of the day struggling to get to grips with the case management system. Every time I get stuck I look for Janine, but when I can't spot her in the grey Formica maze I turn to the neighbour on my right. Her name's Grace and it turns out she's a locum too, though twenty-eight at most. Grace is what I call a tech super-diva but, like Janine, she explains what I'm doing wrong at a speed I can't really keep up with.

After Grace goes for lunch I turn to my left. Nadia, another locum, is closer to me in age and I've already heard her cursing under her breath several times. When I ask her for help she shakes her head and says, 'This bloody system. It's about as counter-intuitive as they come. I reckon I could work at twice the speed on the system we had in my old job.' She looks me in the eye and smiles wearily. 'Welcome to Z City Council, I hope you'll enjoy working here as much as I do ...'

By 3 pm I'm tired of tech-wrestling and have discovered, on a trip to the loo, where they keep the stationery. I help myself to a large pad of paper and two pens, one black, one red. Back at my desk I draw a rudimentary chart, listing the names of Charlotte's cases down the left-hand side. In the next column I write the date of any forthcoming hearing and in the one after that, the state of play with the filing of documents – '17 days late' or '22 days late' or (in just one case) 'everything filed'. Last I write the name of the social worker and any contact details I've been able to dig up. I've worked out how to look up social workers on the system, but generally their contact details are out of date or simply absent. When I look up Jeremy Frick, for example, who is twenty-six days overdue to file a final statement, four care plans and an updated chronology on a case where the final hearing is listed to start the week after next, I get a landline for an office who claim to have no knowledge of him, and a mobile number with just seven digits. Email address? Missing. Name of office he works out of? Missing.

I've gleaned enough information on just six of Charlotte's cases to be able to enter them on my chart. Six down, I tell myself grimly, only eight to go. If one of the eight has a court hearing tomorrow, I'm stuffed. But I'm damned if I'm going to take any flak; the manager must – or should – know what's going on in Charlotte's cases, and she could have saved me hours and hours if she'd written out a little summary next to the case names. I express my irritation to Nadia, in a suitably hushed tone, vaguely wondering if anybody will notice how frequently we put our heads together.

'Huh,' she says, 'I know it's shit but you're a locum, don't forget. They're paying you to put up with having work lobbed at you. Either you catch it and run with it, or you get up and walk away.' She casts her eyes along our row of desks. 'But I'm not sure the permanent staff get treated any better; they just get paid less than us.'

She's right, of course; but I decide to act as if I don't know the deal. So I get up and search for the manager. I spot her sitting on the opposite side of the room from where she told me she'd be, and I fancy I see her wince as I approach. 'Jeremy Frick,' I say in a loud voice, 'no contact details for him and he's twenty-six days late with his evidence! What to do?'

Several heads turn in the desks along the row. Tongues tut, faces sink in hands.

'He's the worst of the lot,' the manager tells me. 'And the most elusive. Call his senior.'

'Who is?' I enquire crisply. Bizarre how I'm expected to navigate this new authority without any kind of map.

'Paul Mettleton. You'll find him on the system.'

I frown. 'Er, I'm having trouble with the system. Could you just …?'

Silent but clearly irritated, she scribbles a number on a Post-it note and thrusts it at me. But when I get back to my seat and try the line, I get the cold, continuous tone for 'unobtainable'.

I get in early the next morning, determined to get the seat on the far side of Nadia, where the drum and click of typing may be a bit less loud. The instant-migraine strip lights are brighter than ever in the almost empty room and pinpoints of pain are already pressing on my forehead. I'm digging in my bag for my painkillers when a young woman at the other end of the row turns to me with tears trickling down her cheeks.

'The sodding system's down!' she wails. 'I've been in since 7.15 trying to issue an urgent application for an EPO but I can't even log on! I hate this goddamn place, nothing works, it's a nightmare!'

Touched by her distress but also energised at hearing the fury in her voice, I get up, introduce myself and ask if I can help. Pink and blotchy-faced, the woman shoots me a look of gratitude. 'Yes please, if you've got magical powers with technology!'

'What time do you need to issue by?'

'Right now. I've got three children who were taken into police protection on Friday morning and the seventy-two hours is up.[1] I need an EPO by 11 am. The dad's got serious mental health issues, and he's found the address of the foster carer and is sitting outside her house in his car, tooting his horn.'

'Have you spoken to IT?'

'They're not answering the sodding phone! I've tried them six times. And this is nothing new. Our system crashes every other day.'

'You may have to go down to court and make the application orally?' I glance at the woman's clothing. She's wearing pale pink dungarees but they're clean and pressed. A sensible judge would hear her dressed like that.

'I'm not qualified. I'm still doing my legal exec training.'[2]

This takes me aback. 'But you've got a caseload?'

'Thirty cases in PLO; I do the pre-proceedings meetings. This one was in PLO too, but last Saturday Dad tried to shoot the dog in front of the toddler so the police took the children into police protection and now we need the EPO.'

Oh my God, I'm thinking. What sort of manager gives an unqualified person thirty cases and then expects her to deal with the fallout single-handed when one of them becomes a full-blown emergency? That would never have happened in the local authorities I've worked in before.

'Who's your manager?' I ask.

'Same as yours – there's only one manager here, but she's not in on a Tuesday.'

This was news to me. 'Someone covers for her?'

The young woman gives me a pitying look, as if my question's naive. 'Not in this place. They don't do "cover" arrangements.'

I'm wondering whether to volunteer to go to court for her, but I need to be at my desk chasing missing statements and hunting down the errant Jeremy Frick. This is my second, and last, day in the office this week. 'So ... what are you supposed to do?'

'I can go to the head of legal, but he's not in yet. And all he'll do is tell me to call IT.'

I ask if she knows where IT are based.

'Ground floor, the door beside the lifts.'

'Go down and grab someone, tell them it's an emergency?'

Looking brighter, she pushes back her chair and makes for the exit.

Back at my desk it dawns on me that while the system's down I can't get very far with chasing missing evidence, so I decide to take a wander round the office. The desks are quickly filling up. Sonia waves and grins as I pass, and then another Black woman appears at my shoulder. She's wearing a calf-length dress with a matching jacket and introduces herself with a warm smile.

'I'm Kemi, Chaser-in-Chief of Missing Evidence. You must be our new locum! I hear you've been having problems with Jeremy Frick ...'

I'm a bit thrown by this. Is she joking? Can a local authority really employ somebody with the brief of chasing evidence, thirty-seven hours a week? I smile and tell her it's not just Jeremy; I've been given a number of cases with evidence long overdue.

Kemi's smile fades. 'Okay, I'm afraid you'll find that it's not that unusual at the moment, our social work teams seem to be struggling. If you give me the names of the cases, I'll do what I can to help.' She looks uneasy, but I can't tell whether that's because she's embarrassed at an outsider getting a glimpse of the mess the social work department's in, or because she's furious to hear that Jeremy Frick has messed up again. I scuttle to my desk and grab the list I made yesterday.

Kemi studies it briefly, then says, 'I'll do what I can. Where were you working before?'

I explain that I'm a barrister who wearied of the bar and wanted a break. She listens with interest, then she leans towards me and lowers her voice.

'Don't quote me, but you may be shocked by the social work practice in this authority. Most of the staff are locums, often from overseas. They go to a social work agency, grab the first post they get offered, then quit after a couple of months. To go travelling, to live in a different part of the country, all manner of reasons.'

'So there's no stable workforce?'

'Almost none. I'd say two months is the average time our social workers remain in post.' She looks at me intently. 'You can just imagine what that's like for the children they're working with.'

Children in care frequently complain of having a series of different social workers allocated to them over time; but a change of social worker every two months is the worst I've heard of.

'Well, good luck,' Kemi goes on, raising her voice again. 'Nice to have you join us.'

The system's still not on, so I go to the kitchen, make a cup of tea and return to my desk. Half an hour later Kemi appears again, clutching a wodge of paper. 'Jeremy's statement,' she says in a tone of triumph, plopping it down on my desk. 'He sent it to me at midnight, before the system went down, and I've printed it out for you.'

I thank her, pick up my red pen and start to read. Immediately I see that he's used the wrong template for the statement. Some years ago, standardised templates were introduced for social work statements with the delightful acronym 'SWET' (social work evidence template). There's one version for initial statements and another for final statements. If the statement wasn't so late I might tell him he has to transfer the information to the correct template, but in the circumstances I decide not to notice his mistake. At least, that is, so long as the content proves okay.

The initial SWET template begins with a series of boxes in which the author has to insert the children's names, dates of birth, current placement status and current legal status. I frown as I read, because two of the first names don't tally with the names I recall from the file on the system, all of which began with 'E' (Erika, Elon, Eliza and Eddy). Beside these names I put a large red question mark, because of course I can't access the file at present. Now to the dates of birth. Three of them look about right, but the baby's date of birth is stated as two years into the future. Another red question mark.

Next I turn to the paragraph Jeremy has written beneath the first heading, which directs the author to 'Set out which court order or order/s are being sought, and why.'

LA seeks int care order in respct all two children. Eliza, Eddy, Jasmine and Tamar placed with patnal grands, who can continue care due living caravan travllr site.

Grandr heart ttack, wife arthrites. Fstr plct sort 4 baby,
give restbite.

I feel my energy draining away. This is possibly the worst social
worker prose I have ever had the misfortune to read. And especially problematic because the document *must* be filed today
and I have no way to contact the author. It looks as if he has
cut and pasted an initial SWET from another case in order to
produce this Frankenstein of a document, then not taken the
trouble to check it over. He should be talking about which *final*
orders he wants, not interim ones, and for *all four* children; and
he should spell out in intelligible terms whether the children
can or cannot reside with the ailing grandparents. Is it just the
baby he wants to place in foster care? And as a respite placement, or more long term?

I read on:

Local authorities seek parentl responty all three child,
decisions promote bst ints. I consider not safe baby retur
car of mother and fath, significant risk of signif harm

By now, Nadia has arrived and is sitting beside me, eating her
yogurt and honey breakfast as she tries, but fails, to boot up
her computer. I slide the offending document across the white
Formica towards her, screwing up my face in disgust as I do so.

She takes a quick glance at it and turns to face me. 'It's
rubbish, isn't it? I'd be embarrassed to file that.'

'Do you know this Jeremy Frick?'

'I think I've heard his name. Quite honestly I don't pay much
attention to who's who in the social work teams, 'cos they
change so fast. One day you get the same social worker in three
or four cases and you think you're getting to know them; next
time you try to contact them, they're gone.'

'Terrible for the children they work with.'

'It's a disaster.'

PART THREE

LOCKDOWN

17

The Horse

About a month before lockdown in early 2020 I'm getting severe pain in my neck from sitting at a badly configured desk in another local authority a couple of hours' drive from home. I ask the manager to have one of the authority's standing desks moved into the team's room, but she refuses to consider this. I lose patience with her attitude to me as a locum – broadly, 'You're not on the staff, you get paid more than us, so keep your mouth shut.' I'm not prepared to sacrifice my health for the sake of the job, so I walk out.

Back at home I resolve that I will never locum again, and write the opening chapter of this book. By now my son's away at university and, in theory, I'm free to radically change my lifestyle. But people are dying in northern Italy in great numbers of a strange virus thought to have originated in China. Within a few weeks the UK is locked down, my son has come home and the most beautiful spring I've ever lived through bursts in the countryside around our cottage.

To begin with I persuade my son to dig a vegetable patch in which I plant potatoes, beans and salad. We go for long walks and later I sit in the garden drinking tea, while he swots for his first-year exams. Once it becomes apparent, however, that the pandemic is not going to blow over in a couple of months, worry starts to set in, both about money and about the sense of isolation I'm likely to feel when my son returns to university. So I contact the Bar Standards Board, register as a sole practitioner and set up my own little chambers in our front room. My plan is to represent parents and children at the newly instituted online court hearings. I'll operate as both barrister and clerk, so I can take as much or as little work as I choose.

Nine months later, during the winter lockdown of 2021, I'm profoundly grateful to be occupied, and earning.

'Tomorrow's going to be a nightmare,' Helen announces from the centre of my screen. Her tired face is framed as ever by her short, chic brown hair. It's the kind of haircut that says, 'I'm a professional, don't mess with me,' but Helen, more than any other lawyer I know, manages to maintain her humanity alongside her legal nous.

We're having a badly needed chat on Zoom at the end of another long January day. 'I've got two final statements to file on two different cases,' she goes on, 'a hearing at eleven in front of Her Honour Judge G' – we exchange grimaces, because G is by far the most difficult judge on our circuit – 'and then I have to explain to my Serbian client why beating up his girlfriend in the street in broad daylight is not going to help persuade the social worker that he should get his son back. Through an interpreter. On the telephone.' She rubs a hand across her forehead. 'WHY do we do this job, Teresa? Are we mad?'

It's a rhetorical question. Helen's a lone parent with a fat mortgage to pay. I no longer have a mortgage but I'm taking all the work I can get in order to keep my mind from dwelling on the fact I'm alone here out in the country, in the coldest cold snap for twenty years.

'What delights await you tomorrow?' Helen asks.

'Not looked properly yet,' I reply, cradling a mug of strong tea in my hands. I've had a three-hour hearing this afternoon and my head's still whirring from delayed access to caffeine.

'Something for Yarvilles,' I go on, opening the new brief on my second screen. 'Contested interim care order. Bruising.'

'Oh, great.' Helen raises her eyebrows in a gesture of irony. 'How many children?'

'Three children subject to proceedings, one with bruising.'

'How old?'

'Baby, three-year-old and six-year-old. Bruising on the three-year-old.' I won't tell her the client's name, but we swap the bare bones of our cases all the time.

'And you're for?'

'The mother. Who says the child was with the father when it happened.'

The look in Helen's eyes tells me she thinks it's time to bring the conversation to a close. She shakes her head and a smile slowly spreads across her face. 'You've got a long evening ahead of you! Much as I hate it, I still prefer my job to yours ... I'll be pouring myself a glass of wine in a minute, while you'll be burning the midnight oil.'

To my way of thinking, Helen's working life as a solicitor representing parents is no easier than mine as a barrister. Locked in her back bedroom, she spends her time battling with the dysfunctional Legal Aid Agency, talking on the phone with distraught clients, chasing the ones who've chosen to run away, representing them in court and briefing counsel for her more complex hearings. She works nine or ten hours a day, without lunch breaks, from Sunday to Friday. (Yes, Sunday. 'I try not to look at my emails on a Saturday,' she told me once, as if this made her an expert in the art of work–life balance.) Unlike me, she mostly doesn't have to work in the evenings; but then I can sometimes pop out for a walk in the middle of the day, and there's much less chasing and cajoling in my job than in hers. Still, she's right that I've got a long evening ahead of me, getting my tired brain around two hundred pages of evidence.

'Okay,' I agree, 'let's call it a day. Talk again soon!' I blow her a kiss and click 'End meeting for all'.

Now I place the guard across the open fire that burns behind my desk, wrap myself in a thick coat, put on my walking boots and set off for a brisk walk along the bottom of the woods, headtorch guiding me around the tree roots. When I reach the gate that leads from the woods into the field, it's time to turn back. I stop for a couple of seconds, enjoy the distant hooting of an owl, breathe in deeply and retrace my steps.

Back home, I feed the cat, watch him squeeze out through the catflap into the darkness, throw a couple of potatoes in the oven and return to my desk. Reaching for a fresh counsel's notebook, I open tomorrow's papers on my screen. When my brain feels overloaded like it does today, I have to make copious notes to force what I read to sink in. Yarvilles' brief contains only the bare minimum of information and soon I turn to the application form in the court bundle for a list of who's who in this new set of proceedings. Slowly, laboriously, I write down the names:

Jordan, six years old
Charlie, three years old – found with grab marks on his
    upper arms
Riley, a baby of six months
Samantha H – mother of all three children – my client –
    age twenty-three
Alfie S – father of the older two – twenty-six
Leo T – father of the baby – no age given
Dawn – paternal aunt – Alfie's stepsister, age thirty-five,
    lone mum to a teenage daughter

Samantha, I gather, split with Alfie some eighteen months ago and now lives with Leo. Alfie also has a new partner, Estelle, who has two small children from a previous relationship. I skim the social work chronology. From five pages spattered with typos and malformed half-sentences, I glean that my new client, who likes to be known as Sam, grew up with a deeply depressed mother and never met her father. She had Jordan at seventeen and Charlie at twenty, while living with Alfie and Dawn on a housing estate on the outskirts of the city. Sam got on well with Dawn and things went okay to begin with; then in 2019 there were a couple of incidents where Alfie assaulted Sam. After the second one, Sam showed up at nursery with a black eye poorly disguised with foundation, and two weeks later Jordan had a long, linear bruise on the back of his calf. A case conference was called and the children were put on child protection plans under the category of physical abuse. Shortly after this, Sam and Alfie parted company, agreeing to take one child each.

Charlie stayed with Sam. Jordan went with Alfie, who quickly moved in with Estelle and her two kids – which might have been fine, except that Estelle's children were, and are, on child protection plans themselves, also under the category of physical abuse. Not a promising situation, you might think, but at this point the local authority, A City Council, saw fit to take Charlie and Jordan off their plans and cease all involvement. I go back to my list of who's who and add Estelle's name beside Alfie's with an asterisk in red biro. She's one to worry about, in the context of the bruising on Charlie.

The story doesn't end there. After a couple of months of sofa-surfing with Charlie, Sam met Leo, moved into his one-bedroom flat in a tower block and promptly got pregnant. I flick forward through the pages to check Leo's date of birth: August 2001. So he's … nineteen. My heart sinks. A moment later I see that he's a care leaver, and it sinks still further.

All child protection lawyers have their prejudices, and I'm no exception. Time and again we've seen that young adults who've recently left the care system tend to find parenting extremely difficult. They've invariably had a poor if not disastrous experience of being parented in their birth families and often a very negative experience in care. Some rare individuals have the extraordinary resilience required to parent well, despite their experiences; but they're few and far between.

A loud miaow interrupts my thoughts as the cat walks back in, his black coat glistening with frost, green eyes searching for mine. I miaow in reply and get up to fetch his towel, keen to dry him before he jumps onto the sofa beside my desk.

On Tuesday of this week, Charlie got his hoodie wet at nursery and when a worker changed it, she found distinct areas of red and purple bruising on both his upper arms, which she thought were grab marks. Following protocol, the nursery manager called social services. When Sam arrived to collect Charlie at 3 pm, she was met by a social worker who asked her to consent to a child protection medical. I scroll down, looking for the medical report, which should be in section E of the bundle.

Electronic bundles are awkward things and, seconds later, instead of the report, a photo of the underside of a child's upper arm appears on the screen, with dark reddish-purple marks near the armpit. I scroll to the next photo, which shows the other arm, bearing similar marks in the same place. My description doesn't capture the horror of what I'm looking at. I half close my eyes and force myself to study the two images, as a wave of nausea washes through my stomach. It's as if someone has taken a fingertip-shaped vice to the child's flesh, and tightened it until hundreds of tiny blood vessels burst beneath the surface.

Wishing I'd never seen these photographs, I take a deep breath and plough on through the bundle until I find the medical report.

At six o'clock on Tuesday evening, Sam told the community paediatrician at the local hospital that Charlie had spent the four days from Friday to Monday evening with Alfie and Estelle. When Alfie brought him home to Leo's at 7 pm on Monday, Sam claimed, she was out 'doing the horse'. (The horse? Is this a typo?) By the time she came in, Charlie was asleep on the sofa. Sam said she simply carried the child to his bed and left him to sleep in his clothes – adding that she daren't undress him for fear of waking him. And on the Tuesday morning, Sam went on, she left the flat before Charlie woke, for an early shift in the supermarket where she worked as a cleaner. It was Leo who got Charlie up and took him to nursery, pushing baby Riley in the buggy.

After Sam had given her account, the paediatrician asked her to remove her son's clothes. Charlie immediately became agitated, running round the room and speaking in an indistinct babble suggestive of a much younger child. When Sam caught him, undressed him and held him still – somewhat roughly, Dr Hemmings noted – the doctor studied the marks on the child's left upper arm, which she described as 'fingertip' bruising measuring four by five centimetres. She also observed a less distinct cluster of bruising on the right arm.

Case law is clear that medics should decline to age bruising on children; all Dr Hemmings would say was that the red and purple colouration suggested the marks might be relatively fresh. She found a number of small, fading yellow and brown marks on other parts of Charlie's body. Most were in bony areas where a child of three could be expected to knock himself in the course of active play, but the marks on the arms were of a different order. I draw a line in red biro around Paragraph 16:

> The large areas of bruising on the inner aspects of both upper arms, accompanied by finger-shaped trail marks, are suggestive of the imprints of a pair of adult hands. As such these areas suggest 'grab marks' and are strongly suggestive of non-accidental injury.

Non-accidental injury or NAI: the words that, when pronounced in writing by a paediatrician, send the stress levels of the child's social worker through the roof. For the local authority lawyer, the words carry the hidden message *get this case into court quickly; if you don't, you could have a more seriously injured child on your hands and in any event you'll be accused of negligence.*

But I'm not a local authority lawyer any longer, I remind myself firmly, I'm back at the bar. It's no longer my job to ensure that all the evidence has been gathered correctly and to get the matter under the nose of a sensible judge. Today my task is to safeguard the interests of the mother. In practice this means I must set aside the distress I feel for the child, while doing everything I can to prevent the removal of both him and his siblings into foster care.

I read on. Following the child protection medical, the social worker persuaded Sam to allow Charlie and baby Riley to be cared for by step-aunt Dawn 'for a couple of days, until we can get the matter before the court'. Jordan, I learn, was already with Dawn: another social worker had visited Alfie to pick him up. (Alfie had been in the middle of a heated argument with Estelle and hadn't raised any objection to Jordan going to his stepsister.)

There's nothing unusual about this. When a child as young as Charlie sustains serious and unexplained bruising, the local authority has to assume that other children in the care of the same adults are also at risk. I wonder whether Estelle's children were left with her and Alfie ...

Now to talk with Sam. Yarvilles' receptionist spoke to her at 10 o'clock this morning and took some basic details, including the important information that Dawn can't continue to care for the children after the coming weekend. Later my instructing solicitor tried to call Sam three times, but her phone was switched off. So it's down to me to get the information from her that I need.

I swivel round in my chair to place a couple of logs on the fire. In my mind I'm running through what the local authority has to prove in order to get interim care orders on these children with a plan of separation from their parents. Interim threshold is clearly met, as is the test for interim removal. With bruising such as this, and uncertainty as to who caused it, I'll get nowhere arguing against removal.

Which means there's only one way in which I may be able to help Sam. As I've already explained, the Children Act 1989 requires local authorities, when 'placing' children outside their families, to prioritise placements with relatives, friends or connected persons over placements with stranger foster carers. My main task this evening is to encourage Sam to think who she can put forward to take on temporary care of her children.

I write a list of the options we need to discuss. It goes like this:

1. Persuade Dawn to change her plans and keep the kids for a few weeks at least, with Sam visiting on a daily basis.
2. Sam to put forward another relative or friend who can care for the children. (Or, better, who can move in with Sam and Leo and supervise their care of all three children, night and day. But this one's a long shot – people who've grown up in care don't tend to have supportive families or reliable friends. And the flat is tiny.)
3. Ask the court to order that Sam go into a residential assessment unit with the children ... without Leo, at least initially. The problem, however, is that Sam is likely to be seen as in the 'pool of possible perpetrators' and therefore not a safe person to be alone with them. It would have to be a unit with twenty-four-hour surveillance.

As I dial Sam's number, I'm imagining a young woman beside herself with worry about how she's going to get her children back; and fearful in the extreme about tomorrow's hearing. But it's not quite like that. The first time I dial, I get the Tesco mobile ansaphone. So I walk to the kitchen, check the spuds, come back and dial again. Same thing. On my third attempt, a man's voice answers. I explain I'm Sam's lawyer and I'd like to speak to her, please. There's a long pause and then a small, child-like female voice says 'Yeah?'

I apologise for phoning in the evening and say it's best we talk now, as there's a lot to think about before tomorrow's hearing.

'Yeah.'

'How're the kids doing?'

'Not seen them.'

'What, not at all? Aren't they with Dawn?'

Silence. 'They are, but I don't go up there.'

'Haven't you been told you can go and visit?'

More silence. 'Yeah, but ... I'm at work all day, and when I get in it's the horse.'

'The *horse*?'

'My friend's horse. She's been in a wheelchair since she had the accident, so I'm looking after it for her. I let it out in the field in the morning, then I go down to muck it out when I get in.'

'I ... see.' Christ, I'm thinking, am I supposed to know about this friend and her accident? And does the horse come first in this young woman's world? I try to explain what's likely to happen in court tomorrow, and ask whether there's any possibility of persuading Dawn to keep the children for longer. No, Sam replies, Dawn's mother's in hospital, got the Covid, so Dawn's got to go up there on Monday to care for Alfie's dad. He's having chemo and he can't keep anything down.

So that's that. One option down, two to go. 'Is there anyone else in your family, or a friend, who could care for them?'

Another silence. 'Not really, no. My auntie, but she lives in Scotland and works full-time.'

'Any friends?'

'Not what I could ask to take the kids, like.' Pause. 'Why can't me and Leo have them back?' The voice is getting stronger. 'It wasn't us what did that to Charlie. Must have been Estelle.'

I take a deep breath and try to explain that although it may well have been Estelle, the court can't be sure until all the evidence has been gathered, and gathering evidence takes a long time, especially in the middle of a pandemic. I tell her I'm very sorry and I know it's really painful to be separated from her kids. She should go and see them whenever she's allowed to; it won't look good if she doesn't visit. Could she go and see them straight from work, perhaps, leave the horse till afterwards?

'Yeh, but it's dark by 4.30. That's why I go straight to the horse.'

'Hmm. But you said you were "doing the horse" at 7 pm on Tuesday, according to the paediatrician. What time do you finish work?'

'All depends. When I'm on early shift I go in at 6.30, finish at two. On a late shift I finish at four.'

'So who cares for Riley while you're working?' I can guess the answer but want her to confirm it.

'Leo. He does them both, Charlie and Riley, and now they're bloody saying he's not safe! What am I supposed to do? Give up work?'

Yes, I think, that would probably have been the safest thing to do. In my experience it's unusual for a young mum from a deprived background with three small kids to work full-time.

I glance again at my list of options. 'Well,' I say, 'you may have to give up work, for a bit. The local authority wants to put the kids – all three of them – in foster care, and you've got to convince them there's a safe alternative. With my help, of course.'

'Not foster care! My kids aren't going to foster care.'

'How about this, Sam. Until it's clear who caused that bruising to Charlie's arms, the court is going to be very worried, frankly, about all four of you – Leo, Alfie, you and Estelle.'

'It was Estelle.'

'I hear that. But the court wants proof. And the judge may say, if you were so worried about Estelle, why did you let Jordan live with her, and Charlie go and stay with her for three days at a time?' By saying this straight out, to a woman I've never met, I know I risk putting her back up. In normal times I'd be sitting with her and be able to judge from her face whether she was ready to be confronted with the reality of her situation. But I can't meet her face to face and we have so very little time in which to prepare, so I take the risk.

I'm half waiting for her to slam the phone down on me, but instead she says, 'Alfie was there all the time. He wouldn't let nothing happen to the boys. He was a sod to me, but he loves his kids.'

In which case, I think privately, we have to wonder what Leo may have got up to while you were doing the horse. I keep that thought to myself. 'Now, what would you say,' I go on, 'if we could persuade the court to let you go into a residential assessment unit? That's a place where they take mums and small children. You'd get a big room or a small flat and they'd watch you while you looked after your children, and they'd write a report on how you are around them.'

'Where's that then?'

'I can't say where, at present. There are a few residential units around the country. It might be local, but more likely in another city.'

'With Leo?'

'To begin with, no, it would have to be just you and the children. It's possible Leo would be allowed to join you after a few weeks, if things went well.' I should add a lot of 'ifs' and 'buts' in relation to the idea of Leo joining her, but I don't. Keep it simple, I tell myself. See how she responds.

'What about the horse? Leo won't do him.'

'You'd have to ask him to. Or someone else. No residential unit's going to have space for a horse.'

'Oh, he's only small, thirteen hands at most. I call him a horse but really he's a pony.' She pauses and I can hear her breathing. 'Ain't nobody's gonna look after him if I'm not around.'

I'm feeling despondent. I try to explain that if Sam can't come up with a living arrangement for the children that the court considers safe, then the judge will order that they go into foster care. And – I'm reluctant to spell this out, but decide I have no option – once the kids are in foster care, it will be difficult to get them back.

'What, even after all the investigation and that?'

'The investigation could take a number of months, Sam. Everything's on a go-slow because of the pandemic. And once the kids are in foster care you may not be able to see them except on a screen.' A lot of kids in foster care are only getting to see their parents on FaceTime or Zoom, because the foster carers are quite understandably afraid of catching Covid.

If someone had said what I've just said to me when my son was young, it would have been a hammer blow. But instead of anything I recognise as distress, I hear a tone of weary defeat in Sam's voice.

'So what am I meant to do?' she asks. I feel a pang of guilt, although it's hardly my fault that she's in this pickle. 'Why can't the kids live with me and Leo?'

I sigh. 'Look, you've told me Leo was alone with Charlie on Monday evening when Alfie brought him home, and alone with him on Tuesday morning after you went to work. So although you're sure Leo wouldn't have done it, the court won't see it like that. The court has to consider the possibility that anyone who was alone with him in those few days could have done it.' Or indeed that a couple who were alone with him could have done it, I tell myself; but it doesn't feel like the best moment to point this out.

'Estelle was alone with him most probably Saturday while Alfie went to the pub to watch the football. He goes every

Saturday.' My heart sinks still further: if Sam knew Alfie was likely to leave the children alone with Estelle, and that Estelle was unsafe around children, why did she let Jordan live with her and Charlie spend the weekend with her?

'Yes, well, the court's going to look very carefully at whether Estelle could have done it,' I reply. 'But at the moment the court can't be sure, and that's the problem we've got.'

I'm weary now. I want to end the call and eat my baked potatoes. 'Please think over our conversation and I'll call you again in the morning,' I say firmly. 'Have you got the hearing link? And are you going to join on a laptop?'

'Ain't got no laptop,' she replies. 'Using Leo's phone; screen on mine's broken.' This piece of information makes me wince. It's bad enough that people can lose their kids in a process that takes place through a screen. When the screen measures ten centimetres by five, it's appalling.

18

Hearing by Video Platform

It's a cold but sunny morning, the first in weeks. By 8 am I'm at my desk, skim-reading the sixty pages of 'strategy'[1] and case conference minutes from the period in 2019 when Sam's older children were put on plans due to the two incidents of domestic abuse and Jordan's linear bruise. I want to be sure there's nothing in there that could be relevant to recent events (and I'm keeping an eye out for mention of a horse). But mainly I'm looking for any hint that Alfie's been rough with either of the children in the past. I find nothing. The only thing of interest is a suggestion that Leo struggles with reading and writing. He went to mainstream school but a student social worker has questioned whether he may have some form of learning disability. For a second I wonder about Sam. Nothing in our conversation last night led me to question her cognitive capacity, but should it have done? No, I tell myself, apart from her obsession with the horse, Sam came over as relatively sharp.

At ten to nine I get up from my desk, unlock the front door and breathe in the sharp, sweet-smelling winter air. A fine dusting of frost sparkles on the grass. It's bitterly cold but the strong, gutsy light fills me with energy. I wave at my neighbour, who's stacking logs in her wood store beside the gate. If we finish in court by lunchtime, I'm going out for a walk. I fetch the Sellotape and stick a sheet of A4 paper to the front door.

COURT HEARING IN PROGRESS. PLEASE DO NOT KNOCK. LEAVE PARCELS ON DOORSTEP

I'm not expecting any parcels, but you never know. Back inside, I click on the link for the pre-hearing discussion and, over the next few seconds, a series of boxes crowd my screen. Here's Alexandra Johnson in her sun-filled garden-shed-cum-office; it's the third time I've been in court with her this week.

'Hiya, Alex,' I greet her. 'Who're you for?'

'Leo.' She raises her eyebrows with an enigmatic smile and flicks her long auburn hair over her shoulder, as if she knows something I don't know. 'You?'

'Mum.'

Ed Adams smiles politely at the bottom of the screen. He's a keen-eyed young man with a wispy beard who's recently joined Alex's chambers. 'Morning,' he says in a tone of forced jauntiness, 'I'm for Alfie.'

'Morning, Ed,' we both reply.

Joanna Pears arrives, representing the local authority. Her blonde hair hangs in greasy straggles to either side of her black-framed spectacles. 'Morning all,' she says flatly. I've heard she's recently had Covid and I can tell she's on her knees with fatigue.

Finally Guy Harrison appears, representing the children. He's short, grey-haired and sturdily built; one of the most experienced care lawyers on our circuit and probably the nicest. I'm always pleased to see him, for Guy believes in treating parents with scrupulous fairness. Not only that, the court orders he drafts are impeccable and he has a sense of humour. Today he's in shirt sleeves with no tie, clutching a mug of coffee.

'Where are we going with this, Joanna?' he asks. 'Have you got a foster placement lined up?'

'Nope,' Joanna replies slowly, 'no such luck'. Her eyes are focused on something we can't see to the side of the screen, and I deduce she's pulling a T-shirt over the head of her small daughter. 'But paternal step-aunt Dawn can keep the children till next Friday. She's found another relative to care for Alfie's dad. Which gives us a few more days to play with ... I'm going to ask the court to adjourn today and re-list us towards the end of next week – assuming your clients will agree to maintain the status quo, of course. Section 20 will be acceptable.'

Alex is still smiling her enigmatic smile. 'I'll talk to Leo, but I doubt if he'll object.'

Good, I think to myself. That gives me and Yarvilles a bit more time to persuade Sam that a residential assessment would be her best option. And to find a residential unit with suffi-ciently close surveillance that the court may agree to it. Joanna's little girl appears for a second in the corner of the screen, opens a door and disappears.

'My client'll be happy with that,' Ed Adams pipes up.

'I'm going to ask for a cognitive assessment of Leo,' Alex adds. 'My solicitor's got concerns.'

Yes, we murmur, good idea. And I go back to interrogating myself about Sam. Could she, possibly, have a cognitive issue? There was nothing in what she said to me last night that raised any doubt in me about her intelligence. I gained the impression that she might be a little emotionally blunted, but ... when you don't meet your client face to face, not even on a screen, how much do you learn about them? I make a mental note to suggest to my instructing solicitor that they set up a video conference with Sam as soon as possible, so we can push her further on the residential assessment idea, and the horse, and watch her care-fully for signs of learning disability. Not that we're experts.

Now Joanna stares straight at me. 'I suppose you know Mum's been offered contact twice and refused?'

'Twice?' I reply, trying to dodge the question. 'I'd like to see a contact plan, to be clear what contact she's been offered. As for the children staying put with Dawn, I'll call my client in a minute, but I can't see why she'd object. Where's the body map,[2] Joanna? We need to see it.'

'And the medical notes,' Guy adds. 'Lets have a direction for disclosure of the children's GP notes.'

'And full police disclosure,' Alex adds.

'Have the parents been interviewed already?' This is news to me.

'Police plan to arrest Leo this afternoon,' Joanna replies, 'Then mother early next week.'

'And Alfie? And Estelle?' Alex and I chorus.

'I don't have more details, but it would seem obvious they have to speak to everyone. They're all four in the pool of possible perpetrators.'

This is as I expected. It's impossible to say exactly when the injury occurred; possibly during the weekend, possibly on Monday evening or even early Tuesday morning. Alfie and Estelle are clearly in the pool, if it's correct that Charlie stayed with them from Friday to Monday; and Leo's in it because he had sole care of Charlie on Monday evening and Tuesday morning. But it's quite reasonable to put Sam in the pool too; she accepts she was at Leo's overnight on Monday night, and who's to say she's telling the truth when she claims the only involvement she had with Charlie was when she carried him from the sofa to his bed, fully clad, and left him there? Now it occurs to me that I omitted to ask Sam where exactly Charlie's bed is, in Leo's one-bedroom flat. In the corridor? Or in the bedroom Sam shares with Leo and – presumably – the baby?

Guy's putting on his tie. 'Who are we in front of this morning?'

Joanna frowns and for a second a glimmer of a smile passes over her features. 'His Honour Judge Y, unfortunately. Or fortunately, Teresa may say.'

His Honour Judge Y is universally disliked by childcare barristers on our local circuit, for a number of reasons, not least his cold, robotic manner. But he's substantially more pro-parent[3] in his thinking than many of our judges.

It's nine thirty and one by one we leave the Zoom to talk to our respective clients. I watch the faces vanish from the screen and stare out the window at my sunlit front garden. The thing that worries me most about this case is baby Riley. If he gets placed in foster care at the end of next week, at just six months old, his bond with Sam will be seriously damaged. The case will run for months, so that by the time it comes to trial – a two-stage process with a gap of many weeks between two lengthy hearings – the bond may be non-existent. It would be very difficult at that point for rehabilitation to Sam to be successful, even if she's fully exonerated, so it's vitally important to get baby and mother reunited at this early stage of the case. I walk to the door and dial Sam's number.

On my fourth attempt, I get through. Sam's voice is as faint and weak as the night before. I explain that Dawn can keep the children for another five or six days, by which time the local authority is likely to have found a foster placement. In the meantime, she absolutely *must* visit the children every day.

'I'm working late tonight,' Sam replies. 'Going in late because of court.'

'Can you see them tomorrow?'

Long silence. 'After I go down the horse, see if I can pop up then.'

Has she given the idea of a residential assessment any thought overnight?'

'Work aren't gonna let me go,' Sam replies in a tone of irritation. 'We're in a pandemic, all leave's cancelled.'

'Sure,' I say, as gently as my own irritation will allow. 'But you have to put the children first. Riley's only six months old and he needs you. I don't want to upset you, Sam, but this is serious. You may have to give up work for the sake of your kids.'

'Can't do that,' she answers in a frosty tone. 'Hay's very pricey these days. Couldn't afford to buy it if I was back on benefits.'

Can't her friend pay for the hay? I decide not to go there and change the subject. 'Are you okay about the children staying with Dawn a few more days? You'll be asked to sign some paperwork.' I try to explain the implications of the children being accommodated under Section 20.

Silence. Then, 'Yeah, with Dawn's all right. But they ain't going to foster care, no way.'

'That'll be next week's battle,' I reply. 'That's why I want you to consider a residential assessment.'

I sense that Sam's silence is now laden with anger. I wind up the conversation and tell her I'll see her in the hearing. Then I email the other legal reps to inform them we're agreeing to the children staying with Dawn under Section 20.

'Can you see and hear me, Ms Thornhill?'

It's three minutes past ten and Ahmed, the court clerk, is checking that everybody who should be in the hearing has joined the video platform and nobody who shouldn't be here has sneaked in.

'Morning,' I reply.

'Who're you for?'

'Mother. Samantha H.' I search the boxes popping up on my screen for a young woman. 'Don't think she's here yet.' As I speak a young couple appear, sitting very close together on a small settee.

'Are you Ms H?' Ahmed enquires. The woman gives a barely audible assent. She has short blonde hair and a large tattoo on the side of her neck.

'And the gentleman beside you …?'

'Leo.' Leo's voice is deep and gruff, contrasting oddly with his slight, boyish frame.

'Represented by me,' Alex pipes up.

I check the remaining boxes on the screen, wondering whether the mysterious Estelle will appear beside Alfie, but no, he's here alone, bearded, young and anxious-looking. For a second my heart goes out to him. And now Ahmed tells us he's locking the hearing. He reads us the rules, spelling out that this is a court hearing, a formal occasion, and that if anyone were to record what is said it would amount to a criminal offence. Each participant must be alone – Leo and Sam excepted – and in a place where they can't be overheard. And will counsel please mute their microphones, to reduce any static.

Before he finishes speaking, a new box appears at the bottom of the screen and His Honour Judge Y comes into view. He's stiff-shouldered, with sharp blue eyes, very short hair and a small, tight mouth.

'Good morning,' he begins in that brusque voice we've all come to dislike so much. 'Let me see, Miss Pears, you're for the local authority; be so kind as to introduce the parties, would you?'

Joanna Pears goes through the names. But just before she gets to Guy Harrison, a miraculous thing occurs. His Honour Judge Y swings through 180 degrees, so that he's hanging upside down, tight lips where the bridge of his nose should be and eyebrows forming a broken line in place of his mouth.

Bloody hell! I mutter to myself, glad my mike is muted. If only I had the bottle to take a screenshot, right now. For a glorious three seconds His Honour hangs there, blissfully unaware of what we're seeing. Then Joanna Pears clears her throat and explains she believes there's a technical problem; and a second later His Honour zips round the remaining 180 degrees to regain his rightful position, eyes uppermost. I glance at my colleagues one by one, checking for evidence of mirth. Alex and Guy are smiling faintly, but it's all so subtle that His Honour doesn't notice.

'We've had productive discussions, Your Honour,' Joanna continues. 'Subject to Your Honour's better view, we have an agreed proposal to put before you. All three children can remain in the care of the paternal step-aunt Dawn G for another week under Section 20, by which time the local authority is very much hoping it'll have a foster placement available. In view of that, I'm not instructed to seek an interim care order this morning. We'd ask the court to list the matter for a contested hearing on Thursday or Friday of next week. And I'm drafting directions for police and medical disclosure.'

Judge Y's features relax momentarily. 'Well, that seems very satisfactory. Much better for the children if they can reside with a family member. Now, let me look at the court diary.'

After a few moments peering at a second screen, he announces that the only court time available is the afternoon of Friday 29 January. We can have ninety minutes, for a hearing which, if not agreed, will require at least a day. I un-mute and point out to His Honour that my client has given me clear instructions to contest, but my comments are swept aside.

'Tell your client,' the judge tells me in a steely voice, 'that she's lucky to get a hearing next week at all. The court lists are dreadfully congested. We'll have to do the best we can in ninety minutes.'

I will certainly not be saying this to Sam H; she's not chosen for her children to be dragged through care proceedings, and she has a right to a fair trial, even in the midst of a pandemic. But, realistically, the lack of court time is unlikely to make any difference: I'm under no illusion that we can win this one.

As the judge draws breath, Alex tells him that she has concerns about her client's cognitive abilities. Will the court grant permission for Leo to undergo a cognitive and capacity assessment[4] by a consultant psychologist, to establish what the position is?

Judge Y holds his head on one side. 'Can your client read and write?' The brusque tone has returned.

'Only with the greatest of difficulty,' Alex replies. 'It's not clear whether that's because he left school at fourteen or for ...' – she searches for a suitable phrase – 'organic reasons.'

'Very well,' the judge replies. 'Cognitive and capacity assessment. I doubt your solicitor will be able to get that done by next Friday, but ask her to do her best.' He gazes ahead of him with a sharp look in his eyes. 'Now, Miss Pears, when you efile[5] the order, send it directly to me, please. The court office are struggling with the volume of work. Anybody else wish to say anything?' One by one we tell him meekly that no, Your Honour, that covers everything.

After the boxes have vanished from my screen I get up, walk to the kitchen and put the kettle on. While I'm waiting for it to boil I try to call Sam three times to check she's understood what's been decided. Three times I get the ansaphone.

19

Snow

On Sunday morning I wake to find snowflakes fluttering past the floor to ceiling windows in my kitchen, covering the patio in a carpet of white. The cat sits close to the glass, his head rising and falling as his eyes follow the flakes with avid attention, but he's not asking to go out. I look at the clock. I need four hours to prep a final hearing for Monday, and I must call my son to ask what he wants for his birthday, but there's time for a sortie. I text my friend Grace in the next village, wrap up warm and set off to meet her in our favourite part of the woods, on a hillside where we're almost guaranteed to be alone. Grace is a teacher in an upmarket girls' boarding school twenty miles away.

We walk and talk for a couple of hours, and Grace tells me about a pupil who worries her, a thirteen-year-old whose wealthy British parents live in Singapore. She was sent to her first boarding school at the age of eight, but as she struggled to settle she was moved after two terms to another school and finally to the one where Grace works. Meanwhile, the father embarked on an affair with one of his colleagues in the merchant bank he directs and the mother left him, setting up home with a lesbian partner who's a well-known artist. In the school holidays the girl and her younger brother fly to Singapore to visit their dad, but mostly he's too busy to spend time with them so he hires a nanny to do the job for him.

'Why don't they stay with their mum?' I ask as we reach the top of a snowy slope.

'Mum doesn't want to see them, as far as I can make out.' Grace turns to me with a grimace. 'Too busy travelling the world with her new partner.'

'Poor girl, no wonder she's unhappy.'

Stamping our feet, we gaze across fields of pristine snow to a line of black skeletal trees.

'She's not just unhappy,' Grace corrects me, 'she's self-harming, really badly. Last week she cut herself all down her arm and they had to rush her to hospital.'

'Bloody hell.' I stare at Grace. 'And the parents? Presumably they've been informed?'

'I assume so. It's for the headteacher to decide at what point to contact the family. But she's not alone, you know. I teach several girls who feel abandoned by their parents. One's anorexic, another one's talking about suicide. Deep down they all seem to feel they're at boarding school because their parents don't love them.'

'It makes me so cross!' I exclaim. 'The parents I work with get taken to court for emotionally abandoning their children.'

'I know. And these girls will have lifelong issues as a result of the neglect they've experienced.'

This is a conversation we have repeatedly. English social policy turns a blind eye to the emotional neglect and sense of rejection many younger children experience when sent to boarding school (I'm told that some teenagers actively enjoy it).

By half twelve I'm tramping homewards. My toes are cold and my breath comes out in a cloud of white. I'm just turning onto the well-walked path above my cottage, when a woman's voice calls my name. I turn, and there, to my astonishment, is Sarah Sherston, her boots covered in snow and her cheeks aglow. Sarah was my favourite social worker when I worked as a locum at M City Council.

'Well, hello!' I cry. 'What are *you* doing here?'

She's got a red knitted hat pulled down over her ears and her black overcoat reaches to her knees; but there's no mistaking the woman I used to sit beside in legal planning meetings. We often saw eye to eye about the children in her cases.

'I live just down the road!' Sarah beams at me. 'Moved here in December.' She's one of those people who went into social work in their forties after a career in something else. Sarah had been a senior manager at Tesco for twenty years before going to college. When our paths crossed, she was a newly qualified frontline social worker, struggling with a massive caseload.

'I must tell you my news!' she goes on, clapping her mittened hands together.

'What?' I've never seen her look so excited.

'I've handed in my notice!'

'Ha,' I reply, 'very well done! What finally triggered that?'

The look of delight on Sarah's face starts to fade. 'It just got worse and worse. Eric, our manager – you remember Eric? – left in the summer. That was a big blow. He was so supportive, you could go to him with any problem and he'd help you sort it out. But management really didn't like him.'

I raise my eyebrows. Eric had a mind of his own, which often brought him into conflict with the people above him.

'Once he'd gone,' Sarah goes on, 'things went from bad to worse. They recruited a new manager who was totally inexperienced. She's awful to work with, really anxious and kind of panicky, so different from Eric. Anya and Jim couldn't stand her, and they both left – remember them?'

I nod. 'Have they been replaced?'

'Management tried, but they just couldn't find anybody. Not even locums.[1] Nobody wants to work for M City Council! And you can hardly blame them … Our team's meant to have six social workers, and now it's down to two, just me and one other, plus a student on placement.'

I shake my head.

'Our caseloads have gone through the roof, and there's no support at all. Last week I was left at nine o'clock at night trying to place two children whose mum was in hospital with Covid. My manager wasn't even answering her phone. It was a bloody nightmare! And the worst thing is, however hard you work, however many extra hours you do – like, sixty hours a week is about normal for me at the moment – nobody *ever* says thank you. Our managers are …' – she lowers her voice as a couple with a child on a sled walk past us – '*shit*. Sorry to use that kind of language, but they really are. *Crap*. I know they're stressed out of their boxes, but they've chosen to be managers and they get paid more than us, and if they could just show some appreciation of how we work our butts off it wouldn't feel so bad.'

'Oh Sarah, it sounds awful.' Standing close to her now, I can see the big dark shadows under her eyes and the lines around her mouth. Sarah's ten years younger than me and last time I saw her she didn't look like this. How frustrating, I think, after chucking in Tesco and spending three years at college, to find the job's hell on earth. 'I'm sure you've done the right thing by resigning,' I go on. 'But what a shame for the team. I don't know how they'll manage without you.'

Her eyebrows flicker. 'Yeah, well, I'm trying not to think about that too much. It feels really awful, like I'm abandoning a sinking ship, and it's going to take a load of children down with it.' Her upper lip starts to tremble. 'I just couldn't go on. I wasn't sleeping. I'd go to bed with my head full of the latest crisis on one of my cases, and four hours later I'd still be awake. It went on like that for about eight weeks, and one day my husband said, "Sarah, this job's making you ill. I don't care about the money. You've got to quit." So I did …'

'Good for you! And … do you have plans?' I'm not sure whether I should even ask this question. 'Back to supermarket management?'

I watch Sarah's face as she takes off her hat, shakes out her thick dark hair and pulls it down again over her ears. 'If only! I look back on that job now like it was a picnic … No, no, I'm staying in social work for the time being, I can't bear to waste the training. But not child protection. I'm looking at something easier, part-time, a children's centre or a family placement team.' She sighs. 'Don't think I'll ever go back to child protection, after the last two years.' I watch as she forces herself to smile. 'So … are you local?'

I point down the hill. 'Just over there, less than half a mile.' I'd invite her to drop in, but indoor visits are forbidden. Instead I take out my phone and ask Sarah for her telephone number, my frozen fingers struggling to hit the keys.

20

Lawrence

I don't really feel like working this afternoon. I can't face the courtroom atmosphere that pervades the front room, so I detach various cables from my laptop and carry it into the kitchen. Here I can sit at the table and sneak glances at my snow-covered patio, when the material I have to read becomes too grim. But it's cold. I get up, open the woodburner, lay a fire and strike a match. Funny how the sight of the orange flames leaping behind the glass gives me such a sense of well-being. Likewise the stack of logs against the wall.

I sit down wearily and open my papers for tomorrow's case. It's expected to proceed as an agreed final hearing, as there's not much that's disputed. I'm for the father, and although I've dealt with the case before, all I can remember is a nasty assault by the mother on the ten-year-old girl.

Three hours later, it's completely dark outside and the woodburner's throwing out a delicious heat. I get up and draw the curtains, thinking good, I can eat and watch the news. I'm about to shut down my laptop when an email arrives from the solicitor representing Sam H.

Hi Teresa

Thought I should let you know we had developments on this one on Friday afternoon. Alfie and Estelle have had a fight – both taken to A&E with cuts and bruises – and split up. Not clear who started it, but sounds like Estelle gave as good as she got. Flat's in Estelle's name so Alfie is homeless and, believe it or not, social worker has agreed to him moving in with stepsister Dawn, Jordan, Charlie and baby Riley!

Sam rang me 5pm Friday – knew all about it – livid that Alfie's with the kids when she's got to see them under supervision. Local authority say they consulted the guardian, who said that so long as Dawn supervises Alfie and doesn't leave him alone with the kids, it's safe. Seems very odd to me! Will try to speak to local authority solicitor first thing tomoz.

Let me know your views?

Cheers
Nicola

I read it once, then twice. What about Estelle's kids, I immediately think, if they're witnessing her getting into fights with her partner? And yes, allowing Alfie to move in with Jordan, Charlie and the baby seems very odd indeed, given that he's clearly in the pool of perpetrators. But it's good if Sam is now actively wanting to see the children. I bash out a quick reply to Nicola, suggesting she write to the local authority solicitor putting on record Sam's objections, and that we make a fuss at the next court date, which is only a week away. It's a case management hearing, at which a fact finding to establish how Charlie got injured will be listed.

* * *

The following afternoon, as I'm writing my attendance note for the final hearing, the phone rings. It's Michelle, the solicitor who briefed me on behalf of Dwayne F more than three years ago. I was still in chambers at the time.

'What a nice surprise!' I exclaim. 'How are you?'

Michelle sounds as rushed as ever. 'Surviving. Had Long Covid all last summer and autumn but I seem to be over it, more or less. And you?'

I know she hasn't rung for a personal chat, so I tell her I'm fine. Which I am, more or less.

'Guess who I heard from two days ago?' she launches in. 'Our favourite client.'

'Dwayne F?' I've often wondered what happened to him.

'He sounded good. His voice was strong, and he seemed more confident. But he's worried sick about Lawrence.'

'Because?'

'The child's utterly miserable, writing letters to his teacher saying he wants to die.'

'Oh no! Is he in the rural placement?'

'He was there six months but he didn't settle, so they moved him back into the city, to a lone foster carer with two little boys of her own.'

'And? No good?'

'Apparently not. He's had two changes of school, one when he went to the country and one when he came back, and the current school say he's completely switched off learning. Which is a terrible shame, because he's bright, like his dad.'

'Is he having contact?'

'Once a month, not enough. But Dwayne has made real progress and is thinking of applying to discharge the care order. I doubt he'll get legal aid, but I thought I'd run it past you.'

Legal aid applications are not something I deal with. 'You'd know best, Michelle, about that.'

'Dwayne would have to satisfy the Legal Aid Agency that he's made substantial changes since the final hearing.'

'What are his circumstances? Does he have his own accommodation?'

'Just been offered a one-bedroom flat. Last week.'

'And what about therapy? I don't suppose he found a way to do it?'

'No therapy. Couldn't afford to pay. But he's working as a delivery driver, so he's off benefits.'

'And the drugs?'

'Drug-free for the last three and a half years.'

'Brilliant! Does Lawrence have the same social worker as before?'

'Different social worker, a man, and they get on much better. He's referring Lawrence to CAMHS.'

CAMHS stands for Child and Adolescent Mental Health Services, the desperately overloaded NHS service tasked with supporting children with mental health issues. Michelle clears her throat and continues, in a tone laden with anger, 'So in about a year, if he's lucky, Lawrence might get some help ...'

'Which is much too long to wait.[1] He must be nine by now? I think you should apply for legal aid and see what happens.'

'That's my view. Will you represent him?'

'Of course, I'd be delighted. Let me know how you get on.'

PART FOUR

LAST DAYS AS
A LAWYER

21

The Cab Rank Rule

On a warm August evening I arrive home after a long day in court and go straight out to water the garden. During all those months of online hearings I forgot how exhausting court work is when your day starts and finishes with an hour's commute, much of it spent in a traffic jam. Now that most of our hearings are attended ones, I'm starting to wonder how much longer I want to do the job ... My son has nearly finished at university, so soon I can pack in legal work and rethink my life if I want to.

But if I do decide to pack it in, there are two cases I must see through to the end. Sam H's final hearing is on Monday and Dwayne's application to discharge the care order for Lawrence is listed in mid-November.

I'm dragging the hosepipe across the grass to the parched potato bed when I receive a call from Henry Ruddock, a solicitor who briefs me frequently. He needs cover for a new care matter, with an initial hearing tomorrow. The client, he says, is a nice woman called Kanchana L. He was going to do the hearing himself, but his wife wants him to attend a family funeral.

Damn, tomorrow is Friday and I was looking forward to a day off, but I don't want to let Henry down, so I agree.

I eat supper in the garden, enjoying my late summer holly-hocks and trying to ignore the flower beds that need weeding. Then I drag myself away and put my plate in the dishwasher. The weather's too lovely to be indoors and I'd like to go for a wander in the woods, but I've got to read the new papers. I sit down at the kitchen table with my laptop, leaving the garden door open beside me.

The client, Kanchana L, is originally from Thailand. She's a masseuse aged thirty-nine and lost her British electrician husband in a road traffic accident eighteen months ago. Early this year she started a relationship with a man called Desmond J, an estate agent in his mid-fifties whom she met on the internet. Some weeks back Kanchana moved with her thirteen-year-old twin daughters – the children of her marriage – into Desmond's spacious suburban home. The girls are now the subject of care proceedings, and the reason is as follows.

Desmond J has three boys from *his* marriage, which ended in divorce fifteen years ago. Since then he's had no contact whatso-ever with his now adult sons or ex-wife. Four months ago, the middle and younger sons went to the police to allege that they'd endured repeated sexual abuse by their father when they were at primary school. Their mother, an emotionally fragile woman, had been dimly aware of what was going on, but preoccupied with her own struggle against breast cancer. She turned a blind eye to the abuse and did not inform the authorities. But when the boys were aged nine, eleven and thirteen, with the breast cancer in remission, she summoned the courage to divorce Desmond and moved with the boys to the other side of the country.

After the allegations were made the police acted promptly, taking detailed statements from the adult sons, and proceeding to arrest and interview Desmond. His response was point-blank denial. He suggested his sons might have developed mental health problems and pointed to their mother's fragility.

In all serious criminal cases, the Crown Prosecution Service is the agency that decides whether the evidence gathered by the police is sufficiently compelling to warrant a prosecution. In this case, despite Desmond's denials, it clearly felt it was; just last week, he was charged with eight counts of anal rape. He's expected to plead not guilty on all counts and the matter will be listed for Crown Court trial to be heard at some point in the next six to nine months.

The standard of proof in criminal cases is higher than in civil cases. A jury in the criminal case can only find Desmond guilty if they are *sure beyond reasonable doubt* that he committed the alleged offences. If the care court is asked to make findings on the same evidence, by contrast, the issue for the judge will be whether it's *more likely than not* that Desmond perpetrated the abuse alleged. This is a lower, civil standard of proof that applies in care proceedings, also referred to as the 'balance of probabilities'.

If a criminal trial is heard prior to the conclusion of the care proceedings, and if the defendant is convicted, the care court can then rely on the conviction as proof of what happened – or, to put it another way, to establish the truth of the allegations and cross the threshold criteria. But it takes many months for a criminal case to be heard and so, rather than wait, the care court has to proceed to try the allegations, to avoid leaving the child or children in limbo. The hearing in which it does this is called a 'fact finding'. Prior to the hearing, the local authority draws up a 'schedule of proposed findings'. After reading the papers and listening to the witnesses, the court makes findings as to which (if any) of the proposed findings are made out.

In a case where the criminal trial has taken place reasonably swiftly but has resulted in a 'not guilty' verdict, the care court may still hold a fact finding, because the standard of proof is lower. So it's possible for an alleged perpetrator of sexual or physical abuse to be found 'not guilty' by a criminal court and yet for findings that he or she perpetrated the abuse to be made by the care court.

In the present case the local authority was alerted by the police to the sexual abuse allegations within a few days of the adult sons speaking to them. Since then a social worker has been working with Kanchana, spelling out the potential risk to her twin daughters if the allegations are true. Kanchana has fluent English and brushed aside the social worker's offer of an interpreter for the meetings. The offer seemed to anger her, and when the social worker repeated it, she explained that – understandably – she didn't want her business being discussed in the Thai community.

The social worker would like Kanchana to separate from Desmond, at least until the criminal trial has taken place; but Kanchana won't hear of it; in every meeting to date, she's been adamant that Desmond is innocent. The sons are lying, she claims, while admitting that she's never met them. The older one has serious mental health problems, and the younger one harbours an irrational and vicious hatred for his father. And in any case, the allegation is one of what Kanchana calls 'gay sex'. Desmond is not gay, she assures the social worker, so why would he want to have sex with young boys? Desmond poses absolutely no risk to her twins and she intends to marry him once 'this stupid business dies down'.

Some weeks back, the social worker persuaded Kanchana and Desmond to sign a voluntary 'safety plan', stipulating that the twins should never be left alone with Desmond. It's not clear whether and to what extent the couple have complied; but Kanchana's attitude has become more and more dismissive. Last week a new social work manager took over responsibility for the case. After a twenty-minute conversation with Kanchana in which he asked for her reaction to Desmond being charged with anal rape and she shrugged her shoulders, he insisted that care proceedings be issued. He wants the court to make an interim care order at tomorrow's hearing, under which the girls will be removed from their mother and placed with their paternal aunt, who has undergone an assessment and been granted temporary approval as a foster carer for the girls.[1] Happily the aunt lives in the same city, so the girls could continue to attend their current school, but all their contact with their mother and Desmond would be supervised. Kanchana, according to the manager, is blind to the risk and therefore incapable of protecting the girls.

I get up from the kitchen table. Sexual abuse cases are something I do my best to avoid, because they trigger difficult feelings about stuff that happened to me as a young woman. I'm annoyed with myself that I didn't enquire more carefully as to what this case was about. Normally I do probe a bit, but Henry's call caught me off-guard.

Moreover, you're not supposed to pick and choose your cases at the bar. You're supposed to follow something called the 'cab rank rule', which means you operate like a taxi, picking up the first passenger in the queue and taking them wherever they want to go. In practice this means representing any client who requests your services in your chosen legal specialism 'without fear or favour'. You're meant to banish any feelings of revulsion you may have about the particular type of case and any doubts about your client's instructions, and simply put them forward to the court. If a criminal barrister is asked to represent someone on a murder charge, for instance, she's not meant to say to herself, 'Can I face the gore?' nor 'Do I think he did it?' Instead she's meant to accept the brief without blinking and take the client's instructions at face value – that he has an alibi or was acting in self-defence, for example – and argue that for all she's worth.

As a care barrister, if you represent an alleged perpetrator of sexual abuse, you're not supposed to think, 'Do I believe the child's account of what happened?' or 'Do I find my client credible?' Again, you're supposed to accept the client's instructions at face value and put them to the witnesses and the court. You can, of course, point out to your client that the story he or she's telling you is one that a court may find difficult to believe; but if they insist that X is what happened, you have to put this scenario forward. And the same applies if, like me, you have the brief to represent the alleged perpetrator's partner. I can – and should – try to warn Kanchana of the likely consequences if she maintains her unstinting support for her new man, but it's she who gives me instructions, not the other way around.

That's all very well and good, and of course I believe that everybody has a right to a fair trial with skilled representation, no matter what they're accused of. But barristers are human beings, not robots. We've all had life experiences, good and bad, and there are times when it's well-nigh impossible to put aside one's feelings in order to do one's best for a client. This is how I feel about sexual abuse cases where I'm asked to represent the alleged perpetrator or their allegedly collusive partner. I know I can't effectively cross-examine a child who says he or she's been sexually abused by an adult; I can't in all conscience put it to him or her that they're lying. In this case it would be a question of cross-examining the adult sons – not as bad as cross-examining a child – but I would still find it difficult. So I do my best to avoid cases of this kind.

I walk over to the sink and fill the kettle. A cup of tea to settle myself.

I sit down again and continue reading. In the four months since the start of the criminal investigation, Desmond's middle son has had a serious breakdown and is now sectioned in a psychiatric hospital. He's unlikely to be well enough to give evidence. Henry thinks that the indictment will be amended to leave 'only' five counts of anal rape, based on the allegations made by the younger son. He too is suffering from stress and has recently dropped out of university, but remains determined to give evidence against his father.

I skim the younger son's statement. It's a detailed description of appalling abuse, which allegedly began when the child was five. Reading a statement is not the same as testing it in cross-examination, of course, but the level of detail is compelling.

> Dad used to drive me to rugby practice on Sunday
> mornings. On the way home he'd turn off the main road
> down a country lane and park in the gateway of a field,
> in a spot well screened by trees. He'd switch off the
> engine, text Mum to tell her we'd stopped at the pub and
> would be a bit late for lunch; then he'd tell me to lie
> down on the back seat ...

My stomach starts to churn and I decide to skip the rest. I don't need the detail for the purpose of tomorrow's hearing.

I sip my tea, thinking about Kanchana who, presumably, has read all this. Or has she? How well can she read documents in English? And if the answer is not very well, has the gist of the content been carefully spelled out to her? This is the first thing I need to check when I meet her. But *if* the case has been properly explained, how's it possible, I ask myself, for this woman to be so convinced that her new partner's sons are lying? She's only known their father four months. And he hasn't spoken with his sons for fifteen years – surely that raises some questions.

I flick to the initial social work statement. The social worker has formed the view that, despite her feisty manner, Kanchana L's a deeply anxious woman, still grieving the loss of her husband and unable to tolerate the thought she may have to bring up her girls alone. I try to imagine what it's like to be Kanchana, thousands of miles from her own family, who apparently were very poor, and recently bereaved but hoping she's found a man who will provide for her and her daughters till they reach adulthood. I feel a flicker of sympathy, followed by a whoosh of dismay. How can the woman – any woman – be cavalier about the risk of her daughters being a target for sexual abuse?

When we meet at court tomorrow, I'll try to persuade Kanchana to think again. Does she really grasp what's alleged against Desmond? And has she tried to imagine what she'll feel if the court orders the removal of her girls, and she only gets to see them twice a week?

Tomorrow's hearing is listed for just one hour. Interim threshold is clearly crossed, with the sons' allegations sufficient to establish reasonable grounds to believe that Kanchana's twins are at risk of suffering significant harm in the form of sexual abuse if an order is not made. Desmond J's denials do not affect this and neither does my client's inability to contemplate that the adult sons may be telling the truth. But one hour will not be long enough for the court to properly consider the arguments for and against removal.

Just as with Baby K in Chapter 9, the court will have to direct itself that 'separation is only to be ordered if the child's safety demands immediate separation'.[2] In recent case law the test for interim removal has been boiled down to two related questions: is removal *necessary*? And is it *proportionate*?[3]

If the local authority is determined to go ahead with its removal application, given the lack of court time, the case will have to be dealt with 'on submissions'. No evidence will be called; instead each of the three lawyers – one acting for the local authority, me for the mother and another for the children – will get a few minutes to try to convince the judge, on the basis of the written evidence, that the test for interim removal is or isn't met; and then the judge will have the challenging task of cobbling together an unappealable judgment and delivering it out loud, all within the hour. And in that way a decision that may well impact the twin girls profoundly will be made. It's madness, but that's the way these things are often done.

The courts claim that the making of an interim order, which is inevitably done at a stage when the evidence is incomplete, 'is not intended to place any party to the proceedings at an advantage or a disadvantage'.[4] This sounds nice and clean and clinical, but in the case of an interim care order sanctioning removal it's highly misleading. I don't dispute that interim care orders are sometimes necessary, in cases where the child or children are at serious risk in the care of the parent; but, whatever the intention, the making of the order generally places the parent from whom the children are removed at a huge disadvantage. Once your children have been removed, it can be extremely difficult to get them back. And the emotional damage that removal may inflict on the children is sometimes, if not always, very deep.

I put down my mug of tea and tell myself I can make a brief submission on behalf of Kanchana without letting the case get to me too much. First, if it turns out Kanchana can't read English, I'll raise the issue of translation. The court shouldn't be asked to make a decision with such far-reaching implications on the basis of documents the mother can't read. This *could* get us an adjournment for the documents to be translated, during which I will urge my instructing solicitor to continue spelling out to Kanchana just how high the stakes are.

If, on the other hand, Kanchana *can* read English, I'll press the point that she says she's been adhering to the safety plan, although she considers it unnecessary. I'll also point out that the girls are still grieving for their father, and that to remove them from their mother at this point could be highly damaging emotionally. I will say that such a step would be disproportionate (although, privately I'm not convinced. To me it looks like a choice of bereavement + separation from Mum, versus bereavement + risk of sexual abuse. I suspect the latter might cause more long-term damage ...).

And after the hearing's over, I tell myself, I'll return the brief. I won't tell Henry the real reason, but sure as hell I'll have a dental appointment on any future date the court throws at us. A *vital* dental appointment that can't be moved. I push back my chair and gaze out the door into the dusk. A silvery full moon hangs low over our long, narrow garden.

Some of us lawyers like to construct a 'case theory' to help us present a case, usually when we find the facts a bit uncomfortable; it's a type of narrative and we know it may prove entirely wrong. By the time I get to court the next morning I've formed a firm hypothesis that Kanchana is a vulnerable woman of little formal education who hasn't been able to read the court papers in English. She doesn't understand the seriousness of the allegations against Desmond J and the fact that the court may order the removal of her daughters. The social workers were mistaken when they took Kanchana's refusal of an interpreter at face value, and have failed to communicate the risks.

As for Desmond J, I see him as quite a threatening figure. There's at least some truth in what his sons have said and I'm glad I won't have to deal with him directly. He's not a party to the proceedings at present because he has no legal relationship with the twins, but very likely he'll be joined as an intervenor.[5]

I find Kanchana and Desmond standing at the door of Court 6, hand in hand. Kanchana's a petite woman in a smart black dress with thick, glossy hair beautifully coiled on the back of her head. Desmond's of middling height, with a red face and neatly clipped greying hair, dressed in a well-cut silver-grey suit. As I walk towards them, Desmond steps forwards and thrusts a hand in my direction. I dodge to avoid it, introduce myself to Kanchana and ask her to follow me.

Kanchana glances at Desmond. 'We like to speak to you together,' she says softly.

'I'm sorry,' I reply, 'but my job is to represent you alone, not your partner, and I must speak with you privately. Mr J is not a party to the proceedings.'

'But the case is all about me!' Desmond J protests. 'I need to speak with you along with Kanchana. I don't have my own brief, do I?' He forces a grin and I see that beneath the bravado he's feeling acutely anxious.

I square my shoulders and shake my head. 'I'm sorry, that's not possible. Please wait here for your partner.' I turn and march swiftly to the nearest consulting room and stand in the doorway. Kanchana hesitates, says something to Desmond and walks towards me, stony-faced. I close the door behind her and we both sit down.

'He didn't do anything,' she blurts out. 'Those boys are lying. He's a good man, Desmond, a very good man.'

Oh dear, I think, as my case theory evaporates before my eyes.

'Those boys are a little bit crazy.' She holds a finger to her temple. 'Not well in their minds. Older one in psychiatric hospital, breakdown. Younger one at home with Mummy. Gave up his studies.'

I gaze at her intently. 'Okay,' I say, 'I understand that's your view, but let me check a few things with you first. Your spoken English is very good, but can you also read in English?'

'Of course!'

'Have you been able to read the social worker's statement?'

'Of course.'

'They didn't have it translated for you, did they?'

'Not needed, I read English.'

'Great, okay, I was just checking. Could you summarise for me what you think the local authority is worried about?'

Kanchana sighs, regarding me as if I'm every bit as annoying as the social worker. Then she summarises the case against Desmond and the local authority's concern for her daughters as precisely as any lawyer might. 'It's all nonsense,' she concludes. 'Desmond's a good man. My daughters love him. They lost their dad but now they have Desmond. We are all very happy.'

'Hmm,' I say slowly. 'I understand that this is your view of the situation. Unfortunately, the local authority sees it very differently. They're very worried about your daughters' safety if they're alone with Desmond. And because you do not share their worry, they're going to ask the court this morning to place your daughters with their aunt, under an interim care order.'

Kanchana looks at me with fury in her eyes. 'They can go to Auntie Sarah! It's okay, I have told them to go. And after Desmond goes to court for the criminal trial, my daughters can return to live with us.'

This takes me by surprise. 'You'll agree to the girls going to their aunt?'

'Why not? She lives close to their school, it's not a problem.'

'You won't be allowed to see the girls much. At most twice a week, with someone watching you and listening to your conversation.'

'Pah, let them watch and listen!'

I stare at Kanchana. 'Wouldn't you prefer to keep the girls with you, but separate from Desmond, at least until this matter has gone through the courts? He may be found guilty and sent to prison, but equally he may not, it's impossible to predict. There'll be a criminal trial and a trial in the care proceedings.'

'I'm not separating from Desmond. He's my fiancé. Girls can go to Auntie.'

We spend the next twenty minutes going over the same ground. I want to be 100 per cent sure that Kanchana has thought it all through and knows the implications of her position. I spell out to her that if she lets her girls go now, she may never be allowed to resume care of them; but she dismisses this idea as ridiculous. Once she's convinced me that she won't be budged from her position, I ask her to wait while I speak with the other counsel.

I find Callum Braddock for the local authority and Eleanor Jack for the children in a room along the corridor. Since Desmond J's not yet been invited to intervene and has no representation, Eleanor has just spoken with him in order to report his position to the court. That's fine, I don't object. But as I walk in, she's regaling Callum with a verbatim account of the conversation. I catch the tail end of it, in which she's imper-sonating Mr J.

'"Believe you me, it'll all come out in the wash. My sons learned to tell porkies at their mother's knee – she was a right basket case, but that's another story – and they're both, let's say, soft in the head. They won't cope when it's put to them they made it up. Put them on the stand, wham into them with the questions and, bang, you'll see their stories collapse, first James then Andrew."' Eleanor completes her performance by making a fist with her right hand and punching it hard into the palm of her left.

I find it hard to suppress a smile as I sink into a chair. 'So,' I turn to Eleanor, 'I assume the guardian's supporting the appli-cation for removal?'

'She sure is.'

'What's your client's position,' Callum asks, 'when she doesn't have Desmond breathing down her neck?'

I clear my throat. 'The whole thing's a pack of lies and Desmond is a *good* man. But we're content for the girls to go and stay with Auntie Sarah; we won't oppose the making of an interim care order.'

Callum tilts back his chair and smiles broadly. 'That's great news! So it's just an agreed order and a few directions.'

By 11.20 we're in front of Her Honour Judge M. She raises her eyebrows when Callum explains that my client will agree to the making of an interim care order and turns to me for confirma-tion. I indicate this is indeed my client's position and that I have explained to her the full implications.

The judge looks puzzled. 'Does your client have fluent English? I see she doesn't have an interpreter with her today.'

'Her spoken English is excellent, Your Honour. And she tells me she has read all the papers without any difficulty. I would, however, ask for the social worker's statement to be translated into Thai.'

Behind me I hear a hiss of irritation. 'Not needed, Your Honour,' my client pipes up. 'I have read the papers. I don't need translation. It's all lies, lies and nonsense. Desmond is a good man.'

The judge looks at her in surprise, then turns back to Callum. 'I assume you're going to ask me to join Mr J as an intervenor? Is he here? Has he had legal advice?'

Before Callum can reply, my client speaks again. 'He is outside the door! He like to come in.'

Now the judge leans forward across her desk and regards Kanchana with a stern expression. 'Please don't shout out, this is a court of law. If you wish to say something, your counsel is here to assist you.'

I swivel round, make eye contact with Kanchana and hold my finger to my lips. She shoots me a withering look, but holds her tongue while the judge makes the interim care order and approves the plan for the girls to be fostered by Auntie Sarah. Next Eleanor gets to her feet and reports in a matter-of-fact tone that she has spoken with Desmond J and he's keen to be joined as an intervenor. The judge thanks her and makes a direction joining Desmond to the proceedings. She directs police disclosure and lists the matter for a case management hearing in two weeks' time.

As we troop out of court, it dawns on me that the date is one which – hooray! – I genuinely can't do, because it clashes with another hearing.

I'm hoping to have another word with my client, but as I reach the lobby I glimpse a red-faced Mr J seizing her by the hand and escorting her, very firmly, into the lift.

22

Fact Finding

In early September I take a few days off to go walking in North Wales with my son. He's become a keen climber at university and takes me up into a disused slate quarry, from where we get amazing views across the mountains to Anglesey. I arrive home on the Sunday afternoon, missing him already and dreading the empty feeling that characterises the cottage these days. Even the cat has taken to wandering off, only returning once I've started to panic about his safety.

I make a cup of tea and take it out to the garden. Most of my summer flowers are over, but the runner beans are heavy with clusters of long, flat, delicious pods. I drag the hosepipe across the grass towards them. The weather's still warm and I'm happy to cool down in the spray as I hold my thumb over the nozzle.

I've set aside this evening to prep Sam H's final hearing. The case has dragged on far longer than it should have done – twenty months – largely due to the pandemic, but also because non-accidental injury cases invariably require a fact finding and often overrun their time frame. Preparation for the fact finding involves the gathering of evidence and, generally, the instruction of at least one expert, who may require anything from six to sixteen weeks to consider the case and write a report. The hearing itself can last from two days to several weeks, depending on the complexity of the case. At its conclusion, just as in a sexual abuse case, the court considers all the evidence and makes findings of fact, or rulings as to how the child came to be injured and – if possible – who is to blame.

Thereafter, unless the findings are successfully appealed, the case is dealt with on the basis that what the court says happened *is* what happened. If the parents are exonerated, threshold is not crossed and the proceedings end. But if one or both parents is found to be responsible either for inflicting the injury or for failing to protect the child, the first question is whether they accept the findings. If they don't, then it is unlikely they will be considered to be safe people to resume care of the child. And even if they *do* accept the findings, often they will be asked to undergo a social work and sometimes a psychological assessment, looking at why the injuries occurred and what changes, if any, the parent(s) have made to ensure that history will not repeat itself. The assessing expert is sent a copy of the court's judgment and must proceed on the basis of the facts found by the court. At the final hearing, some weeks or months later, the court will consider the expert's assessment and the care plan made by the local authority in the light of it, in order to make a decision about the child's long-term future.

My little precis of how fact findings work will make more sense when I tell the story of Sam H's case in more detail.

A week after the initial hearing, when we went back to court – remotely – we were told that Dawn's mother was out of hospital and Dawn was no longer needing to care for her step-father. A valiant woman, Dawn said she was willing to care for all three children for 'as long as it took'. Both the guardian's counsel and I protested about the fact that Alfie was now living with the children, albeit under Dawn's allegedly watchful eye. But for me, acting for Sam, this was not straightforward, because Sam could not offer an alternative carer and she passionately objected to the idea of the children going into foster care.

So I had to be very careful not to rock the boat to the extent that the local authority changed its care plan to foster care. The most I could safely say was that, until the fact-finding established how Charlie had come by his injuries, the local authority should ask Alfie to move out. If Dawn had been willing to consent, Alfie could have been subjected to a court order excluding him from her home,[1] but she was not willing to do so. This left the court with little option but to accept the local authority's assurances that it was closely monitoring the situation.

Sam was fuming by the end of the hearing; but in all our telephone discussions that day, she flatly refused to consider a residential assessment, repeating that she did not want to be away from Leo and could not ask him to care for the horse.

Somewhat reluctantly, the court accepted the local authority's interim arrangements for the children. It joined Estelle as an intervenor and ordered the parents to file statements setting out their accounts of the three days prior to Charlie's bruising coming to light. I urged Sam to make an appointment with Nicola, her solicitor at Yarvilles, so that this could be prepared, stressing the importance of giving her account before she forgot the detail of any falls or mishaps suffered by Charlie, and the times when she claimed he'd been with Alfie and Estelle.

A couple of weeks later, when I read the statement, I saw that Sam's determination to point the finger at Estelle had not diminished. She told more or less the same story she'd told me the night before the initial hearing, but there were new details. She 'knew', from a 'reliable source', that Estelle was in the habit of handling her own children 'very roughly'. Set down in black and white the remark concerned me because it begged the question of why she'd agreed for Jordan to live with Alfie and Estelle, and for Charlie to stay with them every other weekend.

She claimed, however, that Alfie was always present when Charlie was at Estelle's, contradicting what she'd told me about Alfie's regular Saturday trips to the pub.

The other document I was sent with Sam's statement was the cognitive assessment of Leo. After putting him through the usual battery of tests, the psychologist had concluded that Leo had tremendous difficulty processing information at speed, a poor memory, difficulty reading and poor understanding of many common words. His overall IQ was calculated at 63, which meant he was considered to have a mild learning disability. Leo understood in basic terms what the care proceedings were about and had capacity to instruct his solicitor; but in order to participate in legal meetings and court hearings, he needed the assistance of a non-legal advocate.

A few weeks later, the police disclosure arrived. I read the record of Sam's interview with interest and saw she claimed to have long been very worried about the children spending time with Estelle. She had only agreed to Jordan living with Alfie and Estelle because, she said, Estelle had links to drug dealers in the community and Sam was worried about what might happen to her or Leo if she raised an objection. *Really?* I thought. *You put your child at risk for the sake of your own and your partner's safety?*

Shortly after this, Nicola sent me an email from the local authority recording that Sam had telephoned her children's social worker and made a specific allegation against Estelle, saying her 'reliable source' had described witnessing Estelle grabbing one of her own children by the upper arms. *Come on, Sam*, I thought to myself as I read it, *that's just too convenient. Don't forget you're dealing with some quite bright professionals; we can see through this kind of thing.*

Around the same time, a family support worker who'd met both Sam and Alfie years earlier, happened to be in a Kentucky Fried Chicken shop when the pair walked in. Alfie was pushing a buggy in which a baby lay sleeping and Sam had a little boy who looked about three on her shoulders. The FSW left in a hurry, made some notes and telephoned her manager the following morning. When I learned about this I assumed that the local authority would get the matter listed for a further hearing and apply to remove the children to foster care. But I was wrong.

A further interim hearing was due anyway about ten days later. On a hunch, during our pre-court telephone conversation I asked Sam how things were between her and Leo. She was silent for a moment and then replied, in her usual flat tone, 'Split up. Couple of weeks back.'

I feigned surprise and asked her where she was living.

'Still in Leo's flat. Haven't got nowhere else to go.'

'And Leo?'

'Don't know. He walked out the night I told him it was over. He's not been back.'

'So it was your decision to separate?'

Silence.

Worried, I decided I'd better push Sam about the sighting of her and Alfie in KFC and the unnamed 'reliable source' she spoke about in her statement. I knew she wasn't going to like me for this, but if she was playing a game it was my job to warn her that it was unwise.

When I mentioned KFC her tone hardened. 'Not my fault if I happen to go into KFC the same time as Alfie turns up with the kids.'

'Alfie's not supposed to be with the kids unsupervised.'

'He told me Dawn was, like, two steps behind him.'

'Did you see her?'

'I wasn't looking for her.'

'And how come Charlie was on your shoulders?'

'He bloody run at me, didn't he, the moment he saw me. Gave me the biggest hug ever and wouldn't let me go. So I squatted down to say hello and he climbed onto my shoulders. I didn't tell him to, he just did it.'

'Okay, but please try to think how this will look to the local authority, and the court. They may not believe that you just "happened" to go into KFC at the very moment that Alfie turned up there.'

'Alfie does what he bloody likes, Dawn doesn't stop him.'

'So was Dawn there or wasn't she?'

'How would I know?'

The difficulty with this kind of conversation is that the client may start to think that I, their barrister, am acting as if I were the children's social worker. On the other hand, if I don't challenge the client I'm leading them up the garden path as to how likely it is that their story will be believed in court. And when it's a telephone conversation with a person you've never met face to face, it's difficult to judge how to play it.

'The thing you said in your statement, Sam,' I went on, 'about the "reliable source" who told you Estelle was very rough with her kids; that was Alfie, was it?'

Sam sniffed loudly and I sensed her fury. 'I'm not saying who it was.'

A long silence. Then I ask another question: 'How come Alfie's going out and about with the children on his own? What does Dawn think she's doing?'

I was hoping Sam would now admit that Dawn wasn't anywhere to be seen when she 'bumped into' Alfie. By way of response, I got this: 'Dawn's past caring. She knows it wasn't Alfie what hurt Charlie. She's got three small kids in a two-bedroom flat, plus her own daughter, plus Alfie. And she's working.'

Exactly, I say to myself. Poor Dawn. It sounds like a recipe for disaster.

In the Zoom pre-hearing discussion with the other lawyers, Guy Harrison, once again representing the children, demanded to know what the local authority was proposing to do about the placement. It was crystal clear, he claimed, that Alfie and

Dawn had broken the terms of the schedule of expectations they had signed when Alfie moved in, which stipulated that he must never be alone with the children. The choice was simple, Guy claimed: either Alfie had to leave the flat, under a S38A exclusion order to which Dawn must consent; or the children would have to go into foster care. It became obvious in the course of the discussion that local authority counsel agreed with him, but she was having trouble persuading her social worker clients that it was just too risky to leave the current arrangements in place.

As for me, I was very constrained in what I could say. Sam's attitude to Alfie had changed radically and I no longer had instructions to question his presence in Dawn's home. I listened to the discussion in silence, doodling on my counsel's notebook and trying to work out what I was obliged to say about the possibility – or even likelihood – that Sam and Alfie were back together. But before I could say anything at all, local authority counsel announced she wanted to go into a 'break-out room' with her clients. When she emerged fifteen minutes later I thought she looked a little battered. Very hurriedly, she explained that Dawn would now consent to the making of the exclusion order and Alfie would move out.

The court made the exclusion order without hesitation, and I felt relieved; it seemed like a much better solution for the children than foster care. But just one week later, Nicola sent me an email explaining that the placement had broken down. Dawn simply could not cope, solo, with the three children, her own daughter and the demands of her job. Like many people she was working remotely. Although Jordan was attending school, she had really needed the help provided by Alfie. The local authority rushed the matter back to court and sought approval to place Charlie and Riley in foster care under an interim care order. Sam instructed me to oppose, but, given the dearth of alternatives, there was very little I could say. At least Jordan was allowed to stay with Dawn.

In a phone call following the hearing, I explained to Sam I wanted to ask her again if she and Alfie had resumed their relationship, and that I was duty bound to inform the other parties of what she told me. There was a silence and then she said, 'I don't see what difference it makes, T'reeza. I'm with him, yeah, but so what?'

I told her it might make a difference, or it might not, but it was good that she'd told me, and the other parties would appreciate her being up front. Where were they living?

A long silence. Then, 'In a tent down by the canal. I'm not saying where.'

'Oh lord, Sam, I'm sorry. Have you got yourselves on the housing list?'

'No point. Till we get the kids back, we won't have enough points.'

She was right, of course, about the points. Adults with children in their care get priority in local authority and social housing, but parents who are not caring for their children do not.

As for Leo, he'd failed to attend the last two hearings. I asked whether he was back in his flat, but Sam didn't know. From her tone of voice, she didn't much care.

Some weeks after this the expert, a consultant paediatrician, filed her report. In line with the treating paediatrician, she discerned the shapes of adult fingertips in the photographic images of Charlie's bruises. The amount of force required to cause bruising of that severity, she concluded, way exceeded that which would be expected in the course of normal handling of a three-year-old.

The fact finding was originally listed to be heard in August 2021, seven months after the case began. But at the last minute the local authority barrister got Covid. The man who replaced her advised that the evidence should include disclosure of the parties' WhatsApp and text messages for the four-week period beginning on the Friday prior to the injuries being seen. He was right, of course, from the local authority point of view. Sam instructed me to object, and I duly argued that the application was what lawyers call a 'fishing expedition',[2] but the court ruled in favour of disclosure. The fact finding was adjourned and re-listed for November 2021; but it took the various mobile phone providers three months to produce the full set of documents, and the November listing couldn't go ahead either. The younger children had to endure a change of foster placement as a result of the delay, moving to one much further out of town. Sam was offered contact twice a week at a contact centre two bus rides distant, but often called saying she couldn't get the time off work. Leo attended contact assiduously, but sat scrolling on his phone, showing little ability to respond to Riley's cues. Jordan, meanwhile, became more and more settled with Dawn and her daughter.

Once the phone records arrived, Sam's continuing assertion that Charlie's bruising had been caused by Estelle began to unravel. There were 11,000 pages of records, from the phones of Leo, Sam, Alfie and Estelle. In Sam's WhatsApp usage for the Monday evening before Charlie's injuries were spotted by the nursery, the following exchange appeared:

> 20:21. Sam to Lisa (a friend): 'Charlie's being a little sod.'
> 20:27. Lisa to Sam: 'What's up with him?'
> 20:37. Sam to Lisa: 'Winding up Riley.'
> 20:42. Lisa to Sam: 'Get Leo to take him.'
> 20:47. Sam to Lisa: 'Leo's not here. I hate Charlie. He's evil.'

According to the local authority solicitor, there was nothing else of significance in the entire 11,000 pages. Nicola checked, I double-checked, and then we set up a conference with Sam, in person, at Yarvilles' offices. We were half expecting Sam to fail to show, but we were wrong. She arrived, on time, dressed in leggings and a flimsy waterproof, on a cold, wet December afternoon. Her short blonde hair was a little wild, and when she took off the waterproof I saw that the tattoo on her neck extended all the way down her right arm. On her feet she wore a pair of sodden trainers. I told Sam I was glad to meet her at last, face to face.

'Yeah,' she said in a small voice, regarding me with a puzzled stare. 'So what's gonna happen now?'

I told her we needed to look at a passage in the WhatsApp messages from the Monday night before the Tuesday.

'I know,' she cut across me. 'Alfie's solicitor showed him and he went apeshit, hit me across the back of my neck.' She turned her head, revealing a blue-black bruise at the top of her spine.

'Ouch, that looks nasty. I'm sorry, Sam. But we need to know what you say about the messages.' I brought the relevant page up on my laptop screen and read out the exchange with Lisa. Then I looked at Sam. 'You told us Leo was at home with the children that evening and it was you who was out, mucking out the horse. So how do you explain these?' I read a look of anger mixed with shame in Sam's grey-blue eyes. Just like on the phone, she held a long silence before she spoke.

'Leo went out later, after I came in. But I never hit Charlie. He kept poking his fingers into the baby's cheeks, that's a fact. But I never hit him.'

'So … Why didn't you tell us Charlie was awake? You said in your statement he was asleep when you came in.'

'Dunno.'

'And why didn't you tell us Leo went out?'

A shrug of the shoulders.

'Hmm. And why didn't you mention before that Charlie was poking Riley?'

Another silence. Then, 'I never thought it mattered.'

Trying to hide my exasperation, I glanced at Nicola. I was in no doubt that she had explained to Sam just how much every detail of that evening mattered.

'How angry did you get with Charlie?'

This produced a swift response. 'I weren't angry with him.'

'But you said to Lisa, "He's evil."'

'Yeah, he was evil to Riley. But I weren't *angry*.' She pronounced the word with disdain, as if anger was something she never stooped to.

'So how did Charlie get his bruising?' I spoke bluntly, looking straight at her.

'Estelle, I've told you before, it was her.'

'You've told us a number of things before, Sam, that have turned out not to be true. When exactly do you think Estelle hurt him?'

'On the Saturday, when Alfie was at the pub.'

'So you must have seen it when you undressed him for bed on the Monday night?'

'I never undressed him. He slept in his clothes, like I said.'

'But why? Why not undress him?'

Sam's neck was turning a deep red, and for a second I thought she was going to get up and storm out. But instead she turned to me and said, 'Think he fell asleep on the settee.' Then she wrinkled up her nose, as if smelling something bad. 'I don't remember, T'reeza. It's nearly a year ago, innit?'

Nicola and I spent the second half of the conference explaining to Sam that she was going to have a very difficult time when she gave her evidence at the fact finding, which was now listed for April 2022. It was plain from the WhatsApp records that she had lied in both her statement to the court and in her police interview, and this would be used against her by counsel for the local authority and, probably, counsel for Alfie, counsel for Estelle, counsel for Leo and counsel for the guardian. If she insisted that she was not the person who'd hurt Charlie, we would put her instructions forward to the court, but we weren't optimistic that she'd be believed. She should go away, mull over her situation, and consider very carefully whether there was anything else she wanted to tell us about what had happened between her and Charlie on that fateful Monday night.

Just as I was about to say goodbye, it occurred to me to ask whether Sam was still with Alfie, despite the recent assault.

She shot me a look of disgust, as if she thought me a complete fool. 'He ended it, didn't he? He thinks it was me who hurt Charlie.' Pause. 'Which it wasn't, it was Estelle.'

'So ... where are you living now, Sam?'

'Hostel. Down by the station.'

About a week before the fact finding was due to start in April 2022, Nicola learned from the local authority that Estelle's children were no longer on child protection plans. Estelle had a new partner who was seen as a safety factor *and* she had done a drug test, which showed she'd given up crack cocaine. As for Leo, he had become very depressed and would struggle with the task of giving evidence.

Nicola arranged another conference, and again Sam attended. She hadn't contacted Nicola at all during the intervening four months, and her position hadn't changed.

Once it began, the hearing was relatively straightforward, from a legal point of view. Nobody took issue with the expert's conclusions, so the sole issue was which of the four adults had grabbed Charlie.

As the mother of the children, Sam went into the witness box first. She was cross-examined by all five counsel and, as anticipated, they used the WhatsApp messages to show she'd lied in her police and written evidence. When a witness lies in a fact finding, case law dictates that the court must be careful 'to bear in mind that a witness may lie for many reasons, such as shame, misplaced loyalty, panic, fear and distress, and the fact that a witness has lied about some matters does not mean that he or she has lied about everything'.[3] Clutching at straws, I was planning to make much of this principle in my closing submission.

Watching the judge's face, however, I could see that she was taking quite a dislike to Sam as the latter ducked and dived and refused to answer questions about why she'd changed her story. Neither could she explain why she'd called Charlie 'evil'. Sam did a valiant job of retaining her composure, coming over as cold, hard and a little self-righteous. At one point I was willing her to show some emotion, although by now I'd grasped that this young woman's emotions were buried in the bowels of her unhappy childhood. The hours dragged on, and I sensed everyone in the courtroom becoming more and more convinced that Sam was the perpetrator.

Alfie gave evidence next, followed by a very pale-faced Leo (with the help of his non-legal advocate) and finally Estelle. None of the three came over as particularly defensive, nor as reluctant to answer questions – factors that had the effect of bolstering the case against Sam. Leo struggled to understand some of what was put to him, but, when questions were broken down into small chunks, it was clear that he was doing his best to give honest answers. It also became clear that Sam had broken his heart.

At the end of the week the judge gave an exemplary judgment, spelling out that it was for the local authority to prove its case, on the balance of probabilities; and that she had taken account of all the evidence and considered each piece of evidence in the context of all the other evidence, as she was required to do. She had paid very close attention to the evidence of the parents (Sam and Alfie) and of the carers (Estelle and Leo), and she had formed a clear assessment of their credibility and reliability. Sam had lied, but the judge had borne in mind the case law on the significance of lies by a witness. Nevertheless she was satisfied, on the balance of probabilities, that it was Sam who'd caused Charlie's injuries – and this was her finding. Estelle, Alfie and Leo were exonerated.

The matter was adjourned for a fortnight for Sam, Alfie and Leo to mull over the judge's findings. The exclusion order was lifted and Alfie was told he could return to live with Dawn, although Charlie and Riley would remain in foster care. Estelle no longer had a part to play and was discharged from the proceedings.

Three days before the next hearing, Nicola emailed me: Sam had called wanting to appeal against the findings. I had anticipated this and was able to give very clear advice that there were absolutely no grounds for an appeal. If Sam was still not able to accept the findings, Nicola told her, then the court was unlikely to order an expert assessment of her, because she would be seen as continuing to pose a risk to all three children. After a very long silence, Sam whispered, 'Alfie'll have to have them, won't he?' and ended the phone call.

By now Dawn was working in her office three days a week and welcomed Alfie taking over the childcare. Jordan, however, was wary of his dad; he'd formed a tight bond with Dawn and come to see her as his primary carer.

Despite this, at the hearing Alfie put himself forward to take on Jordan's care. When he was asked about Charlie, he said he wasn't sure he could cope with more than one child. The guardian said she wouldn't support him being considered for both children in any event, and made noises about Alfie's failure to stick to the schedule of expectations when he was previously living with Dawn and the children. She would be very concerned about the likely impact of separating Charlie from Riley, after the pair had spent over a year together in foster care with only intermittent contact with their parents. That, we all knew, meant she wanted Charlie and Riley placed for adoption, together. The local authority said this wasn't currently its plan, but it would think things over.

As for Leo, whose expression became ever more desolate, his counsel said he was not putting himself forward to care for Riley, because he knew that without the support of an extended family – he had none – he simply couldn't do it.

I came away from the hearing feeling deeply sad for Leo. I was sad for Sam too, who had not attended, but now accepted that she couldn't and shouldn't compete with Alfie.

This evening, as I settle at the kitchen table, there's not a lot I have to do. I've already read the independent social worker's assessment of Alfie, which says he struggles with his anger and needs to join a programme for male perpetrators of domestic abuse;[4] until he's done this, she couldn't recommend that he become the sole carer for Jordan. The local authority plan is for Jordan to be made the subject of a special guardianship order to Dawn. Alfie can continue to reside in her household, but, should he wish to leave in the future and take Jordan with him, he'll need to go back to court. He'd have to demonstrate a significant change in his circumstances just to get the court's permission to make an application to discharge the SGO[5] and he would struggle to obtain legal aid.

As for Charlie and Riley, the social worker has come round to the guardian's position and wants them adopted, ideally in a joint placement. He's issued an application for placement orders, to be heard tomorrow alongside the care applications. Local authority counsel has drafted a detailed case summary, going through the case law on adoption and setting out the belief of the local authority that, in this sad case, 'nothing else will do'. I stop and consider whether this is right. The case might have worked out very differently if Sam had been able to accept the findings of the court and been willing to look at what had triggered her loss of control. But this was beyond her. As for the two fathers, Alfie is realistic about what he can manage, and accepts the SGO for Jordan and the loss of Charlie, while Leo appears to have given up; and neither Sam nor Leo have any relatives they could have put forward as long-term carers for any of the children. So, I think it's fair to say there are no realistic alternatives and that no, nothing else will do.

I skim-read the social worker's final statement and care plans, which contain little more than what Nicola has told me. Then I read the position statements of the parties, all of whom, unusually, accept the local authority's plans. The hearing won't take long, but it will be painful for Sam. I stand up and walk out into the garden, wondering what I can say on her behalf. She's promised she'll attend tomorrow, and I want to make it as easy for her as I can.

23

Discharge Application

By now it may have struck you that – my son and his friend apart – very few children appear in the pages of this book. That's because, during all my years of practice, I only once came face to face with a child who was subject to proceedings. She was a highly articulate teenager, and we 'met' through a computer screen when I represented her during the pandemic.

Unlike barristers, children panel solicitors who represent guardians do get to meet the children in their cases. They're required to visit the child, accompanied by the guardian, to ascertain the child's wishes in connection with the case. If a young child's wishes conflict with what their guardian thinks is in their best interests, the child's wishes are likely to be communicated to the court, then disregarded, as was the case for Lawrence when he was six. But when an older child, usually a teenager, disagrees with their guardian, the court should be asked to consider whether the child is sufficiently mature to instruct their own solicitor directly. This is canvassed at an interim hearing. If the court agrees, from that point on the guardian has to represent herself and the child's solicitor takes instructions directly from the child.

For me, having spent part of my working life representing parents and part practising as an in-house local authority lawyer, meetings with children were never on the agenda. Despite that, I developed a strong sense of affinity with some of the children in my cases. I tried to imagine what it felt like to be in their shoes (or Moses basket, when the case involved a baby) and I empathised with their suffering.

When I first met Dwayne, just after the fire, I was touched by his stark description of how Lawrence was feeling in the wake of his mother's disappearance. When we failed to persuade the court that Lawrence should be allowed to live with Dwayne, I felt terrible. I wasn't entirely convinced the court's decision was wrong; but I found it almost unbearable to imagine what Lawrence would go through, losing his little brother and sister and being moved to a new foster placement in a strange environment.

Over the next couple of years, Lawrence often came into my thoughts, and Michelle's call brought the case flooding back. To learn that a child with whom you've had dealings is writing notes saying he 'wants to die' is disturbing, to say the least. It's hard not to conclude you've been part of a system that has failed him.

Michelle had a lot of trouble obtaining legal aid for Dwayne. In May 2022 she emailed saying it had finally been granted and she was issuing the discharge application. In July she rang to tell me about the initial hearing, at which she'd represented Dwayne herself. An unfamiliar woman social worker had turned up, announcing that the male social worker Dwayne got on with had left the authority and she'd recently taken over the case. Disappointed, Michelle enquired whether the new worker had met Lawrence, who was now nearly ten. No, not yet. Had she read his files? They were on her desk and on her list of tasks. Did she have a view about the application? The social worker looked embarrassed. Her manager had instructed her to oppose, because Lawrence was now at the top of the waiting list at the local Child and Adolescent Mental Health Services (CAMHS); it was absolutely the wrong moment for him to undergo a change in home circumstances.

Michelle enquired as to what help, exactly, CAMHS were offering. Looking distinctly uncomfortable, the social worker explained that Lawrence's foster carer would be given three sessions with a worker, who would coach her in how to respond to Lawrence's angry outbursts. He was becoming quite awkward to handle, and sometimes behaved unkindly towards the foster carer's own young sons.

Was Lawrence not going to see a therapist himself?

Not at the moment, no; CAMHS didn't always work directly with the child.[1]

When the parties went into court, the district judge ordered Dwayne to file a statement setting out why he felt it was in Lawrence's interests to live with him rather than remain in foster care, what he could offer to Lawrence in terms of housing, school and community, and a summary of Dwayne's own circumstances. The social worker was to file a response three weeks later, followed by a position statement from the guardian.

A week ahead of the final hearing, which is listed for a day and a half, I drive into the city for a conference with Dwayne and Michelle. It's late November but the weather is mild. I'm mulling over what the applicant has to prove on an application to discharge a care order, under S39 of the Children Act 1989. The test has been considered a number of times by the higher courts, most recently in 2021,[2] and the law is clear. The burden of proof is on the applicant (Dwayne) and the standard of proof is the balance of probabilities. The key issue is the child's welfare at the time of the hearing. The local authority does not have to re-prove the threshold it established at the time the care order was made, but neither does the applicant have to prove that threshold no longer applies; questions of harm are addressed in accordance with the relevant parts of the welfare checklist in S1(3) of the Children Act 1989.

If, at the end of the welfare evaluation, the court comes down in favour of refusing the application, it must then consider the parent and child's rights under the European Convention, principally Article 8 – the right to family life – and Article 3 – the right not to be subject to inhuman or degrading treatment. The court must satisfy itself that any interference with Convention rights is both necessary and proportionate. Where the parents' right to family life would conflict with the child's right to family life, the child's interests must prevail. Lastly, it is open to the court to send the child home but substitute a supervision order for the original care order.

Dwayne's sitting in Michelle's waiting room when I arrive, clutching an envelope full of papers. He smiles as he unfolds his long body, stands up and stretches out his hand. I think how well he looks, although his expression's a little tense. Moments later, Michelle ushers us into her room.

'They're bloody changing Lawrence's social worker, again!' Dwayne exclaims as we sit down. 'The new geezer phoned me half an hour ago. That woman we met at court, the one who hadn't even met Lawrence, she's off on maternity leave!'

Michelle rests her elbows on her desk and sinks her head in her hands. 'Did Lawrence ever meet her?'

'Yeah, twice. She went round there right after the hearing, and then she turned up to contact the week before last. Lawrence is still really upset that Dave's gone – the man he had before her – and now he's got to meet another new one. That's four social workers in four years! Who do they think they are?'

Michelle and I exchange glances. Four social workers in four years is not, unfortunately, an unusual experience for a child in long-term care. I had a case once where the child had nine social workers in two years. But I understand Dwayne's indignation. And, given Lawrence's fragile state of mind, it does seem particularly unwise of the local authority to inflict this on him.

'It's rubbish, Dwayne,' I tell him. 'Really bad for Lawrence. But maybe I can use it to bolster your case for discharge of the care order.'

Dwayne sucks his teeth and shoots me a look of cynicism. 'I don't see why my case needs bolstering, T'reeza. I've got a flat, a job, been clean nearly four years. The guardian's supporting me' – this is true, she is – 'and Lawrence is starting to self-harm.'

This last is news to me and Michelle. 'What?' we demand. 'You didn't tell us that!'

'Foster carer found him with a razor blade, scraping it along his arm. He'd pulled his bed out from the wall and was squatting behind it, in the corner.' Dwayne stretches out his arm, pushes his shirt sleeve up to his elbow and drags his finger nails along his skin.

Appalled, I stare at Dwayne. 'Who told you?'

'Foster carer. Texted me. She's all right, is Julie. Knows Lawrence wants to be with me.'

'But when, Dwayne, because it's not in the social worker's statement?'

'Couple of weeks ago.' He pauses. 'And that's not the only thing. Lawrence is changing. His school say he's getting in with the wrong crowd. He's ten, don't forget. Hormones and all that. If this goes on much longer I'm gonna wake up one morning and hear he's joined a gang. He could be on the street running drugs or carrying a knife.'

I listen in silence. Dwayne's a different man from the person I recall from nearly four years ago. He looks healthy, he sounds strong, and he holds himself with an air of self-possession that just wasn't there before. I wonder which judge the final hearing's listed in front of. If only it could be District Judge S, the man who seemed to take to Dwayne at the initial hearing of the care proceedings. I feel sure he would see what I see: a changed man who's ready, more than ready, to take on the care of his troubled but beloved son.

Dwayne looks at me intently, then at Michelle. 'Look, no offence, I know you're both doing your best, but I want to make something really clear. If the court doesn't send Lawrence home this time, I'm not leaving it there. I'm going to my MP. I'm going to the press. I'll take the case right up to the Supreme Court. Europe, even.'[3]

A week later, Dwayne and I arrive at court at the same moment and get into an empty lift. He's smartly dressed in a dark suit with trousers that cover his heels and this time he's wearing a pair of shiny black shoes.

'All right, T'reeza?' he murmurs. 'Sorry if I went a bit over the top last week with you and Michelle … But this is doing my head in, right? I've got to win it, for Lawrence's sake.'

As Dwayne's counsel I'm supposed to 'manage his expectations' – to use an unappealing phrase – but I don't feel like dampening his fire. 'Yes,' I say, 'I get it, Dwayne, you *have* got to win it.'

We find a consulting room, where I leave Dwayne in charge of my laptop while I go in search of local authority counsel. It's a woman today, Elspeth Stuart. She's about my age, with short grey hair, and we've known each other for years. Elspeth looks rather uneasy as she tells me that her clients are still opposed to discharge of the care order. Yes, there has been another change of social worker; no, she doesn't know why they allocated Lawrence to a woman who was about to go on maternity leave; yes, the work with CAMHS is a major factor in their decision that this is not the right time for rehabilitation.

'They want Lawrence to stay put, do they, with his current foster carer? Despite what they say about his behaviour towards her little boys?' I'm not trying very hard to conceal my irritation.

'Stay put?' Elspeth looks even more uneasy and I guess what's coming. 'No, they've identified a new placement for him, with a couple whose own children are grown up. It'll be much better; the child's at an age where he needs a male role model, and these are experienced carers. They won't take any nonsense.'

My jaw drops open. 'The social work statement says Lawrence shouldn't move to his dad just when the work with CAMHS is starting! And now you're telling me they're proposing to move him themselves. *Really*, Elspeth?'

She looks suitably embarrassed but says nothing at all. I hurry back to Dwayne and am recounting this crazy new development when we're called into court. As we hurry across the concourse I mutter to Dwayne, as quietly as I can, 'Don't lose hope. This may just backfire for the local authority. It's an incredibly stupid move on their part.'

The morning's court list had our case in front of District Judge S, but as the court door swings open I glimpse the familiar figure of His Honour Judge P. 'Do come in,' he calls out in his mild, pleasant voice. Hmm, I think. His Honour Judge P's not the most pro-parent judge, but he does try to be fair. I wonder what he'll make of this case. From my place in counsel's row, I see that he's reading something on his tablet and frowning.

A moment later, as Elspeth introduces the parties, I glance round at Dwayne. He's sitting very upright with his jaw clamped, trying to conceal his fury.

Elspeth checks that the judge has read her case summary and goes on to inform him about the new foster carers. I study His Honour Judge P's face closely and am pleased to see the frown lines deepen.

'I see,' he says when she falls silent. 'Or rather, quite frankly, I don't quite see, Ms Stuart. If this young boy needs to stay put in order to benefit from the involvement of CAMHS, why would the local authority want to move him to a new placement at this point in time? Surely that would be as disruptive as returning him to his father?' He casts a glance towards Dwayne, then adds, 'or rather, possibly much more disruptive, given that he has a close relationship with his father.'

Elspeth tries to respond, but His Honour Judge P speaks over her, saying he wants to hear from me and the guardian's counsel before going any further. I get up, standing at an angle so that the judge has a clear view of Dwayne. I summarise Dwayne's position in the most forceful manner I can muster; I'm feeling angry on his behalf, and this is one of those rare occasions when it may be helpful to allow my real feelings to show. I emphasise the sudden change of social worker and the last-minute nature of the proposed change of placement. Both make a nonsense of the reason put forward in the local authority's evidence for its opposition to Lawrence returning to his dad. His Honour Judge P listens politely, making notes.

The guardian's counsel is a tall, middle-aged man I've never met before, called Bill Henderson. We've only spoken briefly, and although the guardian has filed a report recommending that Lawrence return to Dwayne under a six-month supervision order, I'm not quite sure what he's going to say. So I'm thrilled when he tells the court that the guardian is as annoyed as we are about the new social worker and the last-minute proposal to change placement.

When Bill Henderson sits down, His Honour Judge P removes his spectacles and squares his shoulders. 'I'm going to do something which I hardly ever do,' he tells us, 'because in this particular case I feel it is really called for. I've read the papers very carefully and I'm going to give you an indication of the way I see the matter now, at this stage, before hearing from the witnesses.' He pauses, and fixes his gaze on Dwayne. 'My view is that the best interests of this child require that he be returned to the care of his father, subject to a supervision order for a period of twelve months.'

I swivel round and glance at Dwayne. His gaze is firmly on his hands, which are folded in front of him on the desk. They are shaking.

'Now,' His Honour Judge P goes on, 'it's entirely up to the local authority as to whether they want me to hear their witness. I'm perfectly happy to do that, provided it's a good use of court time.' He clears his throat, leaving me in no doubt that he thinks it would be pointless. 'So I'll rise and give you all twenty minutes to consider the matter. Or thirty. Let my clerk know when you're ready to come back in.'

I take my time to leave the courtroom, hoping to overhear what Elspeth is about to say to her clients. But the new social worker and his manager make for the door very fast, leaving their counsel to follow.

For the next thirty minutes Dwayne and I sit opposite each other in our consulting room. Dwayne is visibly torn between anxiety and fury. I tell him I'm cautiously optimistic, but I don't know the team manager and can't predict what she'll do. If she backs down, would he agree to a supervision order for twelve months? It might mean he'd get more support. Yes, of course, he says, he wants all the support he can get.

But if the team manager insists on going ahead with the hearing, I tell him, it's unlikely His Honour Judge P will change his view. We should be okay, although there are no guarantees. Does the local authority have any more surprises up its sleeve? We just don't know. Court rules require that all parties file their evidence well in advance of a final hearing, but that hasn't stopped this local authority pulling a nasty surprise first thing this morning.

'Why am I being treated like this?' Dwayne wants to know. 'Is it because I'm Black? Why can't the local authority see what I've got to offer Lawrence?'

I tell him I don't know. Racism may come into it, of course. A prejudice against lone fathers too. I wish I knew the team manager and social worker, but I've never met them before. It's possible one of them has a bee in their bonnet about any parent with a history of drug misuse.

'But I've been clean *four years*! What more do they want?' Dwayne looks offended and I wish I'd kept my thoughts to myself.

'I suppose they're waiting for Lawrence to go off the rails like I did,' he mutters. 'A bit of self-harm's not enough; they're waiting for him to start doing drugs.'

The time ticks slowly by and the clerk sticks his head round the door to say the local authority has asked for another thirty minutes, which the judge has agreed. Dwayne goes out to get some fresh air, so I go in search of Bill Henderson. I find him sitting in the room opposite, staring at his tablet.

'Don't worry,' he grins, 'the guardian's strongly in favour of your client. She's going to lay into the local authority's muddled thinking if she goes into the witness box.'

'Great.'

Bill points to his screen. 'Have you seen this? President of the Family Division's planning to bring back the twenty-six weeks in earnest, as of January 2023. Strict adherence to the Public Law Outline and a maximum of three hearings per set of proceedings, which includes the final hearing.' He shakes his head with a look of disgust. 'It'll be just like before the pandemic: no experts, no time for careful thought, just a race to the finish.'

'Oh my God, is that right?' I take a step forward and read over his shoulder with a sinking heart the latest 'View from the President's Chambers', in which the current president of the Family Division announces that in the light of delay in deciding care cases that he says has been caused by the combination of an 'unexpected and sustained' 25 per cent rise in the volume of applications since 2015/16 and Covid-19, he's 'embarking on a campaign to exhort, require and expect every single professional, judge, magistrate or staff member in the system to get back to operating the PLO in full and without exception.'[4]

'So we're back,' Bill goes on, 'to the industrial system of child protection. Force each child through the sausage machine at high speed, spew them out the other end and show the world the judiciary are coping. If you get the wrong result for some of the children, nobody's going to notice.'

'And how can anyone say the 25 per cent rise in the volume of care applications was "unexpected"?' I add. 'It's got to be largely the result of austerity. Well, that's my decision made: time to pack it in.'

Bill looks at me with an air of surprise. 'Retire? Really?'

'Yep. I've had enough of this system. It's lost its focus on the needs of children.'

'Good for you, I wish I could do the same.'

By 12.25 there's still no clarity as to what the local authority wants to do. The judge sends out a message that he's adjourning to 2 pm, by which time the local authority must nail its colours to the mast. I try to find Elspeth Stuart, to ask what's holding up her clients' decision-making, but she and they have disappeared into some unknown recess of the building.

At five to two I'm standing at the court door with Dwayne, Bill Henderson and the guardian. We're all expressing our disgust at the stress Dwayne's being put through. Why couldn't the local authority sort out its position before coming to court, like everybody else? And what about the impact on Lawrence, who's well aware that his future's being decided this week? At that moment, a harassed-looking Elspeth speed-walks across the concourse, and signals to me and Bill to follow her to the window.

'I'm so sorry about all this nonsense,' she whispers. 'It's taken me all this time to convince them that their case is hopeless.'

'So are they backing down?'

'Yes, they're backing down. A child arrangements order for Lawrence to live with his dad and a supervision order for twelve months.'

I turn away, meet Dwayne's desperate gaze and hold up my thumb. 'It's all okay,' I mouth, 'you've won.'

The hearing takes less than ten minutes. When Elspeth announces the local authority's new position, His Honour Judge P nods politely. 'I think that's very sensible, if I may say so,' he remarks, as if he has played no role in bringing about their change of heart. Then he turns to Dwayne and his face lights up with a warm, open expression.

'Mr F. I've read about your history with some care, and I have to say I'm most impressed with the hard work you've put in to turn your life around over these last four years. You're clearly devoted to your son and he's lucky to have you as his father. Lawrence will now move to live with you under a child arrangements order and with the support to which he is entitled under a supervision order. I wish you both the happiness you deserve.'

I steal a glance at Dwayne, wondering how he's taking this. On the one hand, I suspect he may feel the judge's words are patronising and that the hope for happiness is unrealistic, given the repeated trauma young Lawrence has been through; on the other, the judge is offering some well-deserved recognition at the end of a long and painful process.

Dwayne's features still bear traces of the anger he has felt all morning, but I see him lean forward and nod at the judge. 'Thank you,' he says in a strong, loud voice. 'We will be happy, Sir. Very happy.'

Epilogue

Writing this book has made me think very hard about our English and Welsh system of child protection,[1] and the role of the Family Court within it.

Child abuse and neglect must be seen in the socio-economic context in which they occur. Britain in 2023 is one of the most unequal societies in the developed world, with eye-watering extremes of wealth and poverty.[2] And in recent years the difficulties faced by the least well-off have been exacerbated by the pandemic, the cost-of-living crisis and a reduction in state support. Where once we had public sector welfare services to be proud of, which helped the poorest groups to parent well – especially public sector housing, the National Health Service, and both statutory and non-statutory children's services operated by social services departments – all have been starved of funds and allowed to deteriorate to a dangerous degree.[3] Sure Start, which became a statutory service in 2009, lost 1,300 of its centres between 2010 and 2020.

In these circumstances, it's hardly surprising that inadequate parenting appears to be on the increase and that the numbers of children in care in England increased by 30 per cent between 2010 and 2023, with an even larger percentage increase in Wales between 2010 and 2022.

Major investment in all our run-down public services would doubtless have a positive impact on the childhood experiences of many. A lot of the children who come before the Family Court in public law cases are being raised by lone mothers, who could parent better if they weren't constantly struggling to keep a roof over their children's heads, food on their plates and money for heating in the pre-payment meter. Many of these women are struggling with their mental health, and it's not hard to see why.

Social work and social workers

Our system of children's social care was designed so that support could be offered to families long before they reached crisis point. But cuts to services in recent years, the exodus of social workers from the profession, and the prioritising of procedure and protocol over face-to-face work with families have meant that, increasingly, intervention only occurs when a child's situation reaches crisis point, by which time care proceedings are seen as the only way forward. Care proceedings are very expensive, as are some of the privately run placements required by the increasing numbers of acutely disturbed older children; the need for both further inhibits local authorities' ability to fund support services for less troubled families who might benefit from them.

In care proceedings, although the Family Court makes the. ultimate decision as to whether a child should be removed from their family, the quality of the court's decision-making is heavily influenced by *the quality of the information* they're given by social workers and the *quality of analysis* in risk assessments. At present, in far too many cases the quality of both information and analysis is poor. This is not usually the individual social worker's fault; it results from insufficiently rigorous recruitment processes for would-be entrants to the profession, inadequate training, poor supervision and support once in practice, and excessive caseloads; but the consequences are serious. In some cases the provision of poor information results in a highly adversarial court hearing in which it falls to the parents' lawyers to ferret out important information about the family's circumstances – or about the local authority's dealings with them – that has been missed from the social worker's statements. This information may cast the case in a new light, suggesting the need for analysis and care planning that is different from what has been put forward by the social worker. In other cases, if the parents' lawyers are less determined to dig out the facts, and if the judge does not ask searching questions him- or herself, the result may be that children are removed from their families where this could and should have been avoided.

I'm not alone in holding the view that many social workers lack the requisite skills. In the government-commissioned Independent Review of Children's Social Care (IRCSC) report *The Case for Change*, published in June 2021, Josh MacAlister, the review chair, says:

> Social workers have to make complex and challenging
> decisions every day, balancing how to protect a child
> from harm, whilst keeping families together where
> possible. We need a system that gives them the skills and
> confidence to do this. Yet, process continues to dominate
> over direct work with families, and decision making and
> risk assessment are too often underpinned by a lack of
> knowledge.[4]

In the national review into the murders of Arthur Labinjo-Hughes (aged six) and Star Hobson (aged sixteen months) during the Covid lockdown,[5] published in May 2022, concern was also expressed about lack of skills and knowledge on the part of social workers. One of the issues in both these cases was the social worker spending insufficient time with the child;

another was a failure to pay attention to information from wider family members.

> Child protection work requires sophisticated relational skills, with practitioners needing to build trust and cooperation with families who can be – or appear to be – reluctant to engage with them, whilst being authoritative and challenging where needed. Professionals need to be able to analyse the engagement of families critically, understanding the signs of parental disengagement and being able to interpret this as evidence when making decisions about a child's safety. Practitioners also need good knowledge and understanding of the factors that might impact on such engagement, for example, different types of domestic abuse including coercive controlling behaviour.[6]

Josh MacAlister was the driving force behind the creation of Frontline, the postgraduate training programme for social workers that opened its doors in 2014. From speaking with Frontline-qualified social workers, I understand that the recruitment process is rigorous, with group exercises, role play and intensive interviewing. Indeed the whole training provided by Frontline sounds very good, with students encouraged to pay careful attention to the challenges of working with a diverse client group and to reflect on how their work may trigger their own unresolved issues. Once the student is on placement, however, the quality of training received depends on the calibre of the supervising social work manager in the local authority in question.

The intention behind Frontline was to create a new generation of highly trained social work managers to lead the profession. As such, it only enrols a few hundred students every year, compared with the approximately 4,000 who enrol for the social work degree.[7] Frontline appears to be an excellent project,[8] but in my view the work is so challenging that *all* child protection social workers need to be very able and highly trained, not just the managers. (Whether all need to be graduates prior to training as social workers is a different issue; given the inequalities in our education system, there's a strong case for recruitment of able students from working-class and ethnic-minority backgrounds who don't possess degrees.)

As to the social work degree, the recruitment process appears to be less rigorous than for the graduate programmes. Many students begin the degree but do not complete it. A social worker I spoke with who had obtained her social work degree in 2019 told me that a large proportion of her cohort of thirty students dropped out. Some quit during the three-year course, others in their first year of work; four years after she qualified, only ten remained in social work. Support for students to process their own issues and understand how these might be triggered by the work was inadequate; and very little guidance was given on how to maintain well-being once in work and how to cope with criticism.

Social worker burnout is a major concern. For several decades social workers have been abandoning the profession in droves, leaving behind a skeletal workforce to cope with ever-increasing caseloads. The press picks up on the cases that go badly wrong, and the negative reputation of the profession hampers recruitment, creating a vicious circle.[9]

This brings me to pay. Social workers are confronted daily with some of the most distressing human suffering occurring in our society. If we want them to do their job well, we must support them properly. In my view 'front-line' children's social workers should be obliged to take a three-month paid sabbatical every three years; and their pay should be much closer to that of doctors. A children's social worker has the emotional and physical well-being of perhaps twenty individual children resting on her shoulders; it's extremely difficult, demanding work, and to get people of the right calibre, the task must be properly rewarded. This of course would require a sizeable increase in government support for local authority funding.[10]

In his IRCSC final report,[11] Josh MacAlister recommends the creation of an Early Career Framework, which would provide ongoing training to social workers during the first five years of their career and, if successfully completed, would be rewarded with higher pay. While it's understood that the government is planning to pilot a version of the framework, it's not clear whether higher pay is on offer.

Power to order local authorities to fund therapy

Given the unavailability of suitable therapy on the NHS for parents in care proceedings, the court must be given the power to order local authorities to fund privately sourced therapy. Again, this would require extra funding for cash-strapped local authorities and extra training for social workers. Social workers are not currently given sufficient training in mental health and in the different types of therapy that could be offered to parents struggling with the effects of trauma. If this were remedied, social workers could make recommendations for suitable therapy without first having to ask the court to instruct a psychologist to advise – a time-consuming, expensive and often fruitless process. The *money saved* could be used to fund the provision of therapy by regulated practitioners operating outside the NHS. The *time saved* should mean that therapy could be offered to a parent from the beginning of the pre-proceedings process, enabling them to engage and benefit before the twenty-six weeks starts to run. Or, even better, it could be offered as a protective measure to parents who are struggling with their mental health, long before they're threatened with care proceedings.

There's also a strong case for parents who lose a child or children at the conclusion of proceedings – whether to adoption, long-term foster care or special guardianship – to be offered counselling to help them deal with the huge loss entailed. Such provision would be more humane than what currently happens, where the parent is abandoned to deal with their grief unsupported. It also might help reduce the high numbers of women who respond to their loss by getting pregnant again quite quickly, without first addressing the issues that led to the removal of the older child or children.

Lack of research

One of the most worrying things about the way the Family Court operates in its public law work is that judges are making decisions without a basis in research. This would not be acceptable in most other fields – imagine the uproar if the NHS were found to be carrying out major procedures such as heart bypass surgery or hysterectomies without there being a basis in medical research establishing when such operations are appropriate and the most effective way of carrying them out.

The research needed is a major project following cohorts of children who have been subject to court proceedings in England and Wales, charting what has happened to them since the court decision. Where the children and their families are willing to participate, the lives of the children should be studied at regular intervals – say at five, ten and fifteen years after the making of the court decision. This could be done so that the report of the research gave families public anonymity, but in such a way that the individual judge who had dealt with their case would know which case he or she was reading about.

I believe many judges would greatly value this information. Their task is often an agonising one, the more so because much of the time they're operating in the dark, or, as it's euphemistically described, 'crystal-ball gazing'. Most judges are decent human beings, who find their work extremely difficult. At a training event years ago I distinctly recall a district judge telling his audience of one hundred odd lawyers and social workers that, after making a difficult decision in respect of a child, he often went home and wept.

There's also a need for very focused research into adoption. Adoption breakdown is not uncommon once adopted children reach their teens,[12] this being more likely in the case of children who were adopted in middle or later childhood. Some research has been done, but more is needed. Judges tasked with making decisions in contested applications for care and placement orders would benefit from up-to-date research into both the factors that tend to result in successful adoptions and those that tend to result in failure.[13]

Twenty-six weeks

While I fully accept that in general delay is not good for children, a system that obliges practitioners to prioritise speed over obtaining the best outcome for the individual child is not conducive to child welfare. Such a system is the product of a brutalist work culture where 'performance indicators' and 'targets' have gained the upper hand over common sense. It may produce nice-looking statistics, but when applied rigidly it will not result in sensitively planned care for traumatised children. Again, I'm not alone in holding this view. In *The Case for Change* we find the following:

> … whilst the 26 week rule has made some impact in reducing drift in cases, it should not be adhered to strictly where rushing proceedings is to the detriment of a child. Over-adherence to the rule can lead to rushed decisions sometimes not allowing time for thorough assessments of parents or potential carers, and may not allow some parents to demonstrate the necessary change required (Masson et al., 2018).[14]

Sadly, it appears that the senior judiciary are not listening. The 'View from the President's Chambers' issued in November 2022, in which the current president of the Family Division announced his campaign to 'exhort, require and expect' every professional in the system to 'get back to operating the PLO in full', will have served to raise the blood pressure of many a social worker, lawyer and judge; but stressed-out practitioners do not perform well and good outcomes cannot be achieved at speed in an environment lacking in resources.

Lack of resources in the system

At present there's a desperate shortage of foster carers. This has been the case throughout my working life, but with the dramatic increase in the numbers of children coming into care, the problem is getting increasingly serious. Alongside this there is an even more desperate shortage of suitable placements for the many youngsters with serious mental health issues who are spending their teens in the care system. Secure units[15] are full to bursting point and in any event cannot cater for very disturbed children. CAMHS is under-resourced and refuses to treat any but the most seriously disturbed, which means children who are actively suicidal.

Add to this a shortage of social workers, a shortage of children's guardians, a lack of experts willing to accept instructions in care cases and insufficient judges, and you have a system where delays are inevitable. Urging the professionals in the system to operate faster will not remedy the situation; and it will drive some to opt for early retirement or a change of career.

Are there any answers?

All the issues outlined above require addressing. In addition, it is interesting to consider the model of family justice offered by the relatively new Family Drug and Alcohol Court (FDAC), which in my view is more humane and seems to be more successful than the conventional Family Court in the particular type of cases it addresses. FDAC was the brainchild of the late Nicholas Crichton,[16] an enlightened and independent-minded district judge who, in the early 2000s, put a lot of time into researching how cases concerning children of substance-abusing parents were dealt with in Australia and the US. In the model he created, a small number of consenting parents selected by their local authority are given the opportunity to address their drug or alcohol addiction during a court process which can last up to twelve months – double the twenty-six-week time frame. The model depends on the court being presided over by a humane judge with excellent communication skills, for – unlike in conventional care proceedings – a key part of his or her task is to form a relationship with the parent or parents in fortnightly informal hearings. Because of this, the system cannot be operated by a series of different judges.

When I sat in the back of Nick Crichton's FDAC in 2014, I was moved to tears by the respect and kindness with which he spoke to parents; and the appreciative response he received from them. He was like a warm and intelligent grandfather, coaxing parents to find strength they did not know they had and to believe in themselves in a way they'd never done before. At the same time, he left nobody in any doubt about his expectation of change, and that it was up to the parent to rise to the challenge.

Parents whose children's cases are heard by FDAC are given intensive support by a team of social workers, substance abuse workers, psychiatrists, domestic violence workers and others. This gives them the best chance of overcoming their substance addiction, generally while the child or children live in temporary foster care. At the hearings, the judge is updated about how things are going and speaks with the parents. The use of lawyers is kept to a minimum, which seems to help create a less adversarial atmosphere and one in which the parent experiences less humiliation and shame than in a standard Family Court hearing.

Parents who have been through FDAC report that, rather than feeling punitive, the process has felt supportive at a crisis point, helping them sustain changes.[17]

A 2023 evaluation by What Works Centre for Children and Families concluded that children whose cases were dealt with by FDAC were more likely to be reunited with their primary carer at the end of the proceedings than children whose cases were dealt with in conventional care proceedings.[18] It also found that a higher proportion of parents who had been through FDAC ceased to misuse drugs or alcohol by the end of the proceedings, compared with parents who had been through conventional care proceedings.[19]

FDAC hearings are cheaper to operate than conventional Family Court hearings, where lawyers are generally the most expensive element. Initially there was a lot of resistance from government to creating and funding FDACs in locations outside London; but by August 2023 there were fifteen FDACs in operation in England and Wales, taking cases from over thirty-six local authorities.[20] There has been talk of adapting the FDAC process so that it can be used in cases where the principal concern is domestic violence; it's not impossible that it could be adapted to cases of emotional abuse, too. For cases of physical or sexual abuse, however, it's much less likely that the model could be made to fit.

I fully accept that most of the changes I advocate would cost considerable sums of taxpayer's money. To those who say it's not affordable, I say this. Better support for families living in poverty plus better children's social care could reduce the high social and economic costs we are currently paying for allowing so many families to fall into crisis. Remember the figures set out in Chapter 1 with regard to the numbers of 'care experienced' adults who do not work or study, who become street homeless, who turn to crime and swell the population of our prisons, and who die prematurely. Quite apart from the human misery involved, lives lived in this way cost the state a lot of money. As one of the wealthiest countries in the world, Britain should strive to do better by its children.

Glossary of Child Protection Jargon

CAFCASS – Children and Family Court Advisory and
  Support Service
CAMHS – Child and Adolescent Mental Health Services
CAO – child arrangements order
CIN – child in need
EPO – emergency protection order
FC – Family Court
FDAC – Family Drug and Alcohol Court
FSW – family support worker
ICO – interim care order
IFA – independent fostering agency
ISW – independent social worker
PLO – Public Law Outline
PPO – police protection order. There is no such order, but
  police can take a child into police protection, i.e. TIPP
PR – parental responsibility
SGO – special guardianship order
TIPP – take into police protection

Notes

Preface – Alice G

1. This is now well documented. *The Case for Change*, an interim report published in June 2021 as part of the government-commissioned Independent Review of Children's Social Care, tells us that 'The more deprived the neighbourhood that children live in, the more likely they are to experience care or child protection …' (p. 23) This is not to say that child abuse is more prevalent in these neighbourhoods, and the authors go on to say, 'The majority of families living in poverty do not maltreat their children and maltreatment is not exclusive to families living in poverty.' (p. 23) https://fdac.org.uk/wp-content/uploads/2021/06/case-for-change.pdf, accessed 26.9.23.
2. Donald Winnicott (1896–1971) was an English paediatrician and psychoanalyst who wrote about child development and the idea of the 'good enough' parent.
3. Barristers' diaries are controlled by clerks, who decide which cases each barrister is to cover in any given week, generally without consulting the barrister.
4. When a child is put on a child protection plan, social workers are expected to closely monitor their well-being. Categories of risk that might be identified in the plan include physical abuse, emotional abuse, sexual abuse and neglect.
5. The view that the age of six is a cut-off point for adoption is not held by social workers in all local authorities in England and Wales; if anything, it's an unusual view.
6. In order to place a child who is subject to a care order with prospective adopters, without parental consent, the local authority has to obtain a 'placement' order.

7. A 'no contact' order is made under the Children Act 1989 S34(4).
8. A parent seeking to discharge a care order is very unlikely to be granted legal aid to pay their costs.
9. S51A of the Adoption and Children Act 2002, which was introduced by the Children and Families Act 2014, now permits applications by birth relatives and certain others for contact with an adopted child. See also Adoption and Children Act 2002 S26.
10. Letters sent via the 'letterbox' scheme are vetted by the local authority before being forwarded. The address of the adopters is kept strictly confidential.
11. The Human Rights Act 1998 makes the provisions of the European Convention on Human Rights applicable in the law of England and Wales. For care lawyers, the most significant provisions are Article 6, the right to a fair trial; and Article 8, the right to family life. Article 3, the right to protection from inhuman or degrading treatment or punishment, is also sometimes relevant in care work.

1: Secrecy, Confidentiality and Why I'm Writing This Book

1. 'Pupillage' is the twelve-month period when a newly qualified barrister is obliged to work under the wing of an experienced barrister for training purposes. During this time the pupil has only a temporary place in chambers, and in the first six months he or she does not have 'rights of audience', which means they cannot speak in court. During the second six months the pupil has rights of audience and can represent clients.
2. Owen Davies KC sat as a circuit judge from 2011 until his retirement from the bench in 2019.
3. A tenant is a barrister who has completed pupillage and acquired a permanent place in a set of chambers.
4. The bar is the heart of the British establishment. In her excellent book *In Black and White* (Endeavour, 2020), the young mixed-race barrister Alexandra Wilson writes movingly about how different she felt from her fellow pupils and how she frequently encountered overt racism. I'm not suggesting that my sense of alienation was anything like as acute as hers, and I take my hat off to her for what she coped with.
5. For more on the connections between poverty and child abuse and neglect see, for example, Naomi Eisenstadt and Carey Oppenheim, *Parents, Poverty and the State* (Policy Press, 2019).
6. The other two are Germany and Poland.

7. https://explore-education-statistics.service.gov.uk/find-statistics/children-looked-after-in-england-including-adoptions, accessed 7.1.24.
8. https://www.gov.uk/government/statistics/children-looked-after-by-local-authorities-in-england-year-ending-31-march-2010, accessed 25.9.23.
9. https://www.gov.wales/children-looked-after-local-authorities-april-2021-march-2022-html, accessed 19.9.23. No figures were available for 2023 at the time of going to press.
10. Wales Centre for Public Policy, *Children Looked After in Wales: Trends*, September 2020, p. 8, https://www.wcpp.org.uk/wp-content/uploads/2020/09/Children-looked-after-in-Wales-Trends.pdf, accessed 4.10.23.
11. https://www.ethnicity-facts-figures.service.gov.uk/health/social-care/adopted-and-looked-after-children/latest, accessed 18.8.23.
12. 'Tackling racial disparity: The journey so far', Home for Good, November 2021, https://homeforgood.org.uk/tackling-racial-disparity-journey, accessed 19.9.23.
13. Josh MacAlister (chair), 'Executive Summary', *The Independent Review of Children's Social Care*, 23 May 2022, pp. 15–16, https://fdac.org.uk/wp-content/uploads/2021/06/case-for-change.pdf, accessed 7.1.24.
14. There are circumstances in which documents can be disclosed to health professionals or counsellors, but in practice this is rarely done without a court order authorising it.
15. See for example Camilla Cavendish, 'Family courts: the hidden untouchables', *The Times*, 7 July 2008, https://www.thetimes.co.uk/article/family-courts-the-hidden-untouchables-sjd0njtks9d, accessed 7.10.2023.
16. Andrew McFarlane in '*Confidence and Confidentiality*: Transparency in the Family Courts', 28 October 2021, paragraphs 21 and 22, https://www.judiciary.uk/wp-content/uploads/2021/10/Confidence-and-Confidentiality-Transparency-in-the-Family-Courts-final.pdf, accessed 7.1.24.
17. https://www.localgovernmentlawyer.co.uk/child-protection/392-children-protection-news/20134-research-finds-major-concern-amongst-children-a, accessed 2.3.2023.

2: Who's Who in Child Protection

1. Children Act 1989 S20.
2. https://www.gov.uk/government/statistics/family-court-statistics-quarterly-october-to-december-2022/family-court-statistics-quarterly-october-to-december-2022#children-act---public-law, accessed 21.9.23.
3. Children Act 1989 S3(1).
4. Children Act 1989 S33(3).
5. *Working Together to Safeguard Children*, 2023, is the current version of the guidance.
6. One of the postgraduate schemes, Step Up to Social Work, instituted in 2010, takes just fourteen months; the other, Frontline, started in 2013, is a two-year course leading to an MSc or a one-year course leading to qualification as a social worker but no MSc; both courses are funded, so that participants get a living allowance and their fees paid. Much of social work training, whichever route is followed, involves placements with different local authorities, where the student assists with real cases for a number of months at a stretch. The profession of social work is regulated by Social Work England in England and the Care Council in Wales.
7. https://www.glassdoor.co.uk/Salaries/newly-qualified-social-worker-salary-SRCH_KO0,29.htm, accessed 12.12.22.
8. https://uk.talent.com/salary?job=social+work+manager, accessed 5.4.2023.
9. A special guardianship order is designed to give the child permanence with a relative or family friend, but without severing their bonds with their birth family. As such it falls midway between long-term foster care under a care order and adoption. See Children Act 1989 S14A.
10. There's been a chronic shortage of 'stranger' foster carers for as long as I can remember. This creates great problems and often results in children being placed with the only foster carer who's available, rather than being carefully matched with the foster carer who can best meet their needs. It also often results in siblings being separated and sometimes in children being sent to live far from their home area.

    Most foster carers are female, and many are lone parents who opt to foster a child or children alongside caring for their own child. There are also some single male foster carers and some foster couples, both gay and straight.

There has for many years been a strong (and arguably misguided) ethos that foster carers should not be paid a salary for what they do, because they should be motivated by a wish to care for children, not by money. Foster carers who work for their local authority (known as 'in-house' foster carers) get paid an allowance in accordance with the age of the child they are caring for. According to government figures, in 2023–24 for foster carers living outside London and the south-east, this will be a minimum of £154 per week for a child of nought to two years, £159 for a child aged three to four, £175 for a child aged five to ten, £199 per week for a child of eleven to fifteen, and £233 for a child aged sixteen to seventeen (https://www.gov.uk/support-for-foster-parents/help-with-the-cost-of-fostering, accessed 10.7.233). Out of the allowance the foster carer is expected to pay for the child's food, clothing, travel, pocket money, toiletries, activity fees and treats.

Around thirty-five years ago a number of independent fostering agencies (IFAs) began operating as commercial enterprises. They generally pay their foster carers more than double what a local authority would pay them, and many people who previously fostered in-house have switched to fostering through an IFA. For obvious reasons, local authorities prefer to use in-house foster carers, but very often none are available and they're obliged to use an IFA.

All foster carers should have access to a fostering support worker tasked with providing them with the support they need to do the job, both practical and emotional; but in practice in-house foster carers often complain about a severe lack of support.

11. The use of children's homes was greatly reduced in the 1990s and 2000s, although in recent years it has increased again. Figures from the Department for Education show that the number of children placed in children's homes grew by 34 per cent between 2009/10 and 2020: see *The Case for Change*, p. 59, https://fdac.org.uk/wp-content/uploads/2021/06/case-for-change.pdf, accessed 25.9.23. Most children's homes are run by private providers.

12. There's an increasing number of older children requiring specialist provision because they have become seriously emotionally disturbed and perhaps suicidal and/or violent as a result of childhood trauma and/or a series of failed social work interventions. Such provision is very hard to find and extremely expensive. In recent years some of these teenagers have been placed in grossly unsuitable provision.

13. Children Act 1989 S31.

14. The Human Rights Act 1998 gives effect to the rights and freedoms guaranteed under the European Convention on Human Rights.
15. The Family Group Conference originated with the New Zealand Maoris, who created the model in response to their children being disproportionately taken into care.
16. Foundations, 'Family Group Conferencing at pre-proceedings stage', June 2023, https://foundations.org.uk/our-work/reports/family-group-conferencing/, accessed 10.10.23.
17. Children Act 1989 S41.
18. The circumstances are that a police constable has reasonable cause to believe that a child would otherwise be likely to suffer significant harm (Children Act 1989 S46). Normally where this occurs the police arrange for the child to go into local authority foster care. The maximum duration is seventy-two hours, after which the child can only be kept away from their parent or carer if a court has made an emergency protection order or interim care order or if the parent agrees to sign consent to S20 accommodation.
19. This process is often referred to as police taking a 'PPO', but in law there's no such creature as a 'Police Protection Order': the correct term is 'taking a child into police protection'.
20. Physical assault, ill-treatment, neglect and abandonment are charged under Section 1(1) of the Children and Young Persons Act 1933 as amended on 3 May 2015 by Part 5 Section 66 of the Serious Crime Act. The harm caused to the child can be psychological.
21. After several years working in public childcare law, most solicitors apply to join the Children Law Accreditation Scheme (formerly the Children Panel). If accepted, this gives them accreditation as suitable people with the requisite level of experience to represent children. They meet the child in the company of the guardian, but take their instructions from the guardian, except in cases where the child disagrees with the guardian *and* is deemed by the court mature enough to instruct the solicitor directly.
22. There's no special training for a newly qualified barrister wanting to practise in child protection. The lawyer may have worked in other areas of law in their early years of practice, but child protection work is so demanding and absorbing that it's difficult to combine it with anything except private family law.

3: Dwayne

1. Form C110A is the form that the local authority completes and sends to the court office to issue proceedings, giving the names of the children, the parents and the social worker, and summarising the grounds for the application.
2. Children in secure accommodation are locked in. Their education and all other activities are provided for on-site. Secure accommodation has to be authorised by either the Family Court or a criminal court. The Family Court can only authorise its use under very strict criteria as to the risk the child poses to her/himself or others, and for limited periods of time.
3. When a woman uses certain drugs while pregnant, there's a risk her baby will be born with withdrawal symptoms, which can be severe and distressing for the baby. This is because while in utero the baby has been accustomed to receiving regular doses of, for instance, crack cocaine, heroin, amphetamines or certain anti-depressants via the umbilical cord, and this supply ceases abruptly at birth. The condition is called neonatal abstinence syndrome (NAS).
4. If the detailed assessment is positive, and if the local authority has concluded the parent should not resume care of the child, it may urge the relative or friend to seek legal advice about the possibility of caring for the child under a special guardianship Order (SGO). Where a child is subject to an SGO, the birth parents who have parental responsibility for the child retain it, but in the event of a disagreement with the special guardian, the latter has the upper hand. So, for example, if the birth mother wants the child to go to a particular school and the special guardian wants to send them to a different school, the special guardian's choice prevails. It is also possible, however, that the local authority believes the kinship carer should care for the child long term under a care order, usually in a situation where the kinship carer is likely to need a lot of support from the local authority.

4: Initial Hearing

1. Tony Blair's father was fostered as a child and then adopted – see 'Blair: Why adoption is close to my heart,' *Guardian*, 21 December 2000, https://www.theguardian.com/society/2000/dec/21/adoptionandfostering.localgovernment1, accessed 6.10.23.

2. In 2005, the figure was 3,770 or 6 per cent of the total number of children who had been in care for more than six months; in 2013 it was 4,010 and in 2015, 5,360. From 2015, however, the numbers began to decline, and in 2022 the figure was 3,000. (Figures from the Department of Education, https://explore-education-statistics.service.gov.uk/data-tables/fast-track/2caf4bf5-4b37-42af-9f6a-08dbca41c6a0, accessed 4.12.23.)

3. 'An Action Plan for Adoption: Tackling Delay', Department for Education, 2011, https://assets.publishing.service.gov.uk/media/5a7a3eab40f0b66a2fc00f13/action_plan_for_adoption.pdf, accessed 4.12.23.

4. Re B (Care Proceedings: Appeal) 2013 UKSC 33.

5. Ibid., para 33, from the judgement of Lord Wilson.

6. Ibid., para. 76, from the judgement of Lord Neuberger, quoting Lady Hale (now Baroness Hale).

7. Ibid., para 77, from the judgement of Lord Neuberger, again quoting Lady Hale.

8. Ibid., para 77, from the judgement of Lord Neuberger.

9. Ibid., para 77, from the judgement of Lord Neuberger.

10. Re B-S 2013 EWCA Civ 1146.

11. Ibid., para. 30, from the judgement of Sir James Munby.

12. Ibid., para. 34, from the judgement of Sir James Munby.

13. Ibid., para. 44, from the judgement of Sir James Munby.

14. Ibid., para. 26, from the judgement of Sir James Munby.

15. Adoption and Children Act 2002 S1(2).

16. The adoption welfare checklist, set out in the Adoption and Children Act 2002 S1(4), requires the court to consider a number of welfare issues, including the child's wishes, needs, the effect on them of becoming an adopted person, any harm they have sustained and, most importantly for Dwayne, the following:

(f) the relationship which the child has with relatives, with any person who is a prospective adopter with whom the child is placed, and with any other person in relation to whom the court or agency considers the relationship to be relevant, including:

(i) the likelihood of any such relationship continuing and the value to the child of its doing so,
(ii) the ability and willingness of any of the child's relatives, or of any such person, to provide the child with a secure environment in which the child can develop, and otherwise to meet the child's needs,
(iii) the wishes and feelings of any of the child's relatives, or of any such person, regarding the child.

6: The Psychologist's Evidence

1. A placement order is made under the Adoption and Children Act 2002 S21 and allows the local authority to place the child with any prospective adopters chosen by the local authority. By S21(3)(b) the court may make a placement order against the wishes of both the parent who has PR or the guardian if it is satisfied that the parent or guardian's consent should be dispensed with. This provision is subject to S52(1)(b) of the same Act, which requires that the court be satisfied that the welfare of the child requires the consent to be dispensed with.

2. 'Triple P' is short for Positive Parenting Program (or Programme in the UK). Devised in Australia, it's now available in twenty-five countries around the world, both via attended groups and on-line. According to the programme's website: 'The Triple P – Positive Parenting Program is one of the most effective evidence-based parenting programs in the world, backed up by more than thirty-five years of ongoing research. Triple P gives parents simple and practical strategies to help them build strong, healthy relationships, confidently manage their children's behavior and prevent problems developing.' https://www.triplep.net/glo-en/home, accessed 10.7.23.

3. When I was first in practice, legal aid paid for a solicitor's clerk to attend court with counsel. Their role was to take notes, especially when counsel was questioning witnesses, and to provide badly needed support to the client. This enabled counsel to give her full attention to the legal process.

4. PAUSE is a charity that works to improve the lives of women who have had, or are at risk of having, more than one child removed from their care. Their vision is 'of a society where women who experience the removal of children into care are given the best possible support, so that it never happens more than once'. See https://www.pause.org.uk/about-us/, accessed 11.10.23.

5. Mothers returning to court within five years of previous care proceedings make up 20 per cent of the parents in care proceedings. See *The Case for Change*, p. 51, https://fdac.org.uk/wp-content/uploads/2021/06/case-for-change.pdf, accessed 26.9.23.

6. It's difficult to get definitive information about this. See, however, the *NHS Talking Therapies Manual*, last updated in February 2023, the cover of which bears the title *The Improving Access to*

Psychological Therapies [IAPT] *Manual*, despite the fact that IAPT no longer exists. On p. 14, Table 2, which is headed 'NICE-recommended psychological interventions', the following is offered as a 'Low-intensity intervention' for depression: 'Individual guided self-help based on CBT, Computerised CBT, Behavioural Activation, Structured group physical activity programme'. These will be delivered by Psychological Wellbeing Practitioners (PWPs), who are not even qualified counsellors let alone psychotherapists. It appears that patients have to have tried some of these 'low-intensity interventions' and failed to respond before they will be offered a 'high-intensity' intervention. The latter, for people deemed to be suffering 'mild to moderate' depression, includes 'CBT (individual or group) or interpersonal psychotherapy (IPT); Behavioural Activation; Couple therapy; Counselling for depression or Brief psychodynamic therapy'. For those with 'moderate to severe' depression the offer is a number of different types of CBT, one offer of IPT combined with medication or, for those with post-traumatic stress disorder (PTSD), Eye Movement Desensitisation and Reprocessing. The criteria that a patient has to satisfy to be offered 'interpersonal psychotherapy' remains a mystery. However, it appears that the patient has to try the 'low-intensity' interventions first before moving on to the 'high-intensity' ones, and this in itself, combined with lengthy waiting lists, is likely to mean that a parent in care proceedings will never be offered an effective course of psychotherapy sessions within the twenty-six-week time frame.

7: The Timescale of the Child

1. See the report of the Family Justice Review, chaired by David Norgrove, which reported in November 2011. This expressed concern about the impact on children of delay, and analysed the causes both in terms of social work processes *and* court processes, including a perceived over-reliance on the use of experts. https://assets.publishing.service.gov.uk/government/uploads/system/uploads/attachment_data/file/217343/family-justice-review-final-report.pdf, accessed 10.7.23. See also 'The Impact of and Avoidance of Delay in Decision Making', a summary of key research messages assembled by the Department for Education-funded Research in Practice, https://fosteringandadoption.rip.org.uk/wp-content/uploads/2014/04/Impact-of-avoidance-and-delay.pdf, accessed 10.7.23.

2. The guidance was formally known as the 'Protocol for Judicial Case Management in Children Act Cases'.
3. Children Act 1989 S32(1)(ii) and S32(5).
4. Children and Families Act 2014 S13(6).
5. The designated family judge is the lead judge for a geographic court area, which may include several counties.
6. In this context, Lord Wilson's insistence that everything must be done to 're-build the family' is not adhered to in practice – see Chapter 3 and *Re B (Care Proceedings: Appeal)* 2013 UKSC 33 at para. 33.
7. Figures from https://www.cafcass.gov.uk/about-us/our-data, accessed 7.10.23.
8. For most parents who have lost a child in care proceedings, there's no support whatsoever; and indeed the local authority is not legally required to provide support. The loss of a child to adoption can leave a parent suicidal; and often the same parent is hauled before the Family Court a few years later, after the birth of their next baby, presenting with all the same problems that she had at the time of the first set of proceedings.

8: In the Woods

1. Vicarious trauma is a well-recognised phenomenon. The British Medical Association describes it as follows: 'Vicarious trauma is a process of change resulting from empathetic engagement with trauma survivors. Anyone who engages empathetically with survivors of traumatic incidents, torture, and material relating to their trauma, is potentially affected, including doctors and other health professionals.' See https://www.bma.org.uk/advice-and-support/your-wellbeing/vicarious-trauma/vicarious-trauma-signs-and-strategies-for-coping, accessed 26.9.23.
2. There are small signs that this ethos is beginning to change. See Camilla Wells, 'Why we need to create a trauma-informed legal community', *Counsel*, August 2023, https://www.counselmagazine.co.uk/articles/why-we-need-to-create-a-trauma-informed-legal-community-#:~:text=Vicarious%20trauma,can%20be%20extreme%20and%20relentless, accessed 26.9.23.
3. A formal meeting between a barrister and their client is referred to as a 'conference', often abbreviated to 'con'.
4. Such an application is made under Part 25 of the Family Procedure Rules 2010, which deals with expert evidence in court proceedings. A residential assessment is a type of expert assessment, and the resulting report is treated as expert evidence.

5. If the parent has a learning disability, as many of the parents who come before the care courts do, good practice requires that they be assessed under a specialised methodology adapted to their needs. There are several such methodologies, of which the most commonly used is the Parenting Assessment Manual or PAMS assessment, which has to be carried out by a specially trained social worker. PAMS assessments were invented by clinical psychologist Sue McGaw in 1999. They use minimal amounts of text and rely heavily on cartoons to communicate ideas.
6. Children and Families Act 2014 S13(6).

9: Baby K

1. Lawyers say a case has gone 'part heard' when a hearing takes longer than the time frame allotted to it. When this happens it can cause havoc for barristers' clerks, who have to re-jig their barristers' diaries to ensure every hearing is covered. One of the unhappy results is that clients don't always get the barrister they were expecting turning up to court to represent them – instead they get a stranger.
2. A cognitive assessment is carried out by a consultant psychologist with the aim of establishing whether the parent has any form of learning disability and, if so, in which areas; and what assistance s/he may require in order to participate in court proceedings. These may include the services of a (non-legal) advocate or intermediary tasked with ensuring s/he understands what's being said; the use of simple language by the lawyers and judge during hearings; and frequent breaks during which the advocate can check the parent's comprehension.
3. See the Children Act 1989 S38 and S31.
4. Except, for example, in a case where the mother has consumed certain street drugs or excessive alcohol during the pregnancy, thereby causing the baby harm in utero that will manifest at birth.
5. DNA tests are commonplace in care proceedings whenever there is uncertainty as to a child's paternity. Usually the costs are shared between the parties, with Legal Aid paying the contribution of each of the legally aided parties.
6. Children Act 1989 S1(1).
7. Children Act 1989 S1(5).
8. Stated by Mr Justice Ryder in *Re L (A Child)* 2008 1FLR 575.
9. A parent and child foster placement is a foster placement that takes in both mother and baby. The foster carer is tasked with

close observation of the mother's parenting and must step in if she considers the care to be unsafe. In the initial stages the mother is not usually permitted to leave the placement alone with the baby; and in most cases the baby is subject to an interim care order.

10. See, for example Sue Gerhardt, *Why Love Matters: How Affection Shapes a Baby's Brain* (Routledge, 2014).
11. *Re C (A Child) (Interim Separation)* 2019 EWCA Civ 1998, at para. 2.
12. Some of the new courthouses built in the early 2000s were mothballed within a few years, with all hearings for a large geographical area being listed at a central location. Apart from the appalling waste of taxpayer's money this entailed, it has meant that some parents in public law proceedings have to travel very long distances at their own expense to attend court hearings. For parents living on state benefits, the costs can be prohibitive.
13. A stay is an order that preserves the status quo. When a court orders the separation of a child from their parent, if it's arguable that the court has made an error of law, the parent's lawyer can apply for a stay, which means the removal will not take effect until the appeal has been heard.

11: Final Hearing

1. As a single man, Dwayne will have been on a very low 'band' under the local authority scheme for prioritising people according to housing need. If a court order were made placing a child in his care, he would most likely be placed in the top band and be able to bid for available properties.
2. After completing its parenting and any other assessments, the local authority social worker has to file a 'final' care plan for each child subject to proceedings. This will cover with whom the child is to live, any support services to be offered (such as play therapy) and the proposed arrangements for contact with family members. The court is obliged to consider the 'permanence' provisions of the care plan before making a final order: Children Act 1989 S31(3)A(a). Permanence provisions are defined by the Children Act 1989 S31(3B) as:

(a) such of the plan's provisions setting out the long-term plan for the upbringing of the child concerned as provide for any of the following:

(i) the child to live with any parent of the child's or with any other member of, or any friend of, the child's family;

(ii) adoption;

(iii) long-term care not within sub-paragraph (i) or (ii);

(b) such of the plan's provisions as set out any of the following:

(i) the impact on the child concerned of any harm that he or she suffered or was likely to suffer;

(ii) the current and future needs of the child (including needs arising out of that impact);

(iii) the way in which the long-term plan for the upbringing of the child would meet those current and future needs.

3. By 'stranger adoption', lawyers refer to adoption by a family or individual who is initially a stranger to the child; as opposed to adoption by a relative or step-parent, which also sometimes occurs.

12: A Country Home with Horses

1. The full welfare checklist in the Children Act 1989 S1(3):

(a) the ascertainable wishes and feelings of the child concerned (considered in the light of his age and understanding);

(b) his physical, emotional and educational needs;

(c) the likely effect on him of any change in his circumstances;

(d) his age, sex, background and any characteristics of his which the court considers relevant;

(e) any harm which he has suffered or is at risk of suffering;

(f) how capable each of his parents, and any other person in relation to whom the court considers the question to be relevant, is of meeting his needs;

(g) the range of powers available to the court under this Act in the proceedings in question.

2. A child arrangements order (CAO) under the Children Act 1989 S8 deals either with the living arrangements for a child or the contact arrangements, or both. In the past a 'lives with' child arrangements order was known as a Residence Order and, in the distant past, as a 'custody order'. A CAO is a private law order, meaning that it does not confer any power on the local authority.

3. A supervision order is made under the Children Act 1989 S31 for an initial period of twelve months but it may be extended to last a maximum of three years. It gives the local authority the power to 'advise, assist and befriend' the child (CA89 S35). Lawyers often say that a supervision order 'has no teeth'; but a child subject to a supervision order may have more resources made available to them than a child who is not subject to one. The order can only be made if threshold criteria are met.

14: Anxiety Levels Rise

1. The system of placing the names of children considered to be at risk of significant harm on the 'child protection register' was subsequently replaced by the placing of such children on 'child protection plans'. In both cases the decision was, and is, made by a vote taken at a child protection conference.

2. In her 2011 report 'The Munro Review of Child Protection', commissioned by the then secretary of state for education Michael Gove, Professor Munro described child protection as 'a defensive system that puts so much emphasis on procedures and recording that insufficient attention is given to developing and supporting the expertise to work effectively with children, young people and families'. https://assets.publishing.service.gov.uk/government/uploads/system/uploads/attachment_data/file/175391/Munro-Review.pdf, p. 6, accessed 10.5.23.

   A similar observation was made by Josh MacAlister in *The Case for Change*, a 2021 interim report in his government-commissioned Independent Review of Children's Social Care. He said: 'If we consider that the greatest value of social work is in the interaction between social workers and children and families, then it should be an ongoing source of alarm that 1 in 3 of all social workers in children's services do not work directly with children or families (Department for Education, 2021a). Even those in direct practice spend less than one third of their time with families (Department for Education, 2020a). This is a staggering misuse of the greatest asset that children's social care has – its social workers.' *The Case for Change*, p. 77, https://fdac.org.uk/wp-content/uploads/2021/06/case-for-change.pdf, accessed 25.9.23.

3. *Re M (A Minor) (Care Order: Threshold Conditions)*, 1994, 3 WLR 558.

4. The Victoria Climbié Inquiry: Report of an Inquiry by Lord Laming, published January 2003, https://assets.publishing.service.gov.uk/media/5a7c5edeed915d696ccfc51b/5730.pdf, accessed 3.10.23.

5. The aim of Every Child Matters was described by the government as 'to ensure that every child has the chance to fulfil their potential by reducing levels of educational failure, ill health, substance misuse, teenage pregnancy, abuse and neglect, crime and anti-social behaviour among children and young people'. Under the auspices of Every Child Matters the programme of

Sure Start centres, begun in 1998, was expanded. Centres were opened in the poorest areas of England and Wales with the aim of providing support to pre-school children and their parents.

6. The first serious case review (SCR), overseen by Sharon Shoesmith, then director of children's services for the London Borough of Haringey prior to her sacking, was published in November 2008; it was subsequently judged to be inadequate and a second SCR was held, chaired by Graham Badman. This reported in May 2009. One of the conclusions was that Haringey Children's Services' expectations of the mother in terms of her duty to care for and protect her child were too low; another was that the social workers involved in the case had been too willing to accept the mother's lies and obfuscations as to the cause of Peter's recurring injuries. The comments on the legal service provision are at para 3.22.5 of the report of the second review, see https://assets.publishing.service.gov.uk/government/uploads/system/uploads/attachment_data/file/595135/second_serious_case_overview_report_relating_to_peter_connelly_dated_march_2009.pdf, accessed 1.5.2023.

7. 'Between 2012–13 and 2019–20, spending on non-statutory children's services decreased by 35% in real terms' – figure given in *The Case for Change*, p. 11, based on information from the Department for Education. https://fdac.org.uk/wp-content/uploads/2021/06/case-for-change.pdf, accessed 27.9.23.

15: Duty

1. S47 of the Children Act 1989 reads:

Where a local authority –
… (b) have reasonable cause to suspect that a child who lives, or is found, in their area is suffering, or is likely to suffer, significant harm, the authority shall make, or cause to be made, such enquiries as they consider necessary to enable them to decide whether they should take any action to safeguard or promote the child's welfare …

(3) The enquiries shall, in particular, be directed towards establishing –
(a) whether the authority should –
(i) make any application to court under this Act;
(ii) exercise any of their other powers under this Act;

2. Sexual Offences Act 2003 S9(2)(a) and S13(1).

16: The Locum

1. Where a police constable has reasonable cause to believe that a child would otherwise be likely to suffer significant harm, s/he has the power under Children Act 1989 S46 to take the child into police protection for up to seventy-two hours. Normally where this occurs the police arrange for the child to go into local authority foster care. After the seventy-two hours expire, the child can only be kept away from their parent or carer if a court has made an emergency protection order or interim care order or if the parent consents to S20 accommodation.
2. A legal executive is not a fully qualified lawyer.

18: Hearing by Video Platform

1. A 'strategy' meeting is an emergency joint meeting between a child's social work team and the police, called by the local authority in the wake of an incident of serious concern.
2. The body map is an outline drawing of a child onto which the examining doctor marks the exact location of injuries, with descriptive labels.
3. In conversation between ourselves, lawyers frequently refer to particular judges as being 'pro-parent' or 'pro-local authority', based on our experiences arguing cases in front of them. Judges are only human, the same as lawyers, and it's often possible to discern a particular pattern to the attitudes a given judge adopts.
4. Where it is ordered, a capacity assessment is conducted by the same consultant psychologist who conducts the cognitive assessment. He or she is tasked with deciding whether the subject has the intellectual capacity to give instructions to their lawyer, as defined by the Mental Capacity Act 2005 Sections 2 and 3. If the conclusion is that they do not, then the official solicitor will be asked to represent the parent. In practice this can lead to inordinate delays in the conduct of the proceedings.
5. To 'efile' an order means to file it electronically, by email.

19: Snow

1. According to Josh MacAlister in *The Case for Change*, children's social work relies on locums or 'agency' staff at an inordinately high rate. On p. 79 he writes, 'The full-time equivalent (FTE) agency worker rate remains at around 15% (Department for

Education, 2021a), far higher than comparable professions, such as the 7% of agency staff in adult social care (Skills for Care, 2020).' https://fdac.org.uk/wp-content/uploads/2021/06/case-for-change.pdf, accessed 9.10.23.

20: Lawrence

1. CAMHS have notoriously long waiting lists, and in most parts of England and Wales will only see children with the most acute mental health disturbances.

21: The Cab Rank Rule

1. Such assessment takes place under Regulation 24 of the Care Planning Placement and Case Review Regulations 2010.
2. This is a quote from Lord Justice Thorpe's decision in *Re LA (Care: Chronic Neglect)* 2009 EWCA Civ 822.
3. Lord Justice Peter Jackson in *Re C (A Child)* 2019 EWCA Civ 1998.
4. Ibid.
5. When the allegations at the core of a set of care proceedings involve a person who is not a party (that is, not a parent of the child or children concerned), that person is usually invited to 'intervene' in the proceedings. This means they are entitled to participate in any fact finding and to have legal representation in order to contest the allegations against them. If findings of a serious nature are made against a non-party, this may result in restrictions on the contact they'll be permitted to have with their own children or the children of their partner; for this reason, they must be given an opportunity to defend themselves.

22: Fact Finding

1. S38A of the Children Act provides that, in certain circumstances, when a court is making an interim care order, it can include an exclusion requirement directed at a person living in the child's home whose continued presence would put the child at risk of significant harm; but this can only be done if there's another person living in the home who's able to care for the child and if that person consents to the exclusion.
2. Lawyers use this term to describe an application for disclosure where the applicant fails to specify what documents they are looking for. It was apt in this case, where the local authority was

simply hoping that something of relevance might turn up in the messages; but the application was nevertheless granted.
3. *R v Lucas* [1981] QB 720.
4. Such programmes do exist, but they can be hard to access and some have long waiting lists.
5. Children Act 1989 S14D(3)(b) and S14D(5). SGOs are not intended to create temporary living arrangements for children.

23: Discharge Application

1. Cases where CAMHS works with a child's carer rather than directly with the child are not unusual. While there may sometimes be merit in this, it does not take account of the frequency with which children in foster care are obliged to move placements, especially when their behaviour is perceived as 'challenging'. It is likely that the decision to proceed in this way is influenced by resources, or rather the lack of them.
2. *TT (Children: Discharge of Care Order)* 2021 EWCA Civ 742.
3. Dwayne is referring to the European Court of Human Rights.
4. 'A View from the President's Chambers', 29 November 2022, https://www.judiciary.uk/guidance-and-resources/a-view-from-the-presidents-chambers-november-2022/#:~:text=The%20single%20focus%20of%20this,Family%20Procedure%20Rules%202010%2C%20PD12A, accessed 4.12.23.

Epilogue

1. For a detailed account of the numerous flaws in our current system of children's social care – a topic that's broader than but includes child protection – I cannot recommend the interim report of the Independent Review of Children's Social Care (IRCSC), *The Case for Change*, highly enough. See https://fdac.org.uk/wp-content/uploads/2021/06/case-for-change.pdf, accessed 28.9.23.
2. According to the Equality Trust, writing in 2022, 'The UK has one of the highest levels of income inequality in Europe, although it is less unequal than the United States', https://equalitytrust.org.uk/scale-economic-inequality-uk, accessed 19.9.23.
3. Non-statutory children's services lost 35 per cent of their funding during austerity. See *The Case for Change*, p. 72, citing figures from the Department for Education, https://fdac.org.uk/wp-content/uploads/2021/06/case-for-change.pdf, accessed 28.9.23.

4. *The Case for Change*, June 2021, p. 11. See https://fdac.org.uk/
wp-content/uploads/2021/06/case-for-change.pdf, accessed
26.9.23.
5. This was carried out by the Child Safeguarding Practice Review
Panel. See https://www.gov.uk/government/publications/national-
review-into-the-murders-of-arthur-labinjo-hughes-and-star-
hobson, accessed 29.9.23.
6. Ibid., para. 12.15, p. 88.
7. Independent Review into Children's Social Care final report,
p. 237, https://assets.publishing.service.gov.uk/media/
640a17f28fa8f5560820da4b/Independent_review_of_children_s_
social_care_-_Final_report.pdf, accessed 7.1.24.
8. Frontline has however been criticised by some social work
academics for allegedly providing insufficient academic training
and for costing more to the state than other types of social work
education. See Five years of Frontline in Community Care, https://
www.communitycare.co.uk/2018/10/03/five-years-frontline-
impact-debate-future-fast-track-social-work-training/, accessed
11.10.23.
9. See the interim report of the Independent Review of Children's
Social Care, chaired by Josh MacAlister, https://fdac.org.uk/
wp-content/uploads/2021/06/case-for-change.pdf, accessed
4.12.23
10. The Independent Review of Children's Social Care, in its final
report in May 2022, called for a government investment of £2.6
billion. See https://assets.publishing.service.gov.uk/government/
uploads/system/uploads/attachment_data/file/1141532/
Independent_review_of_children_s_social_care_-_Final_report.
pdf, accessed 4.12.23.
    In response, the Conservative government provided just £200
million, or approximately 13 per cent of that sum. The
government response document was entitled 'Stable Homes, Built
on Love', https://assets.publishing.service.gov.uk/government/
uploads/system/uploads/attachment_data/file/1147317/
Children_s_social_care_stable_homes_consultation_
February_2023.pdf, accessed 4.12.23.
11. See https://assets.publishing.service.gov.uk/government/uploads/
system/uploads/attachment_data/file/1141532/Independent_
review_of_children_s_social_care_-_Final_report.pdf, accessed
4.12.23.
12. A 2014 University of Bristol research project found that teenagers
were ten times more likely to experience an adoption breakdown
than young children. See https://www.communitycare.co.

uk/2014/04/09/adoptions-ten-times-likely-break-teenage-years-finds-study/, accessed 11.10.23.

13. See Alan Rushton, 'Outcomes of adoption from public care: research and practice issues', Cambridge University Press online publication, January 2018, https://www.cambridge.org/core/journals/advances-in-psychiatric-treatment/article/outcomes-of-adoption-from-public-care-research-and-practice-issues/C481AB8A0FF29F14ADDB6E711C9D6E57, accessed 15.8.23.

14. *The Case for Change*, June 2021, p. 46, https://fdac.org.uk/wp-content/uploads/2021/06/case-for-change.pdf, accessed 26.9.23.

15. A secure unit is a residential establishment where children aged thirteen to seventeen who satisfy certain criteria are locked in. Children aged under thirteen can only be placed in a secure unit with the specific prior approval of the secretary of state.

16. Nicholas Crichton, 1943–2018.

17. 'What Works Centre for Children and Families – Evaluation of Family Drug and Alcohol Courts', August 2023, https://foundations.org.uk/our-work/reports/family-drug-and-alcohol-courts/#:~:text=Key%20findings&text=A%20higher%20proportion%20of%20FDAC,(4.2%25%20versus%2023.8%25), accessed 4.12.23.

18. Ibid., 52 per cent versus 12.5 per cent.

19. Ibid., 33.6 per cent versus 8.1 per cent.

20. In all there are currently 339 local authorities in England and Wales.

Acknowledgements

This book would not have seen the light of day without the encouragement and input of many friends and former colleagues, some of whom gave their time reading drafts and making comments at various stages of the writing process. I hugely appreciate their help, but take full responsibility for the contents of the book and of course for any errors.

Grateful thanks are due to Enzo Bavetta, Emma Crichton Miller, Helen Crocker, Mark Frith, Celia Hart, Chloe Harkness, Joanna Hughes, Nikki Kenna, Jeff Kenna, Claudia Lank, Julia Mortimer, Christine Roberts, Colin Robinson, Sarah Stott, Judith Trustman, Elizabeth Veats, Catherine Wilson, Sara Robertson-Jonas and Orna Ross.

Thanks also go to several others who prefer not to be named; their input has been significant, too.

Lastly, many thanks to my editor Ajda Vucicevic and my agent Jane Graham Maw.